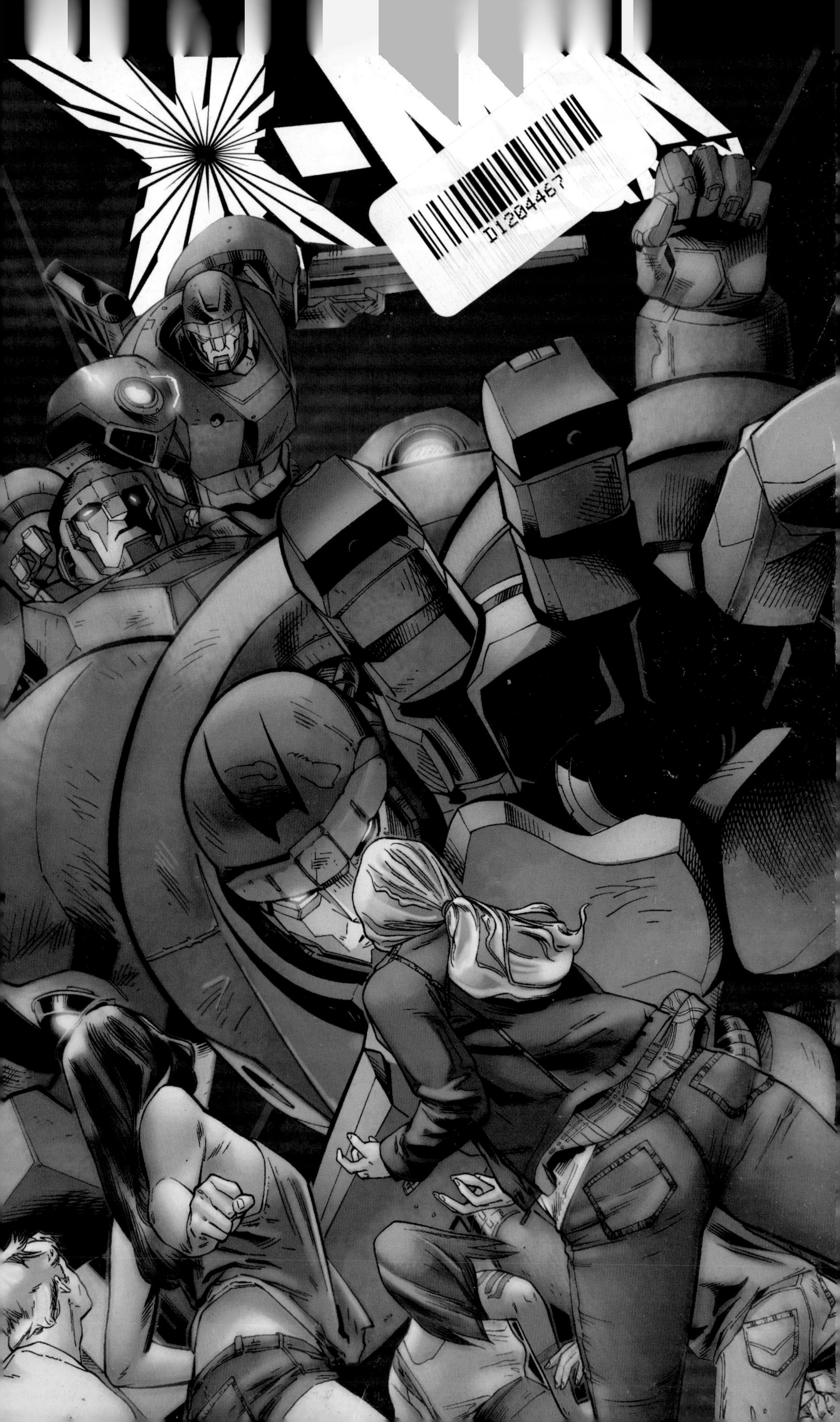

COLLISION

WRITER: Mike Carey

PENCILER: Clay Mann
with Tom Raney

INKER: Jay Leisten
with Tom Raney & Sandu Florea

COLORIST: Brian Reber

LETTERER: Virtual Calligraphy's Cory Petit

COVER ART: Leinil Francis Yu

ASSISTANT EDITOR: Jake Thomas

EDITOR: Daniel Ketchum

CONSULTING EDITOR: Nick Lowe

BONUS HANDBOOK PAGES

HEAD WRITERS/COORDINATORS: Jeff Christiansen & Mike O'Sullivan

WRITERS: Mike O'Sullivan & Jeph York

PAST WRITER: Eric J. Moreels

PRODUCTION: Joe Frontirre

COLLECTION EDITOR: Jennifer Grünwald

EDITORIAL ASSISTANTS: James Emmett & Joe Hochstein

ASSISTANT EDITORS: Alex Starbuck & Nelson Ribeiro

EDITOR, SPECIAL PROJECTS: Mark D. Beazley

SENIOR EDITOR, SPECIAL PROJECTS: Jeff Youngquist

SENIOR VICE PRESIDENT OF SALES: David Gabriel

EDITOR IN CHIEF: Joe Quesada

PUBLISHER: Dan Buckley

EXECUTIVE PRODUCER: Alan Fine

X-MEN LEGACY: COLLISION. Contains material originally published in magazine form as X-MEN LEGACY #238-241. First printing 2011. Hardcover ISBN# 978-0-7851-4668-1. Softcover ISBN# 978-0-7851-4
Published by MARVEL WORLDWIDE, INC., a subsidiary of MARVEL ENTERTAINMENT, LLC. OFFICE OF PUBLICATION: 135 West 50th Street, New York, NY 10020. Copyright © 2010 and 2011 Marvel Characters,
rights reserved. Hardcover: $19.99 per copy in the U.S. and $22.50 in Canada (GST #R127032852). Softcover: $14.99 per copy in the U.S. and $16.99 in Canada (GST #R127032852). Canadian Agreement #406
All characters featured in this issue and the distinctive names and likenesses thereof, and all related indicia are trademarks of Marvel Characters, Inc. No similarity between any of the names, characters, persons,
institutions in this magazine with those of any living or dead person or institution is intended, and any such similarity which may exist is purely coincidental. **Printed in the U.S.A.** ALAN FINE, EVP - Office of the Pre
Marvel Worldwide, Inc. and EVP & CMO Marvel Characters B.V.; DAN BUCKLEY, Chief Executive Officer and Publisher - Print, Animation & Digital Media; JIM SOKOLOWSKI, Chief Operating Officer; DAVID GABRIEL,
Publishing Sales & Circulation; DAVID BOGART, SVP of Business Affairs & Talent Management; MICHAEL PASCIULLO, VP Merchandising & Communications; JIM O'KEEFE, VP of Operations & Logistics; DAN CARR, Exe
Director of Publishing Technology; JUSTIN F. GABRIE, Director of Publishing & Editorial Operations; SUSAN CRESPI, Editorial Operations Manager; ALEX MORALES, Publishing Operations Manager; STAN LEE, Ch
Emeritus. For information regarding advertising in Marvel Comics or on Marvel.com, please contact Ron Stern, VP of Business Development, at rstern@marvel.com. For Marvel subscription inquiries, please call 80
9158. **Manufactured between 1/10/2011 and 2/7/2011 (hardcover), and 1/10/2011 and 8/8/2011 (softcover), by R.R. DONNELLEY, INC., SALEM, VA, USA.**
10 9 8 7 6 5 4 3 2 1

PREVIOUSLY:

After a hard-fought battle against an army of mutant-slaying Nimrod Sentinels, the X-Men have saved both the city of San Francisco and the mutant messiah, Hope, from certain destruction at the hands of the super-Sentinel Bastion. With Hope safely amongst their number and a resurgence of the mutant species imminent, the X-Men turn their eyes to the future...

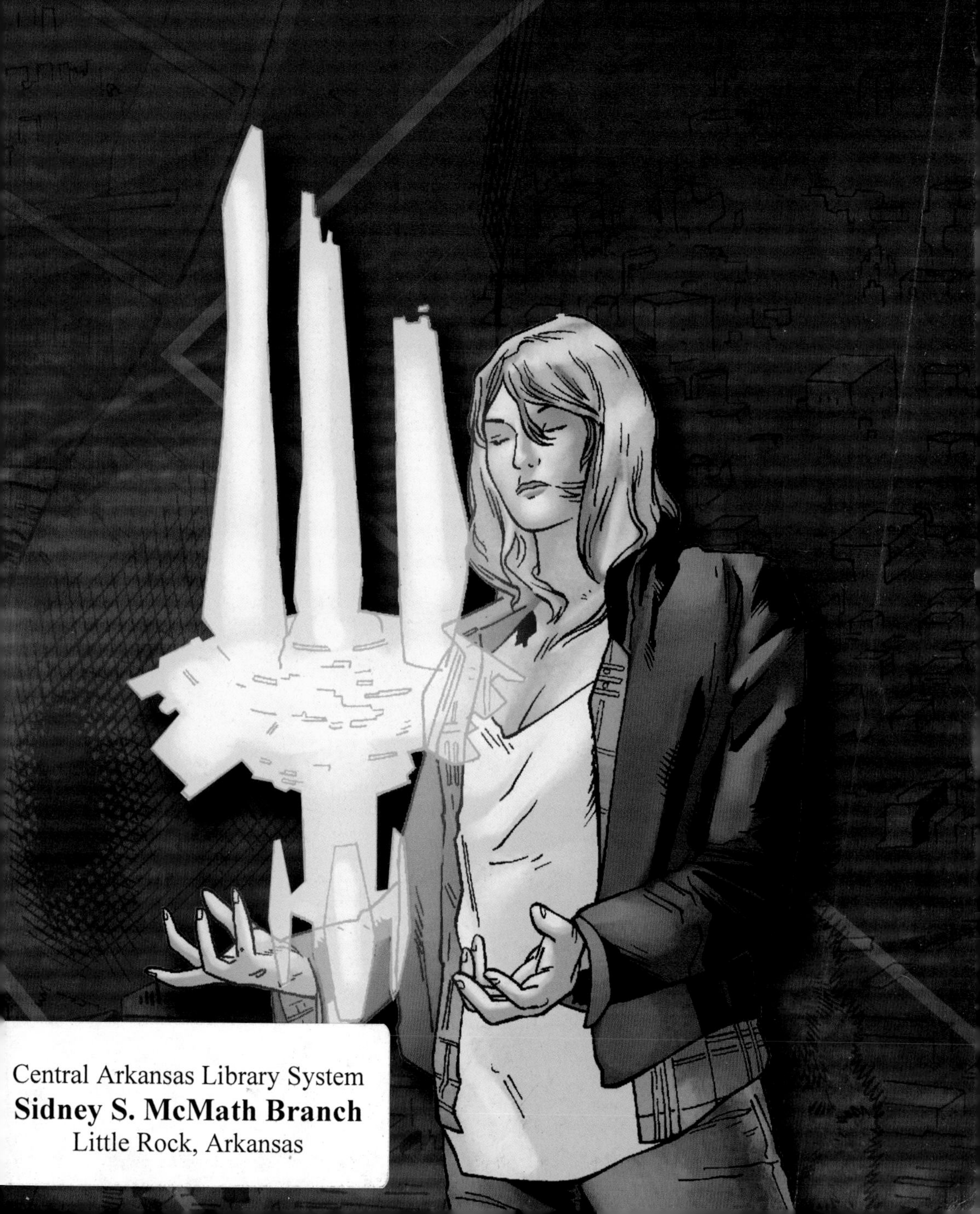

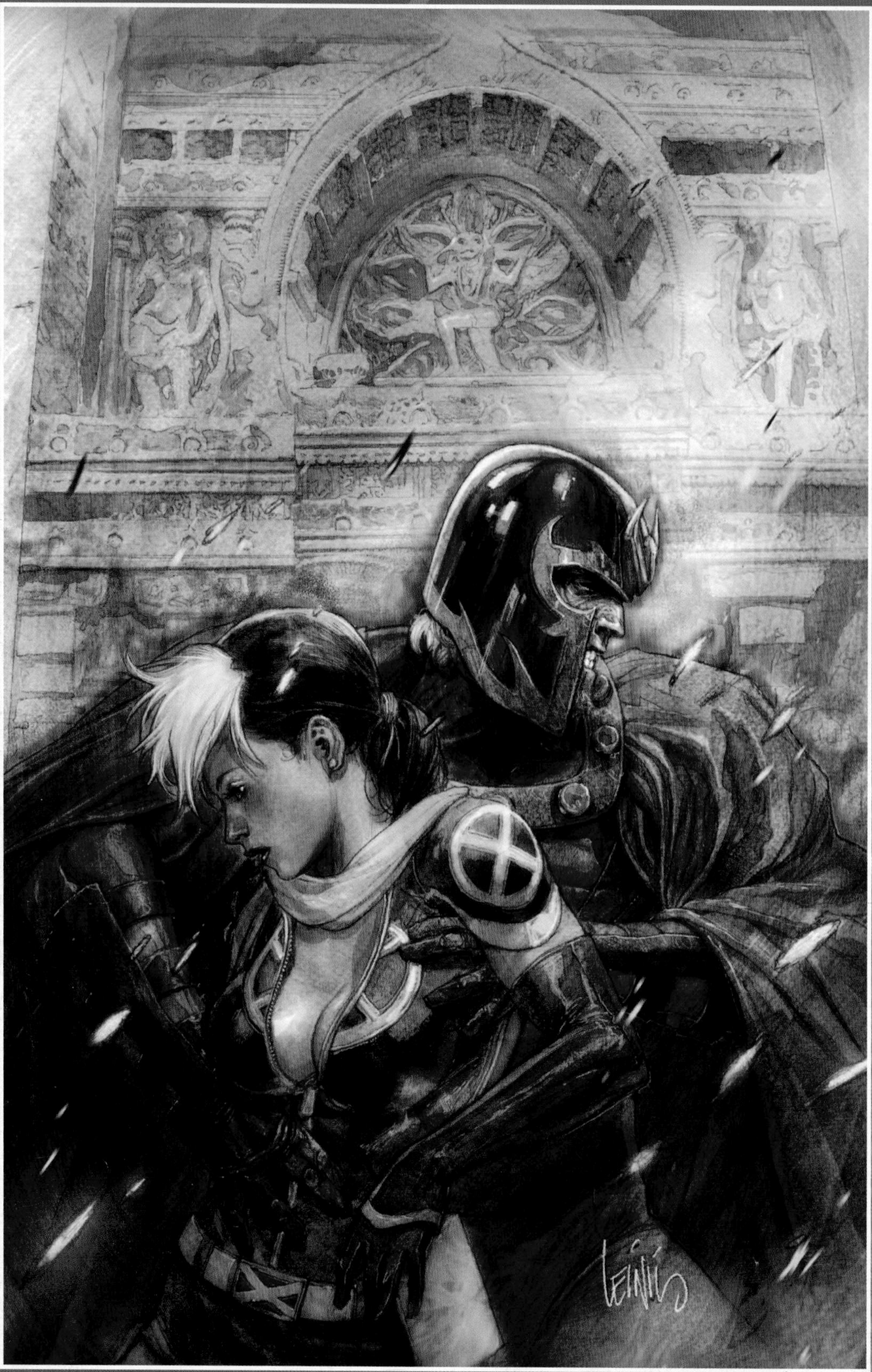

#238

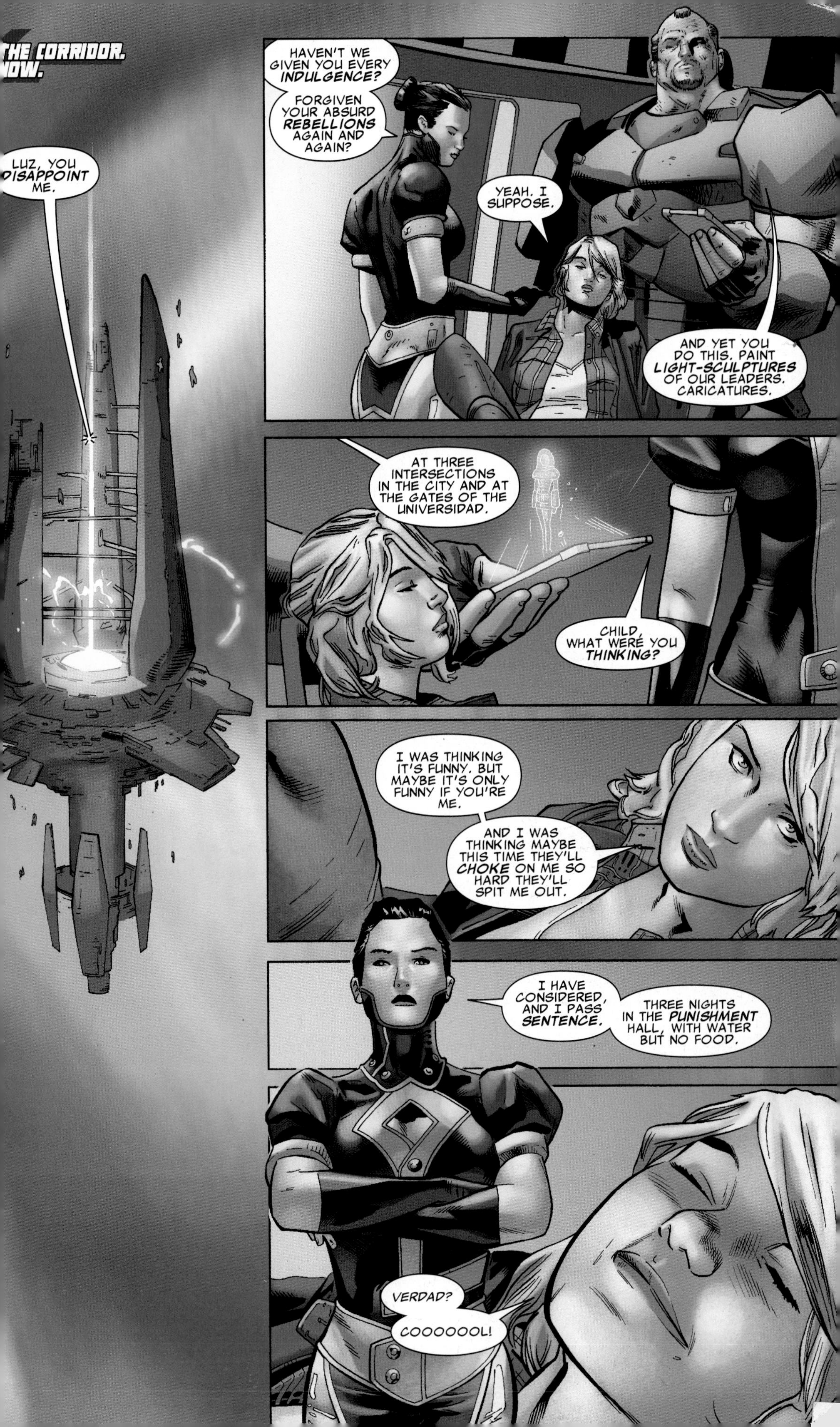
THE CORRIDOR.
NOW.
LUZ, YOU DISAPPOINT ME.
HAVEN'T WE GIVEN YOU EVERY INDULGENCE?
FORGIVEN YOUR ABSURD REBELLIONS AGAIN AND AGAIN?
YEAH. I SUPPOSE.
AND YET YOU DO THIS. PAINT LIGHT-SCULPTURES OF OUR LEADERS. CARICATURES.
AT THREE INTERSECTIONS IN THE CITY AND AT THE GATES OF THE UNIVERSIDAD.
CHILD, WHAT WERE YOU THINKING?
I WAS THINKING IT'S FUNNY. BUT MAYBE IT'S ONLY FUNNY IF YOU'RE ME.
AND I WAS THINKING MAYBE THIS TIME THEY'LL CHOKE ON ME SO HARD THEY'LL SPIT ME OUT.
I HAVE CONSIDERED, AND I PASS SENTENCE.
THREE NIGHTS IN THE PUNISHMENT HALL, WITH WATER BUT NO FOOD.
VERDAD?
COOOOOOL!

ANGELFIRE IS ALMOST READY TO GO ONLINE.

YOU KNOW THE CITY NEEDS *ENERGY*--AND YOU'LL HAVE A PLACE IN THE *THIRTY.* AREN'T YOU PROUD OF THAT?

YEAH, I'M THE HAPPIEST *COG* ON THE WHOLE WHEEL.

USE THIS TIME TO REFLECT. YOU'RE TOO *OLD,* NOW, FOR THESE 'CHILD-GAMES.

IT'S NOT A *GAME,* CORREGIDORA. IT'S *ART.*

IN THAT CASE, I APOLOGIZE. YOUR SENTENCE IS EXTENDED TO *SEVEN* NIGHTS.

NOTIFY HER *TEACHERS.* IF THIS HAPPENS AGAIN, THEY'LL BE PUNISHED TOO.

YES, BELOVED SISTER.

AND HAVE HER *PSYCH PROFILE* SENT TO MY FOCAL SPACE.

AT ONCE.

OKAY.

LET'S SEE WHAT WE CAN *DO* HERE.

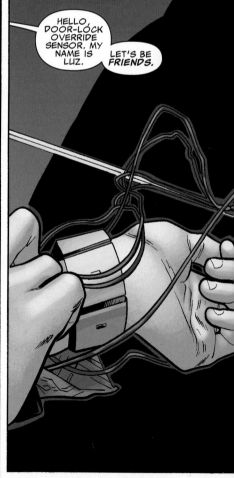

HELLO, DOOR-LOCK OVERRIDE SENSOR. MY NAME IS LUZ.

LET'S BE *FRIENDS.*

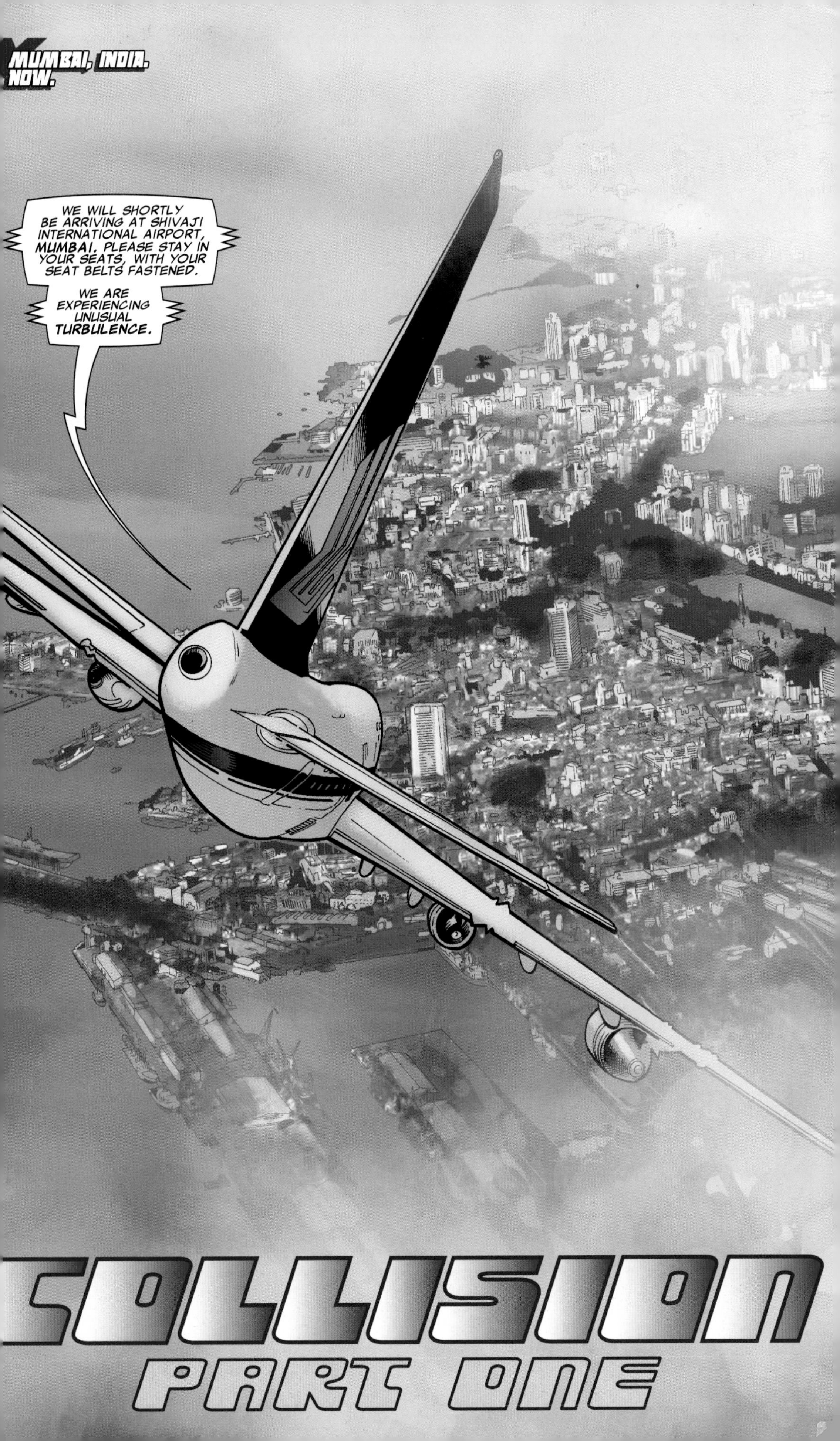
MUMBAI, INDIA. NOW.
WE WILL SHORTLY BE ARRIVING AT SHIVAJI INTERNATIONAL AIRPORT, MUMBAI. PLEASE STAY IN YOUR SEATS, WITH YOUR SEAT BELTS FASTENED.
WE ARE EXPERIENCING UNUSUAL TURBULENCE.
COLLISION
PART ONE

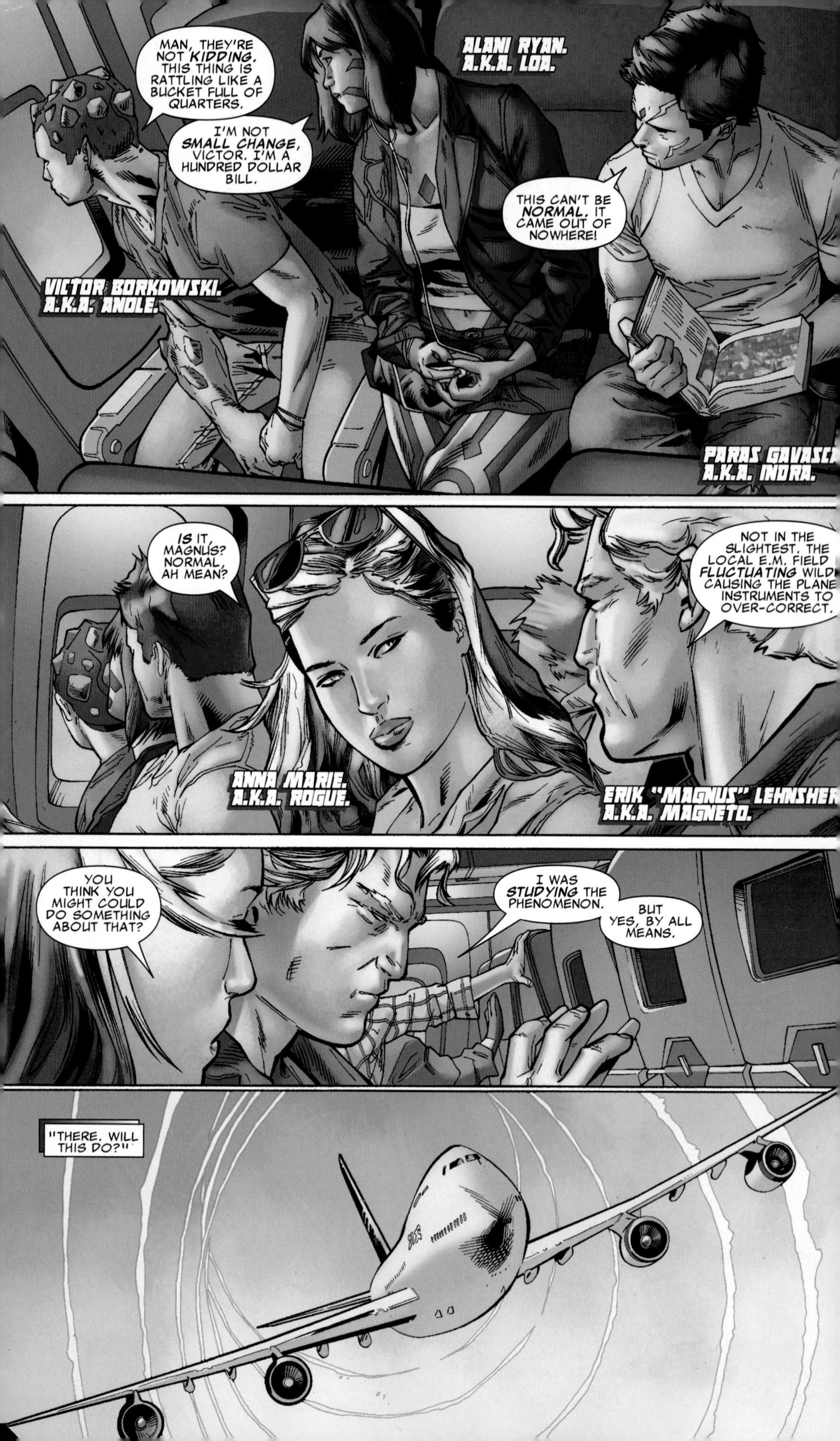

MAN, THEY'RE NOT KIDDING. THIS THING IS RATTLING LIKE A BUCKET FULL OF QUARTERS.
I'M NOT SMALL CHANGE, VICTOR. I'M A HUNDRED DOLLAR BILL.
ALANI RYAN. A.K.A. LOA.
THIS CAN'T BE NORMAL. IT CAME OUT OF NOWHERE!
VICTOR BORKOWSKI. A.K.A. ANOLE.
PARAS GAVASC A.K.A. INDRA.
IS IT, MAGNUS? NORMAL, AH MEAN?
NOT IN THE SLIGHTEST. THE LOCAL E.M. FIELD FLUCTUATING WILD CAUSING THE PLANE INSTRUMENTS TO OVER-CORRECT.
ANNA MARIE. A.K.A. ROGUE.
ERIK "MAGNUS" LEHNSHER A.K.A. MAGNETO.
YOU THINK YOU MIGHT COULD DO SOMETHING ABOUT THAT?
I WAS STUDYING THE PHENOMENON.
BUT YES, BY ALL MEANS.
"THERE. WILL THIS DO?"

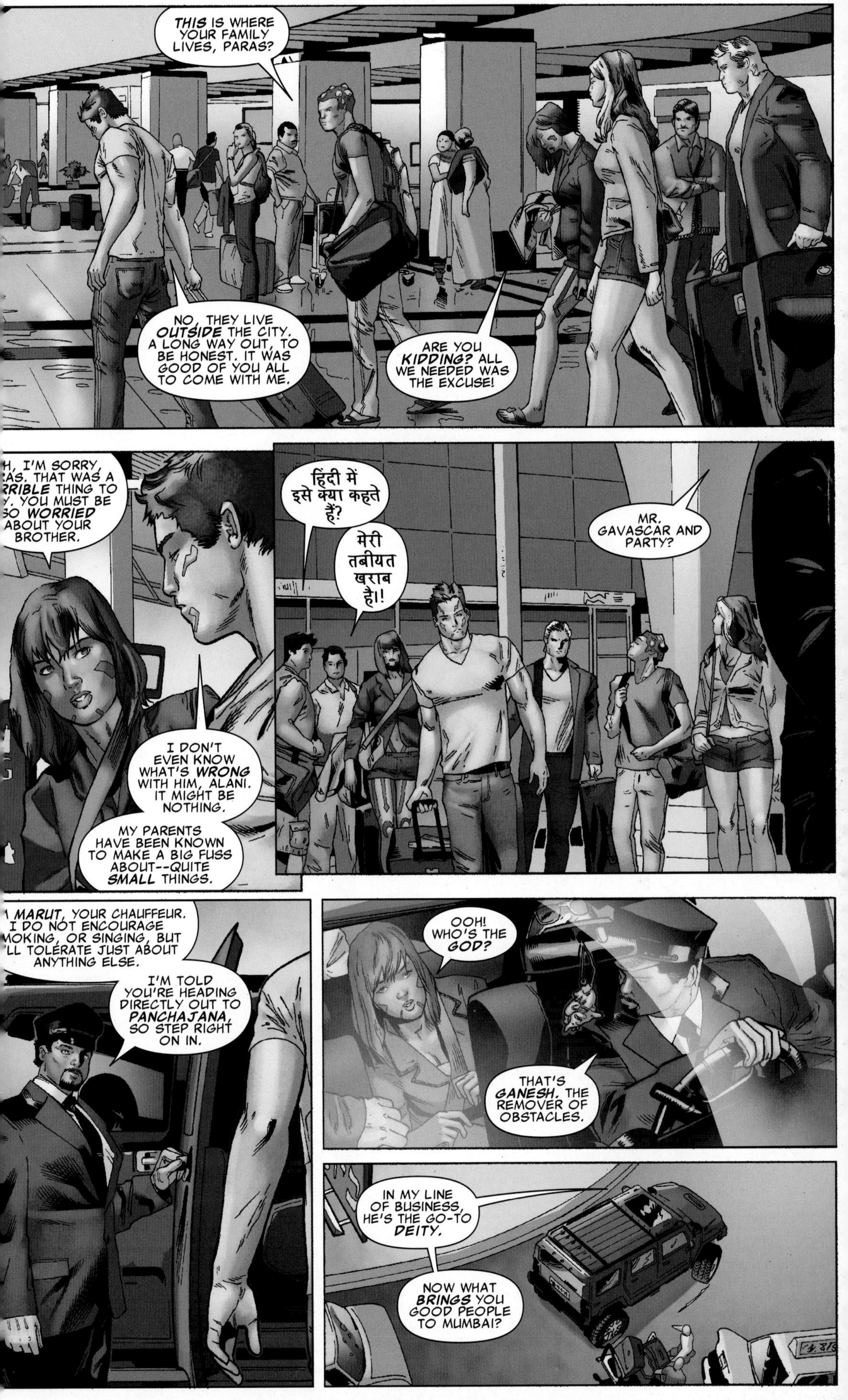
THIS IS WHERE YOUR FAMILY LIVES, PARAS?
NO, THEY LIVE OUTSIDE THE CITY. A LONG WAY OUT, TO BE HONEST. IT WAS GOOD OF YOU ALL TO COME WITH ME.
ARE YOU KIDDING? ALL WE NEEDED WAS THE EXCUSE!
H, I'M SORRY, RAS. THAT WAS A RRIBLE THING TO Y. YOU MUST BE SO WORRIED ABOUT YOUR BROTHER.
I DON'T EVEN KNOW WHAT'S WRONG WITH HIM, ALANI. IT MIGHT BE NOTHING.
MY PARENTS HAVE BEEN KNOWN TO MAKE A BIG FUSS ABOUT--QUITE SMALL THINGS.
हिंदी में इसे क्या कहते हैं?
मेरी तबीयत खराब है।!
MR. GAVASCAR AND PARTY?
I MARUT, YOUR CHAUFFEUR. I DO NOT ENCOURAGE MOKING, OR SINGING, BUT 'LL TOLERATE JUST ABOUT ANYTHING ELSE.
I'M TOLD YOU'RE HEADING DIRECTLY OUT TO PANCHAJANA, SO STEP RIGHT ON IN.
OOH! WHO'S THE GOD?
THAT'S GANESH. THE REMOVER OF OBSTACLES.
IN MY LINE OF BUSINESS, HE'S THE GO-TO DEITY.
NOW WHAT BRINGS YOU GOOD PEOPLE TO MUMBAI?

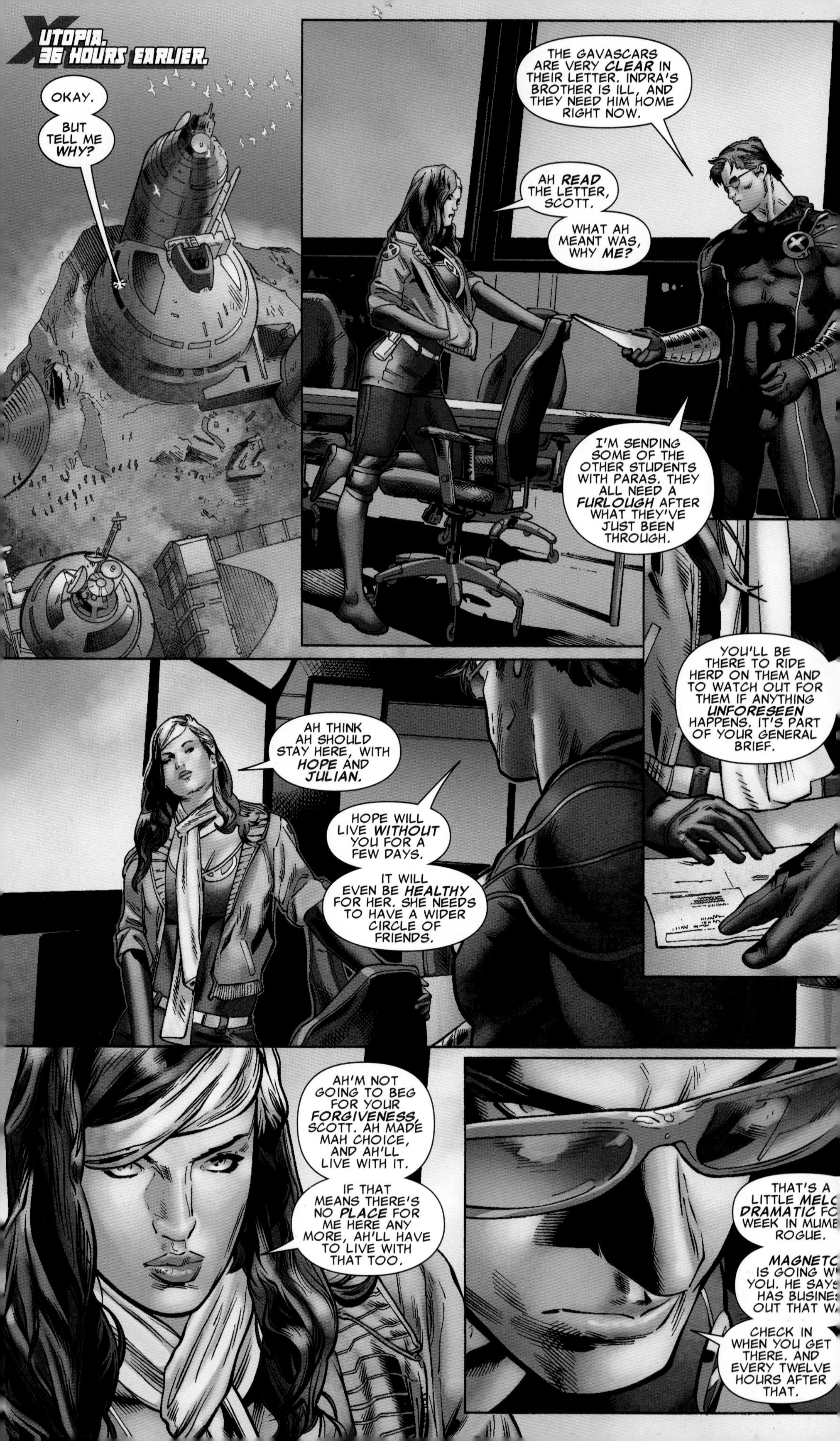
UTOPIA. 36 HOURS EARLIER.
OKAY.
BUT TELL ME WHY?
THE GAVASCARS ARE VERY CLEAR IN THEIR LETTER. INDRA'S BROTHER IS ILL, AND THEY NEED HIM HOME RIGHT NOW.
AH READ THE LETTER, SCOTT.
WHAT AH MEANT WAS, WHY ME?
I'M SENDING SOME OF THE OTHER STUDENTS WITH PARAS. THEY ALL NEED A FURLOUGH AFTER WHAT THEY'VE JUST BEEN THROUGH.
YOU'LL BE THERE TO RIDE HERD ON THEM AND TO WATCH OUT FOR THEM IF ANYTHING UNFORESEEN HAPPENS. IT'S PART OF YOUR GENERAL BRIEF.
AH THINK AH SHOULD STAY HERE, WITH HOPE AND JULIAN.
HOPE WILL LIVE WITHOUT YOU FOR A FEW DAYS.
IT WILL EVEN BE HEALTHY FOR HER. SHE NEEDS TO HAVE A WIDER CIRCLE OF FRIENDS.
AH'M NOT GOING TO BEG FOR YOUR FORGIVENESS, SCOTT. AH MADE MAH CHOICE, AND AH'LL LIVE WITH IT.
IF THAT MEANS THERE'S NO PLACE FOR ME HERE ANY MORE, AH'LL HAVE TO LIVE WITH THAT TOO.
CHECK IN WHEN YOU GET THERE. AND EVERY TWELVE HOURS AFTER THAT.

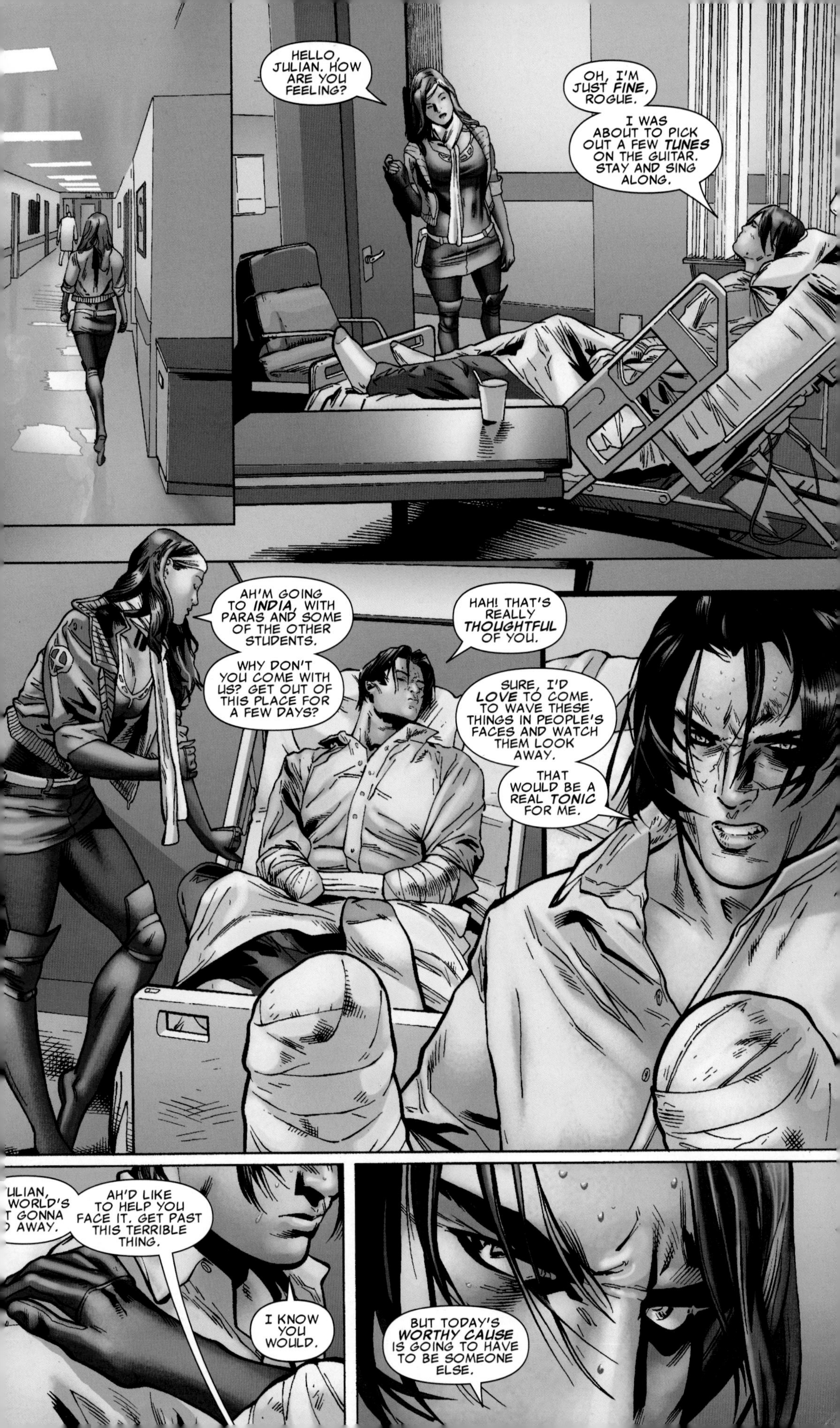
HELLO, JULIAN. HOW ARE YOU FEELING?
OH, I'M JUST FINE, ROGUE.
I WAS ABOUT TO PICK OUT A FEW TUNES ON THE GUITAR. STAY AND SING ALONG.
AH'M GOING TO INDIA, WITH PARAS AND SOME OF THE OTHER STUDENTS.
WHY DON'T YOU COME WITH US? GET OUT OF THIS PLACE FOR A FEW DAYS?
HAH! THAT'S REALLY THOUGHTFUL OF YOU.
SURE, I'D LOVE TO COME. TO WAVE THESE THINGS IN PEOPLE'S FACES AND WATCH THEM LOOK AWAY.
THAT WOULD BE A REAL TONIC FOR ME.
ULIAN, WORLD'S T GONNA AWAY.
AH'D LIKE TO HELP YOU FACE IT. GET PAST THIS TERRIBLE THING.
I KNOW YOU WOULD.
BUT TODAY'S WORTHY CAUSE IS GOING TO HAVE TO BE SOMEONE ELSE.

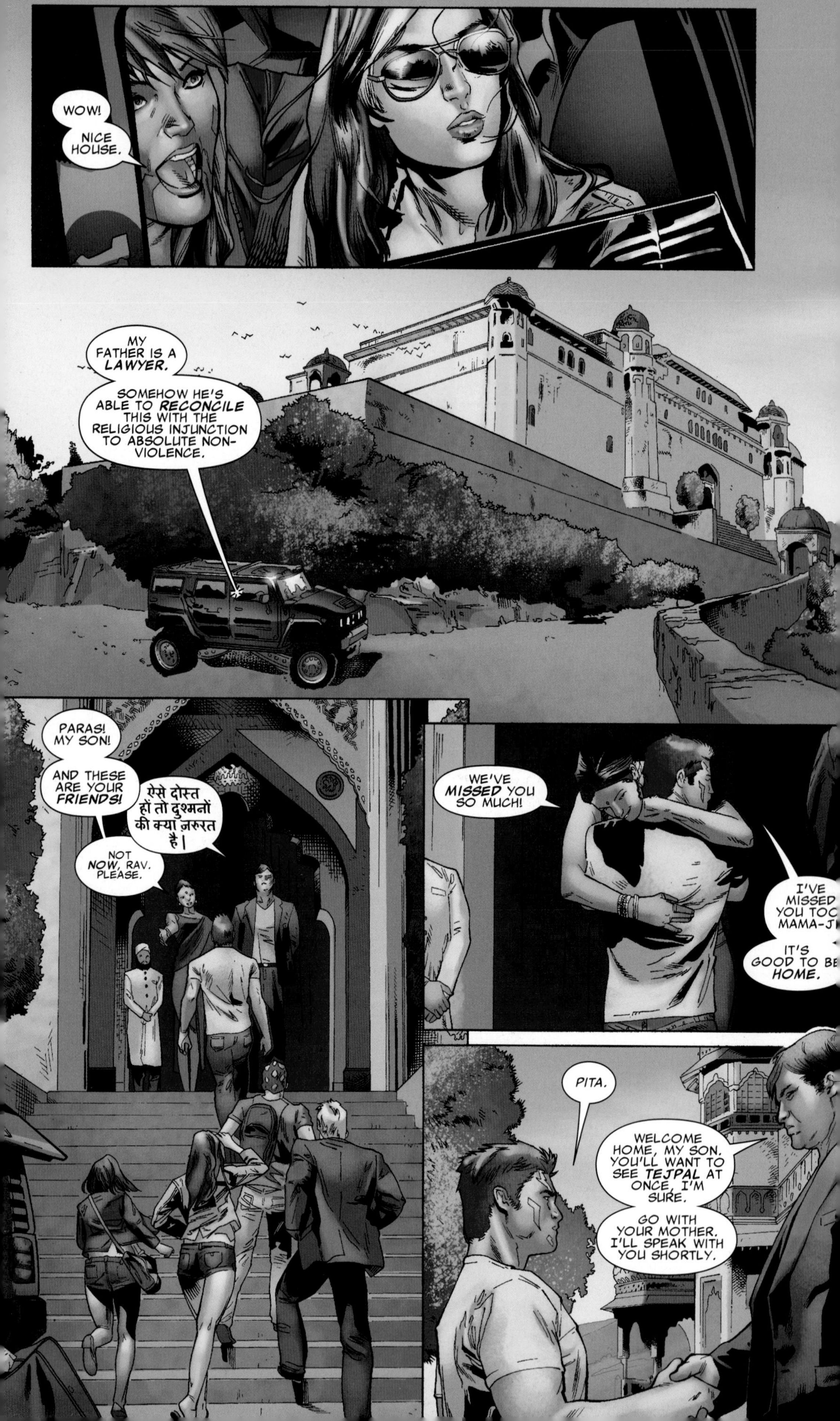
WOW!
NICE HOUSE.
MY FATHER IS A LAWYER.
SOMEHOW HE'S ABLE TO RECONCILE THIS WITH THE RELIGIOUS INJUNCTION TO ABSOLUTE NON-VIOLENCE.
PARAS! MY SON!
AND THESE ARE YOUR FRIENDS!
ऐसे दोस्त हों तो दुश्मनों की क्या ज़रुरत है।
NOT NOW, RAV. PLEASE.
WE'VE MISSED YOU SO MUCH!
I'VE MISSED YOU TOO MAMA-JI
IT'S GOOD TO BE HOME.
PITA.
WELCOME HOME, MY SON. YOU'LL WANT TO SEE TEJPAL AT ONCE, I'M SURE.
GO WITH YOUR MOTHER. I'LL SPEAK WITH YOU SHORTLY.

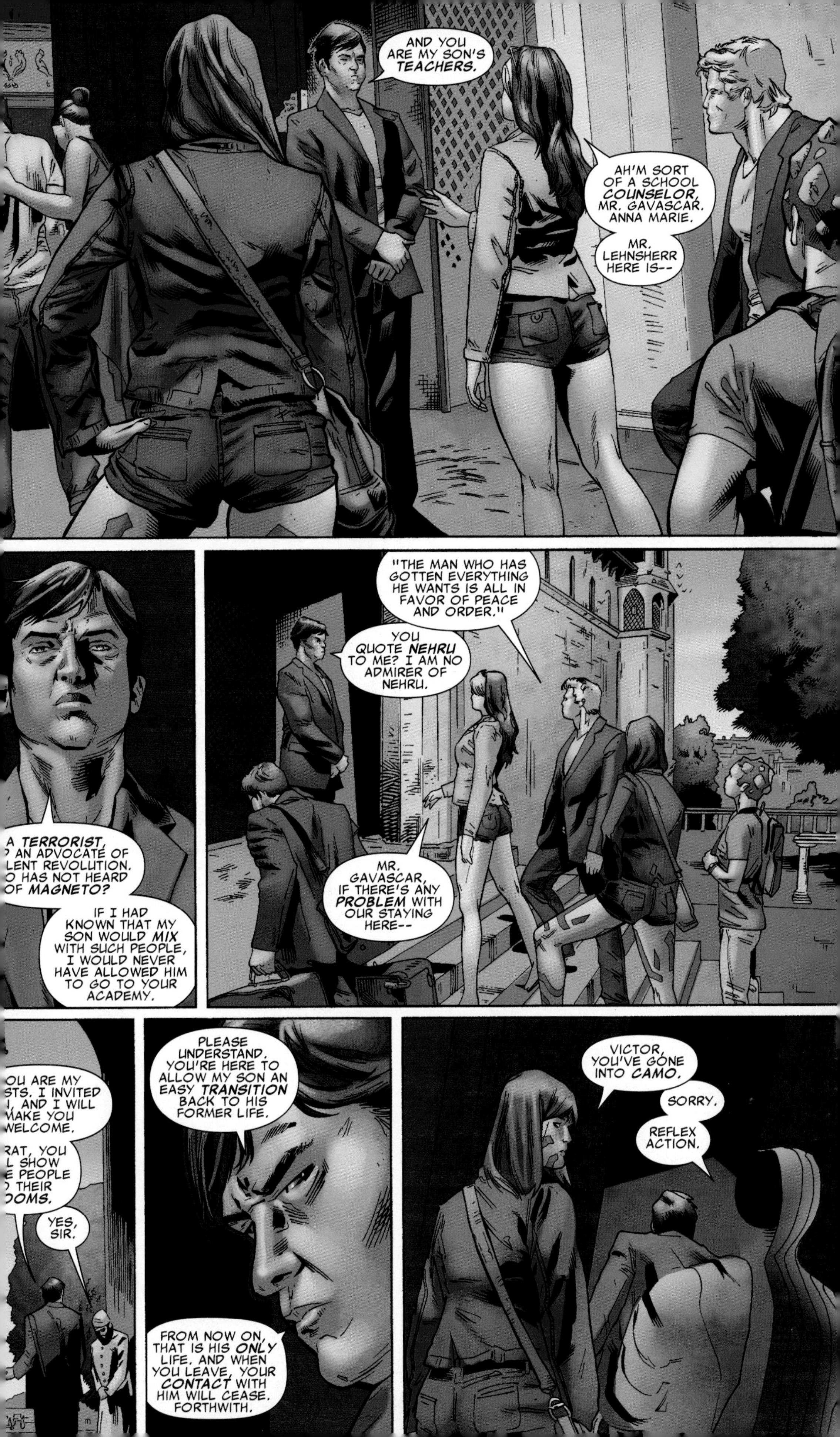
AND YOU ARE MY SON'S TEACHERS.
AH'M SORT OF A SCHOOL COUNSELOR, MR. GAVASCAR. ANNA MARIE.
MR. LEHNSHERR HERE IS--
A TERRORIST, AN ADVOCATE OF LENT REVOLUTION. O HAS NOT HEARD OF MAGNETO?
IF I HAD KNOWN THAT MY SON WOULD MIX WITH SUCH PEOPLE, I WOULD NEVER HAVE ALLOWED HIM TO GO TO YOUR ACADEMY.
"THE MAN WHO HAS GOTTEN EVERYTHING HE WANTS IS ALL IN FAVOR OF PEACE AND ORDER."
YOU QUOTE NEHRU TO ME? I AM NO ADMIRER OF NEHRU.
MR. GAVASCAR, IF THERE'S ANY PROBLEM WITH OUR STAYING HERE--
OU ARE MY STS. I INVITED I, AND I WILL MAKE YOU WELCOME.
RAT, YOU L SHOW E PEOPLE O THEIR OOMS.
YES, SIR.
PLEASE UNDERSTAND. YOU'RE HERE TO ALLOW MY SON AN EASY TRANSITION BACK TO HIS FORMER LIFE.
FROM NOW ON, THAT IS HIS ONLY LIFE. AND WHEN YOU LEAVE, YOUR CONTACT WITH HIM WILL CEASE. FORTHWITH.
VICTOR, YOU'VE GONE INTO CAMO.
SORRY.
REFLEX ACTION.

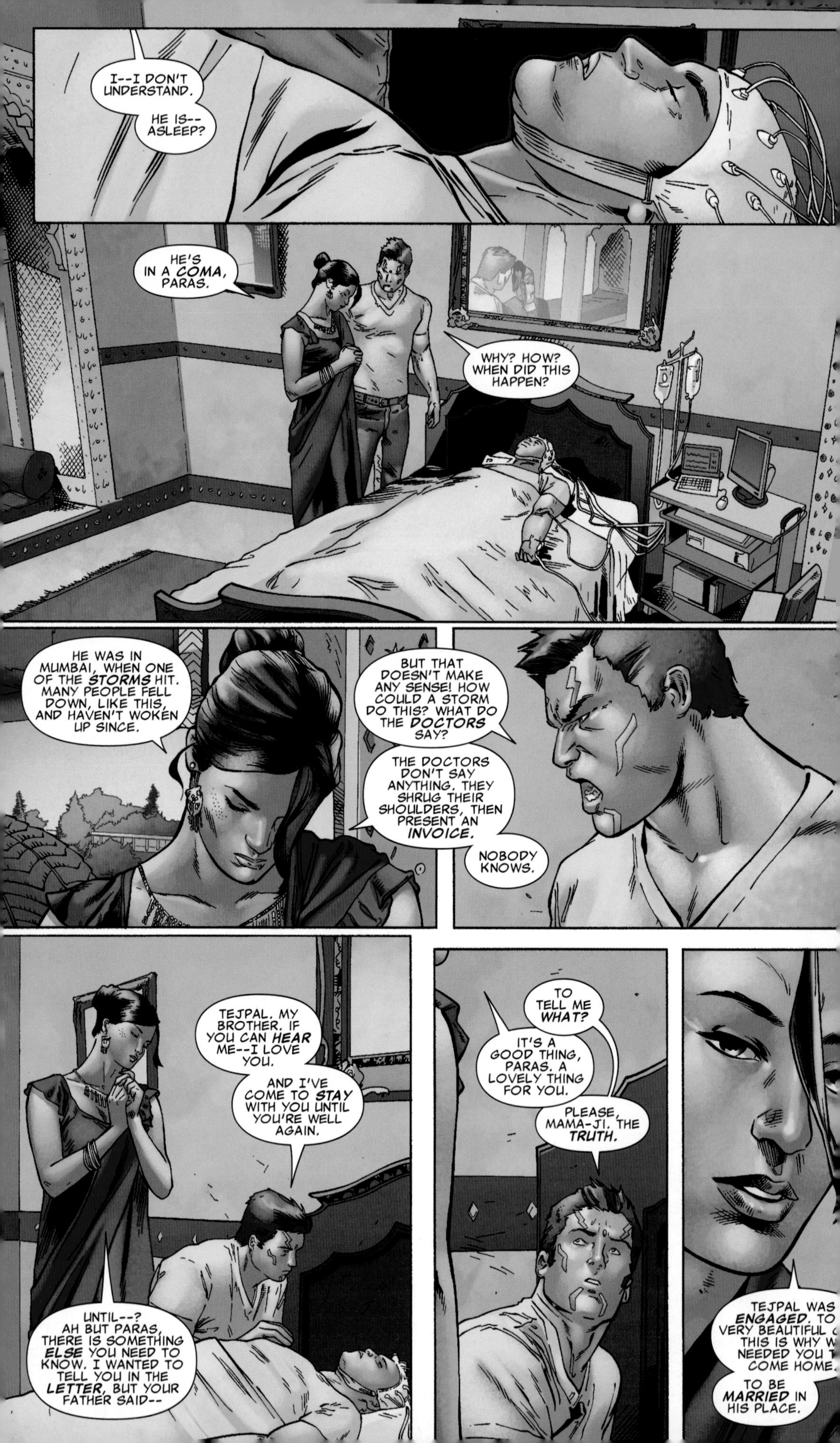
I--I DON'T UNDERSTAND.
HE IS-- ASLEEP?
HE'S IN A COMA, PARAS.
WHY? HOW? WHEN DID THIS HAPPEN?
HE WAS IN MUMBAI, WHEN ONE OF THE STORMS HIT. MANY PEOPLE FELL DOWN, LIKE THIS, AND HAVEN'T WOKEN UP SINCE.
BUT THAT DOESN'T MAKE ANY SENSE! HOW COULD A STORM DO THIS? WHAT DO THE DOCTORS SAY?
THE DOCTORS DON'T SAY ANYTHING. THEY SHRUG THEIR SHOULDERS, THEN PRESENT AN INVOICE.
NOBODY KNOWS.
TEJPAL. MY BROTHER. IF YOU CAN HEAR ME--I LOVE YOU.
AND I'VE COME TO STAY WITH YOU UNTIL YOU'RE WELL AGAIN.
UNTIL--? AH BUT PARAS, THERE IS SOMETHING ELSE YOU NEED TO KNOW. I WANTED TO TELL YOU IN THE LETTER, BUT YOUR FATHER SAID--
TO TELL ME WHAT?
IT'S A GOOD THING, PARAS. A LOVELY THING FOR YOU.
PLEASE, MAMA-JI. THE TRUTH.
TEJPAL WAS ENGAGED. TO VERY BEAUTIFUL
THIS IS WHY W NEEDED YOU COME HOME.
TO BE MARRIED IN HIS PLACE.

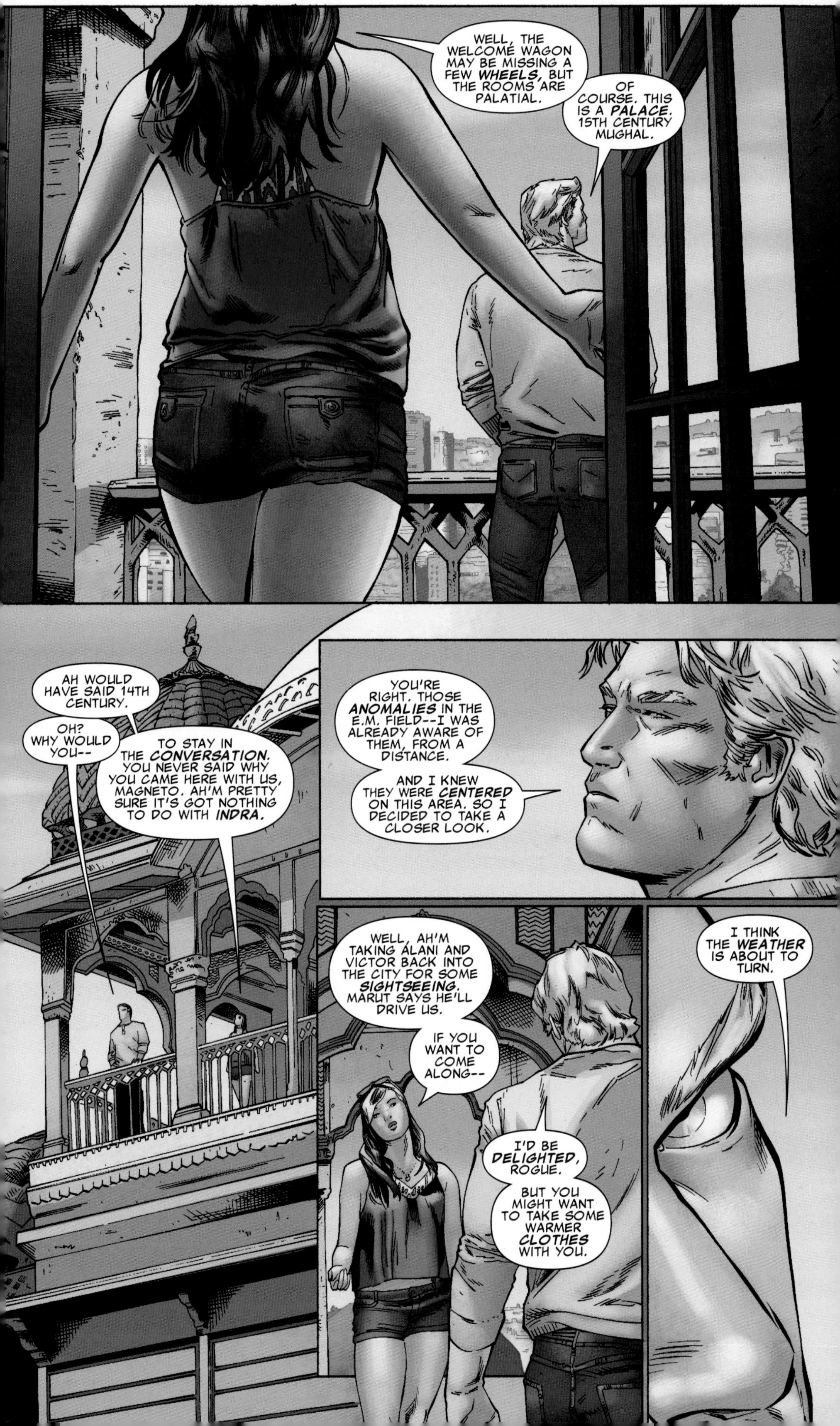
WELL, THE WELCOME WAGON MAY BE MISSING A FEW WHEELS, BUT THE ROOMS ARE PALATIAL.
OF COURSE. THIS IS A PALACE. 15TH CENTURY MUGHAL.
AH WOULD HAVE SAID 14TH CENTURY.
OH? WHY WOULD YOU--
TO STAY IN THE CONVERSATION. YOU NEVER SAID WHY YOU CAME HERE WITH US, MAGNETO. AH'M PRETTY SURE IT'S GOT NOTHING TO DO WITH INDRA.
YOU'RE RIGHT. THOSE ANOMALIES IN THE E.M. FIELD--I WAS ALREADY AWARE OF THEM, FROM A DISTANCE.
AND I KNEW THEY WERE CENTERED ON THIS AREA, SO I DECIDED TO TAKE A CLOSER LOOK.
WELL, AH'M TAKING ALANI AND VICTOR BACK INTO THE CITY FOR SOME SIGHTSEEING. MARUT SAYS HE'LL DRIVE US.
IF YOU WANT TO COME ALONG--
I'D BE DELIGHTED, ROGUE.
BUT YOU MIGHT WANT TO TAKE SOME WARMER CLOTHES WITH YOU.
I THINK THE WEATHER IS ABOUT TO TURN.

CORREGIDORA--

COME IN, MARTILLO. IT'S MY TURN TO MONITOR THE ANCHOR TONIGHT.

DOESN'T IT AMUSE YOU THAT A CITY AS MAGNIFICENT AS OURS SHOULD BE TETHERED LIKE A BALLOON TO THE SIDE OF ITS PARENT UNIVERSE?

BELOVED SISTER--I HATE TO DISTURB YOU AT YOUR LABORS.

LUZ HAS *DISAPPEARED* FROM HER CELL.

ESCAPED, YOU MEAN? THEN *TRACK* HER AND PUT HER BACK.

WE READ HER IN THE VENTS, BUT SHE'S TOO CLOSE TO THE *MEMBRANE* TO BE PURSUED.

PROBABLY SHE'LL *RETURN* WHEN SHE REALIZES THAT THERE'S NO ESCAPE THAT WAY.

EXCEPT THAT THERE *IS.*

WELL, ONLY IF--

YOU'RE NOT *SUGGESTING* THAT SHE WOULD--

YOU FORGET, MARTILLO. LUZ IS AN ARTIST. PRACTICALITIES DON'T *CONCERN* HER OVERMUCH.

THERE! SHE INTENDS TO *JUMP*, AND TAKE HER CHANCES.

SHE KNOWS WE CAN'T *FOLL* SHE BELIEVES S HAVE TIME TO G GROUND, ON *OTHER* SIDE OF MEMBRANE.

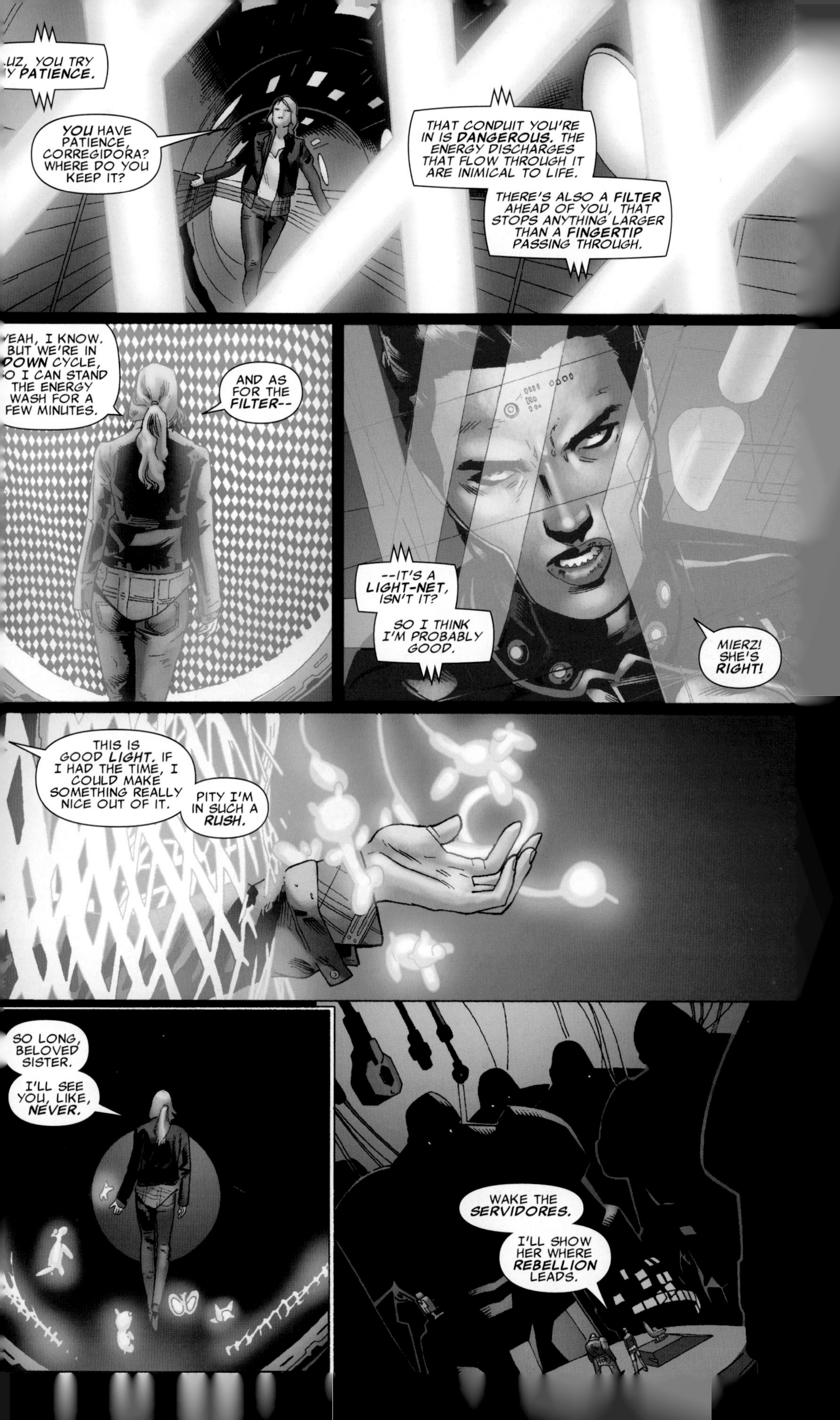

..UZ, YOU TRY ..Y PATIENCE.
YOU HAVE PATIENCE, CORREGIDORA? WHERE DO YOU KEEP IT?
THAT CONDUIT YOU'RE IN IS DANGEROUS. THE ENERGY DISCHARGES THAT FLOW THROUGH IT ARE INIMICAL TO LIFE.
THERE'S ALSO A FILTER AHEAD OF YOU, THAT STOPS ANYTHING LARGER THAN A FINGERTIP PASSING THROUGH.
..EAH, I KNOW. BUT WE'RE IN ..DOWN CYCLE, ..O I CAN STAND THE ENERGY WASH FOR A FEW MINUTES.
AND AS FOR THE FILTER--
--IT'S A LIGHT-NET, ISN'T IT?
SO I THINK I'M PROBABLY GOOD.
MIERZ! SHE'S RIGHT!
THIS IS GOOD LIGHT. IF I HAD THE TIME, I COULD MAKE SOMETHING REALLY NICE OUT OF IT.
PITY I'M IN SUCH A RUSH.
SO LONG, BELOVED SISTER.
I'LL SEE YOU, LIKE, NEVER.
WAKE THE SERVIDORES.
I'LL SHOW HER WHERE REBELLION LEADS.

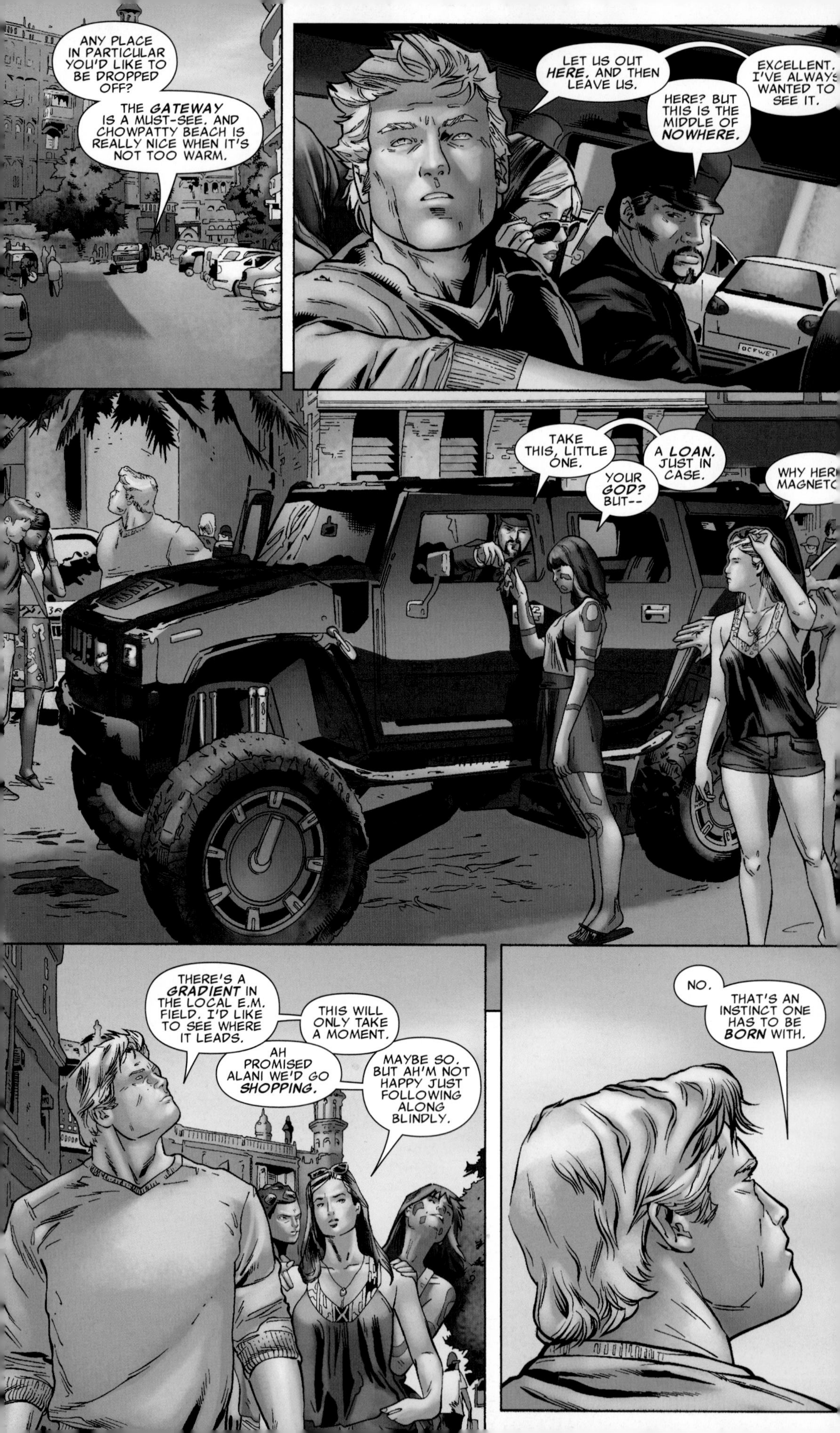
ANY PLACE IN PARTICULAR YOU'D LIKE TO BE DROPPED OFF?
THE ***GATEWAY*** IS A MUST-SEE. AND CHOWPATTY BEACH IS REALLY NICE WHEN IT'S NOT TOO WARM.
LET US OUT ***HERE***, AND THEN LEAVE US.
HERE? BUT THIS IS THE MIDDLE OF ***NOWHERE***.
EXCELLENT. I'VE ALWAYS WANTED TO SEE IT.
TAKE THIS, LITTLE ONE.
YOUR ***GOD?*** BUT--
A ***LOAN***. JUST IN CASE.
WHY HER MAGNETO
THERE'S A ***GRADIENT*** IN THE LOCAL E.M. FIELD. I'D LIKE TO SEE WHERE IT LEADS.
THIS WILL ONLY TAKE A MOMENT.
AH PROMISED ALANI WE'D GO ***SHOPPING***.
MAYBE SO. BUT AH'M NOT HAPPY JUST FOLLOWING ALONG BLINDLY.
NO.
THAT'S AN INSTINCT ONE HAS TO BE ***BORN*** WITH.

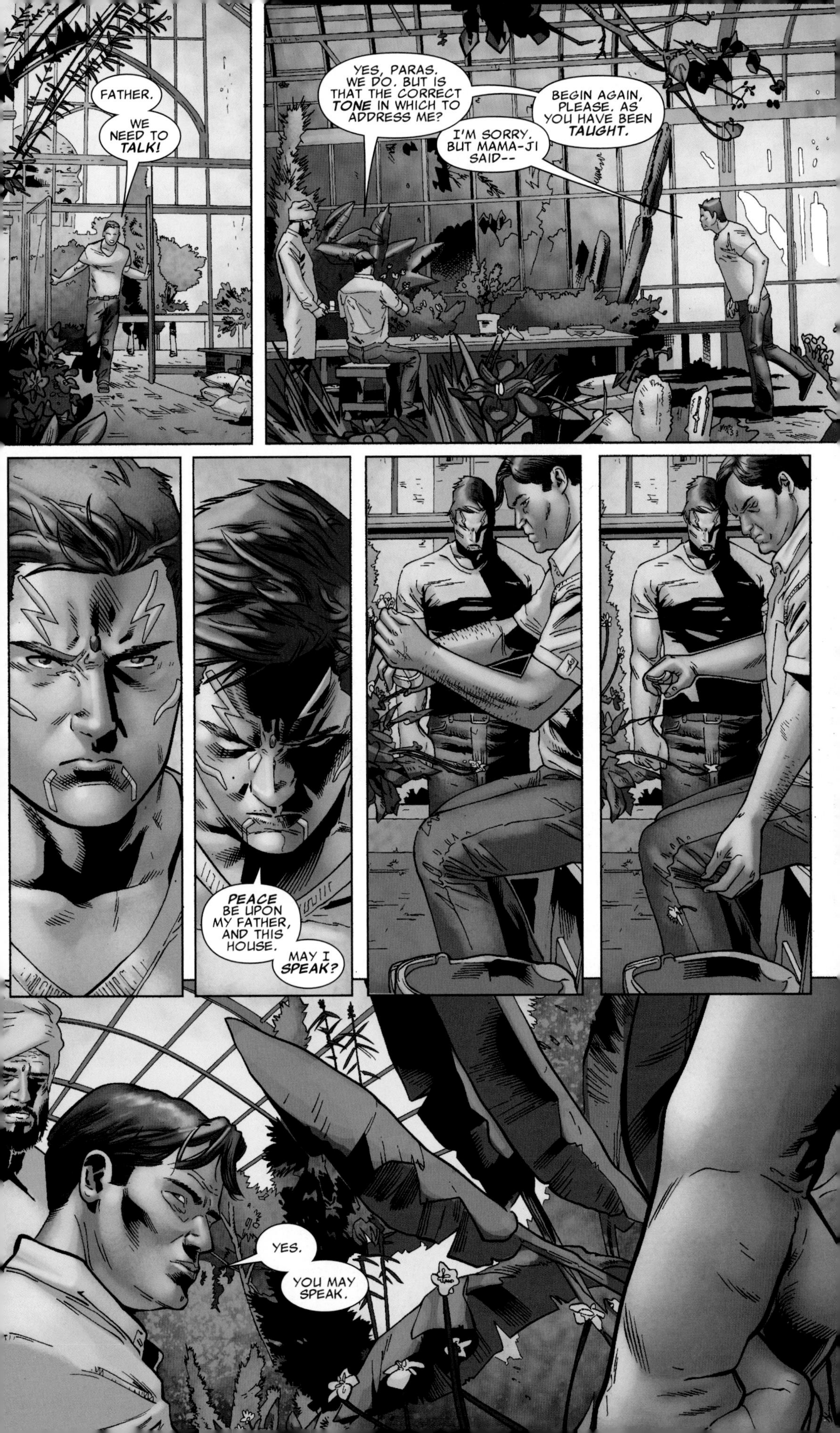
FATHER.
WE NEED TO TALK!
YES, PARAS. WE DO. BUT IS THAT THE CORRECT TONE IN WHICH TO ADDRESS ME?
I'M SORRY. BUT MAMA-JI SAID--
BEGIN AGAIN, PLEASE. AS YOU HAVE BEEN TAUGHT.
PEACE BE UPON MY FATHER, AND THIS HOUSE.
MAY I SPEAK?
YES.
YOU MAY SPEAK.

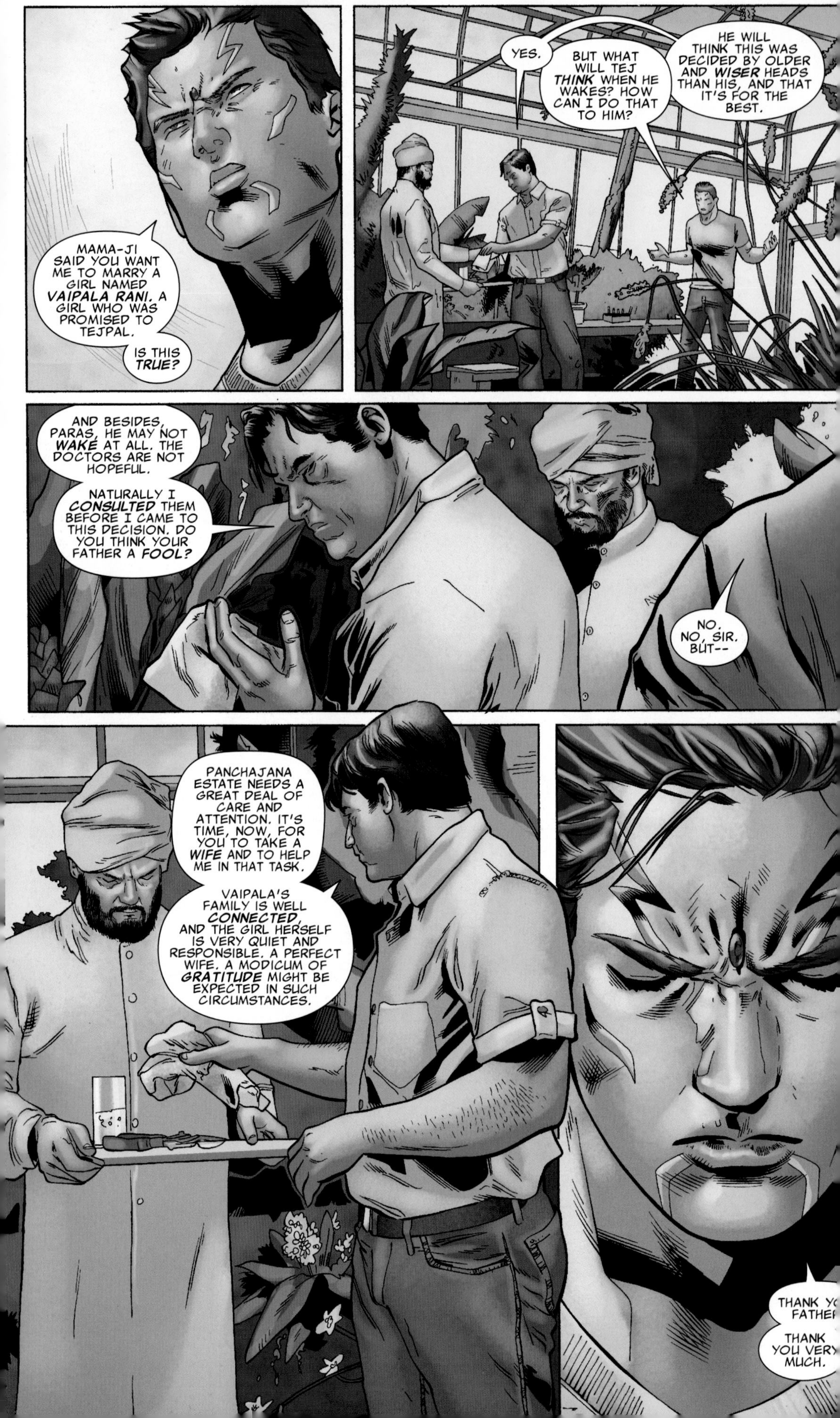
MAMA-JI SAID YOU WANT ME TO MARRY A GIRL NAMED VAIPALA RANI. A GIRL WHO WAS PROMISED TO TEJPAL.
IS THIS TRUE?
YES.
BUT WHAT WILL TEJ THINK WHEN HE WAKES? HOW CAN I DO THAT TO HIM?
HE WILL THINK THIS WAS DECIDED BY OLDER AND WISER HEADS THAN HIS, AND THAT IT'S FOR THE BEST.
AND BESIDES, PARAS, HE MAY NOT WAKE AT ALL. THE DOCTORS ARE NOT HOPEFUL.
NATURALLY I CONSULTED THEM BEFORE I CAME TO THIS DECISION. DO YOU THINK YOUR FATHER A FOOL?
NO. NO, SIR. BUT--
PANCHAJANA ESTATE NEEDS A GREAT DEAL OF CARE AND ATTENTION. IT'S TIME, NOW, FOR YOU TO TAKE A WIFE AND TO HELP ME IN THAT TASK.
VAIPALA'S FAMILY IS WELL CONNECTED, AND THE GIRL HERSELF IS VERY QUIET AND RESPONSIBLE. A PERFECT WIFE. A MODICUM OF GRATITUDE MIGHT BE EXPECTED IN SUCH CIRCUMSTANCES.
THANK YO FATHE
THANK YOU VERY MUCH.

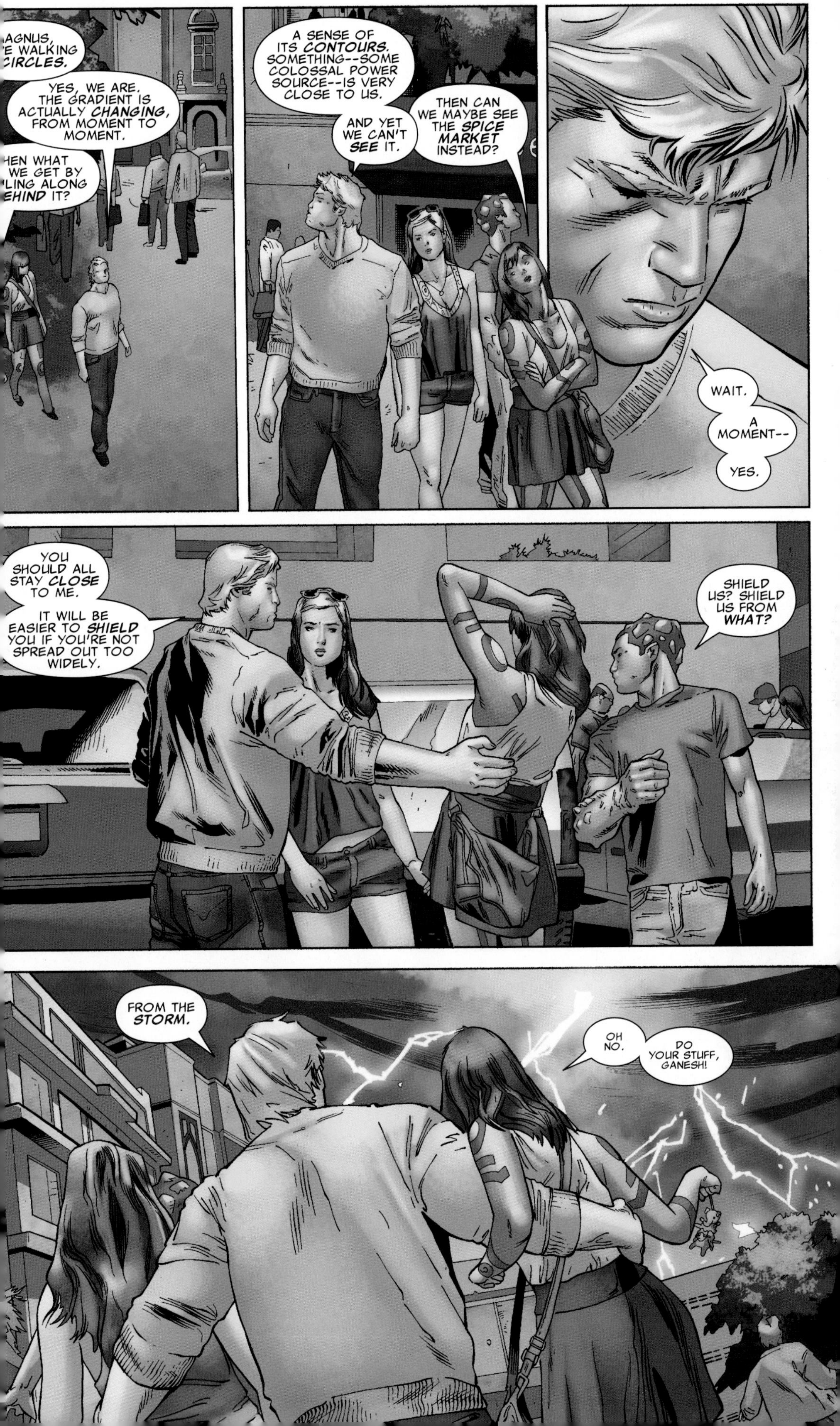

AGNUS, 'E WALKING CIRCLES.
YES, WE ARE. THE GRADIENT IS ACTUALLY CHANGING, FROM MOMENT TO MOMENT.
HEN WHAT WE GET BY 'LING ALONG EHIND IT?
A SENSE OF ITS CONTOURS. SOMETHING--SOME COLOSSAL POWER SOURCE--IS VERY CLOSE TO US.
AND YET WE CAN'T SEE IT.
THEN CAN WE MAYBE SEE THE SPICE MARKET INSTEAD?
WAIT.
A MOMENT--
YES.
YOU SHOULD ALL STAY CLOSE TO ME.
IT WILL BE EASIER TO SHIELD YOU IF YOU'RE NOT SPREAD OUT TOO WIDELY.
SHIELD US? SHIELD US FROM WHAT?
FROM THE STORM.
OH NO.
DO YOUR STUFF, GANESH!

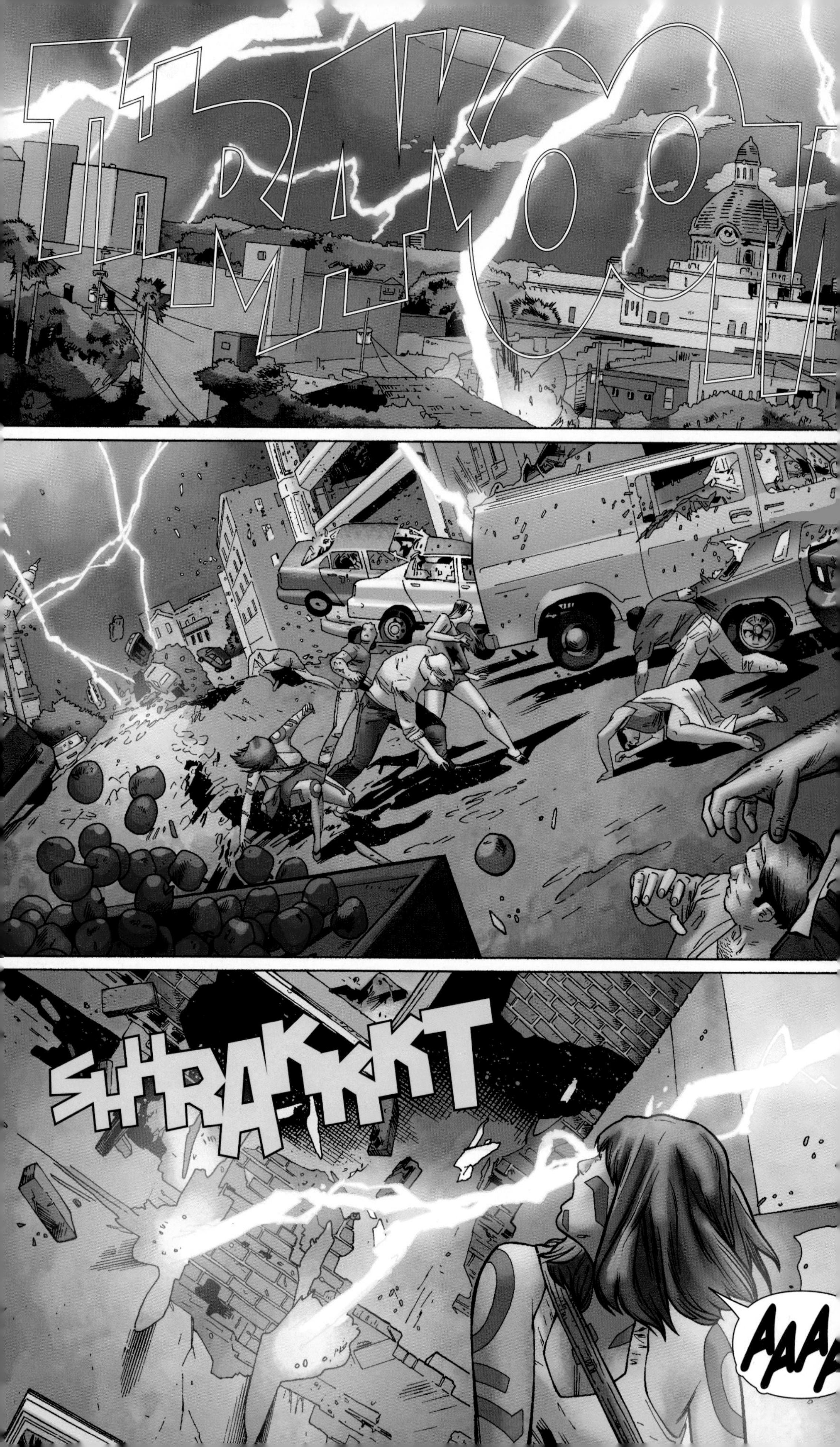

THRAKOOOM
SHRAKKKT
AAA

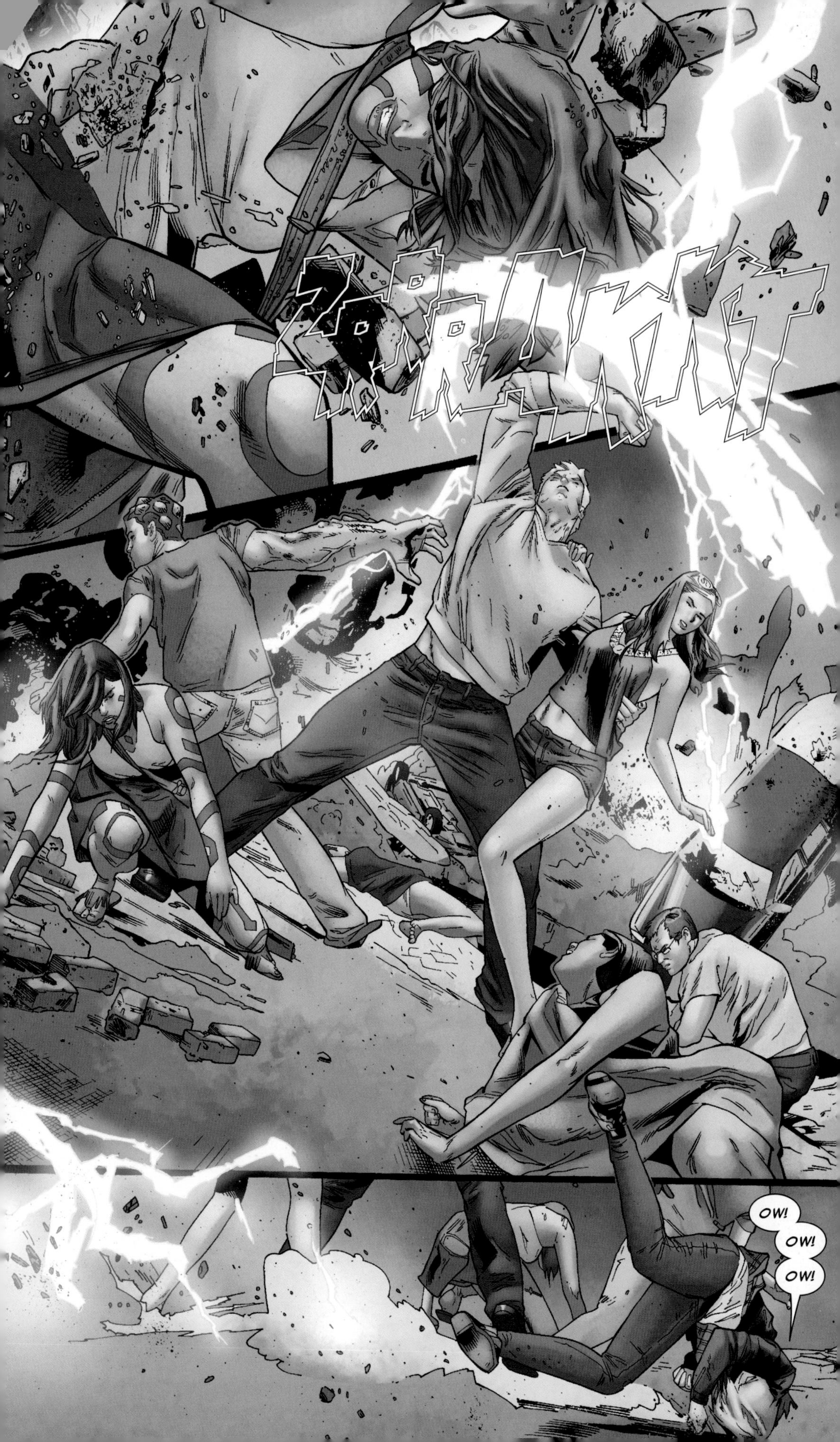
OW!
OW!
OW!

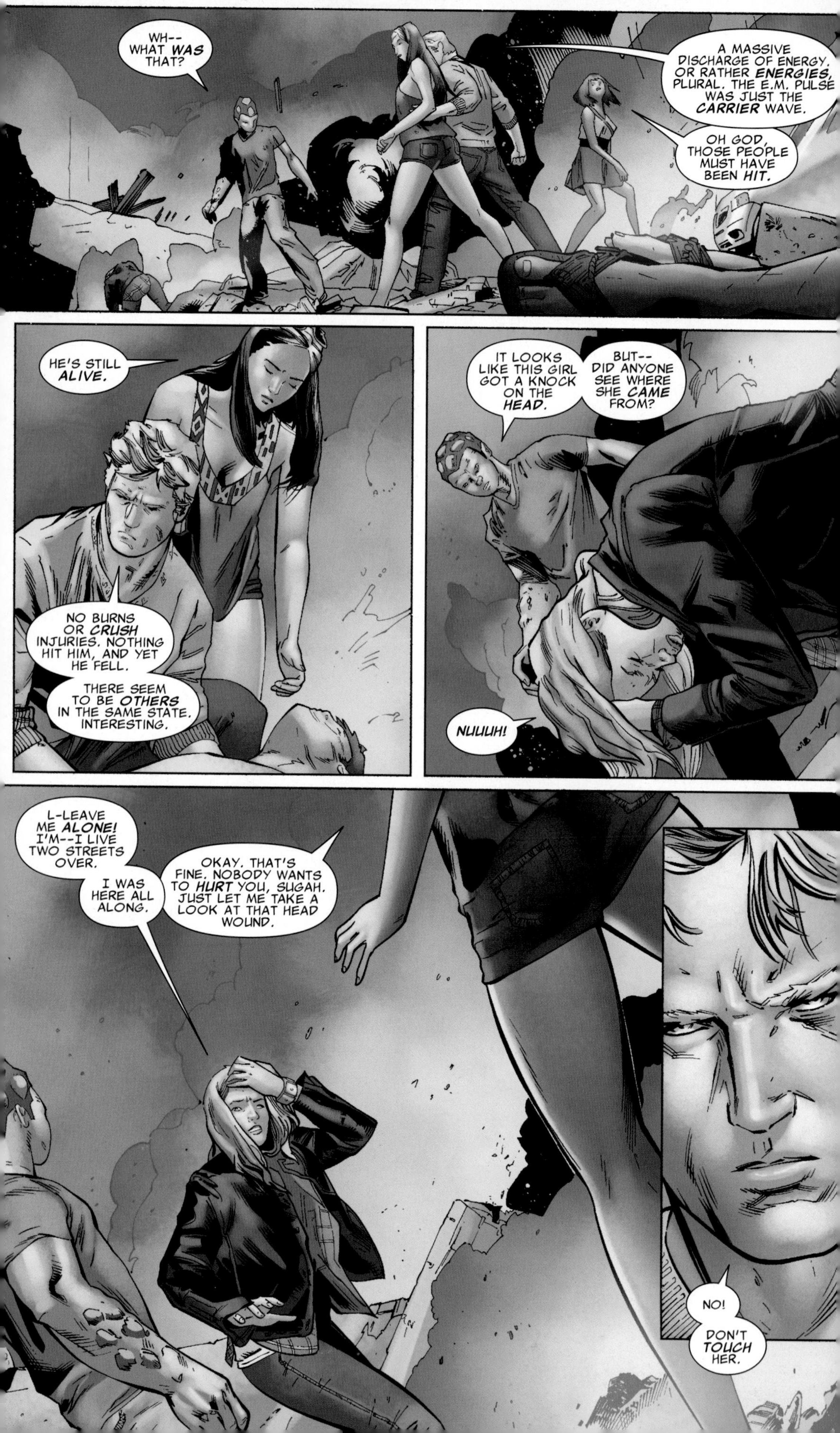
WH-- WHAT WAS THAT?
A MASSIVE DISCHARGE OF ENERGY. OR RATHER ENERGIES, PLURAL. THE E.M. PULSE WAS JUST THE CARRIER WAVE.
OH GOD, THOSE PEOPLE MUST HAVE BEEN HIT.
HE'S STILL ALIVE.
NO BURNS OR CRUSH INJURIES. NOTHING HIT HIM, AND YET HE FELL.
THERE SEEM TO BE OTHERS IN THE SAME STATE. INTERESTING.
IT LOOKS LIKE THIS GIRL GOT A KNOCK ON THE HEAD.
BUT-- DID ANYONE SEE WHERE SHE CAME FROM?
NUUUH!
L-LEAVE ME ALONE! I'M--I LIVE TWO STREETS OVER.
I WAS HERE ALL ALONG.
OKAY. THAT'S FINE. NOBODY WANTS TO HURT YOU, SUGAH. JUST LET ME TAKE A LOOK AT THAT HEAD WOUND.
NO!
DON'T TOUCH HER.

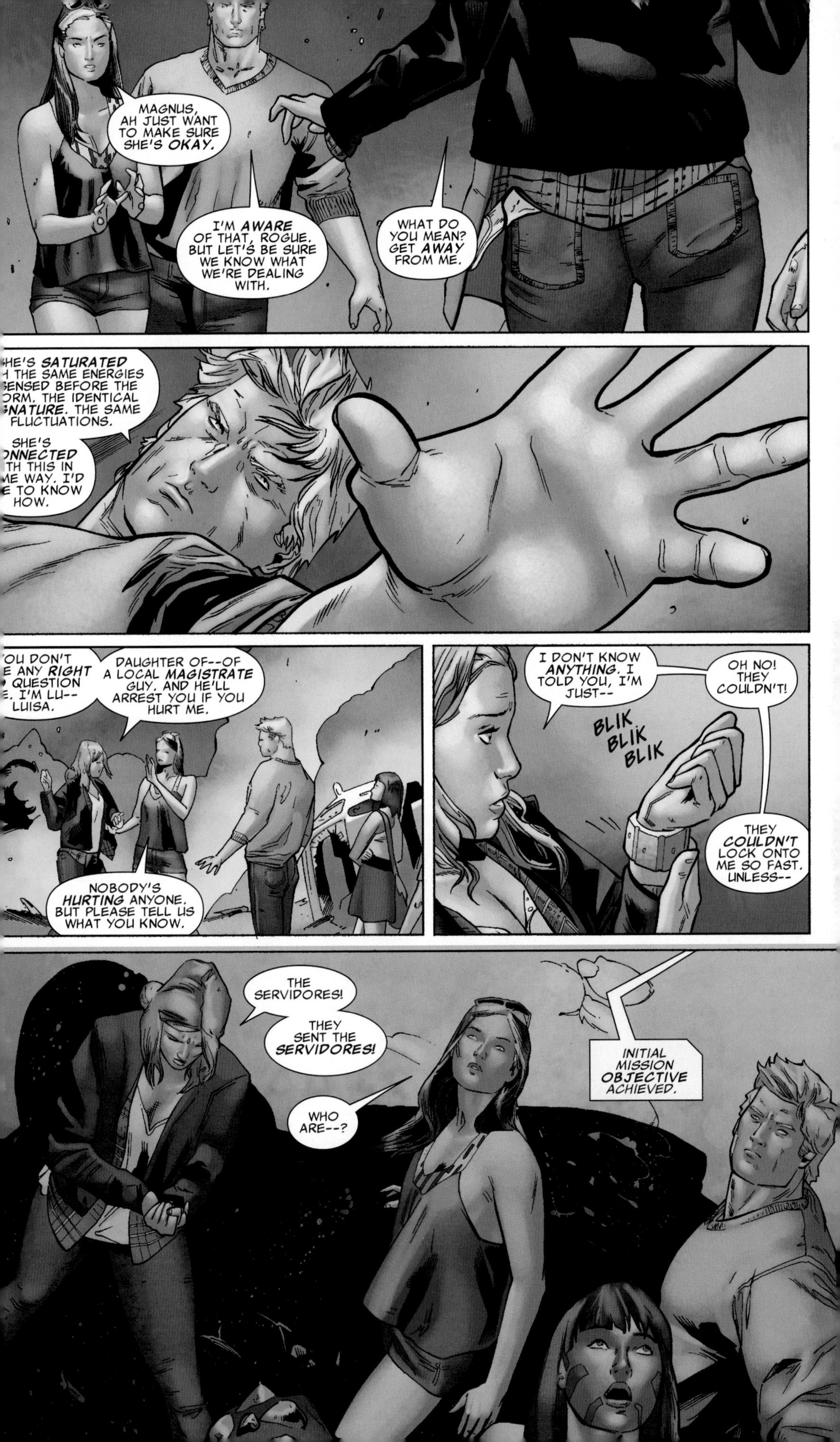
MAGNUS, AH JUST WANT TO MAKE SURE SHE'S OKAY.
I'M AWARE OF THAT, ROGUE. BUT LET'S BE SURE WE KNOW WHAT WE'RE DEALING WITH.
WHAT DO YOU MEAN? GET AWAY FROM ME.
HE'S SATURATED H THE SAME ENERGIES SENSED BEFORE THE ORM. THE IDENTICAL NATURE. THE SAME FLUCTUATIONS.
SHE'S ONNECTED TH THIS IN ME WAY. I'D E TO KNOW HOW.
OU DON'T E ANY RIGHT QUESTION E. I'M LU-- LUISA.
DAUGHTER OF--OF A LOCAL MAGISTRATE GUY. AND HE'LL ARREST YOU IF YOU HURT ME.
NOBODY'S HURTING ANYONE. BUT PLEASE TELL US WHAT YOU KNOW.
I DON'T KNOW ANYTHING. I TOLD YOU, I'M JUST--
BLIK BLIK BLIK
OH NO! THEY COULDN'T!
THEY COULDN'T LOCK ONTO ME SO FAST. UNLESS--
THE SERVIDORES!
THEY SENT THE SERVIDORES!
WHO ARE--?
INITIAL MISSION OBJECTIVE ACHIEVED.

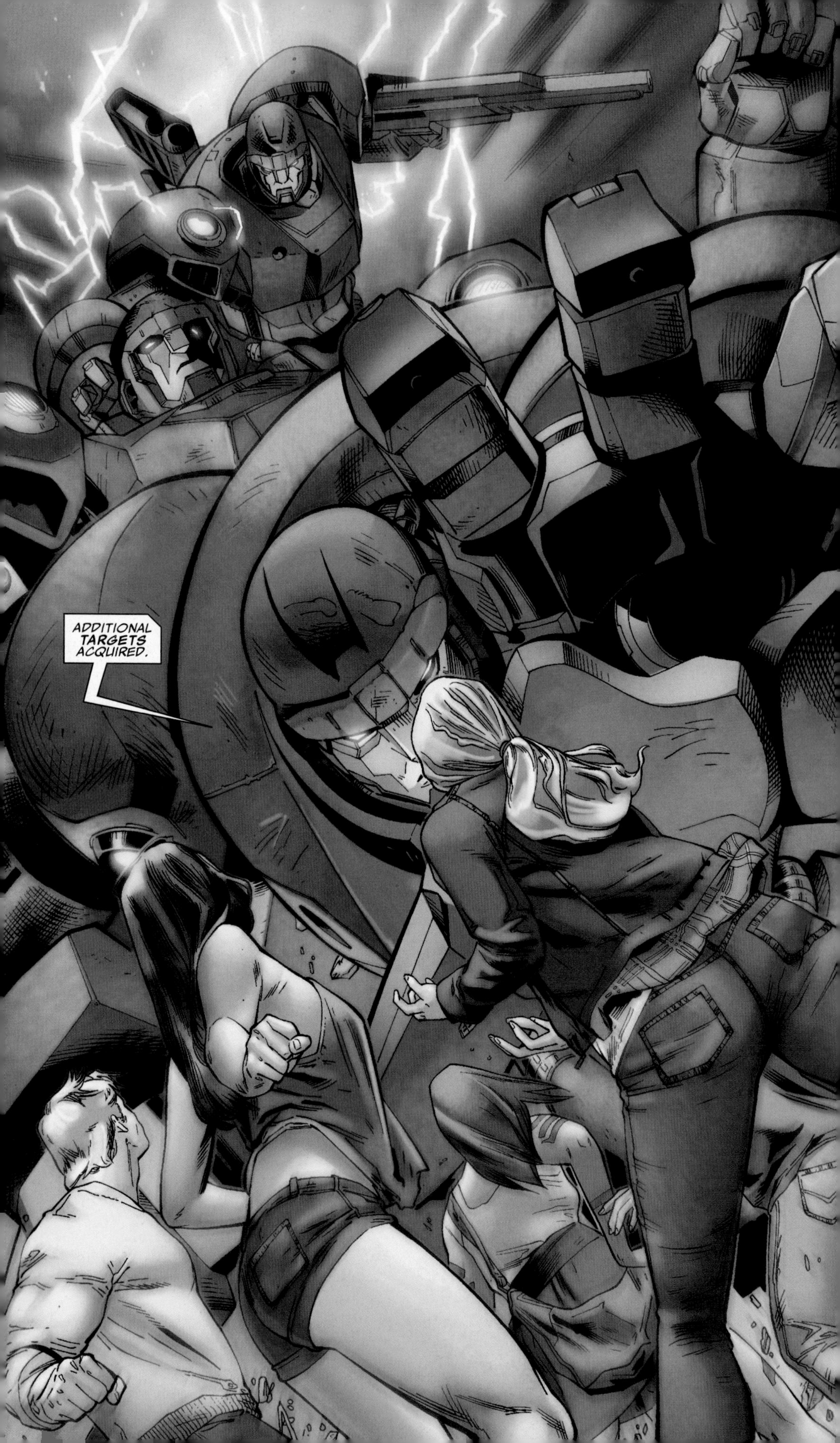
ADDITIONAL TARGETS ACQUIRED.

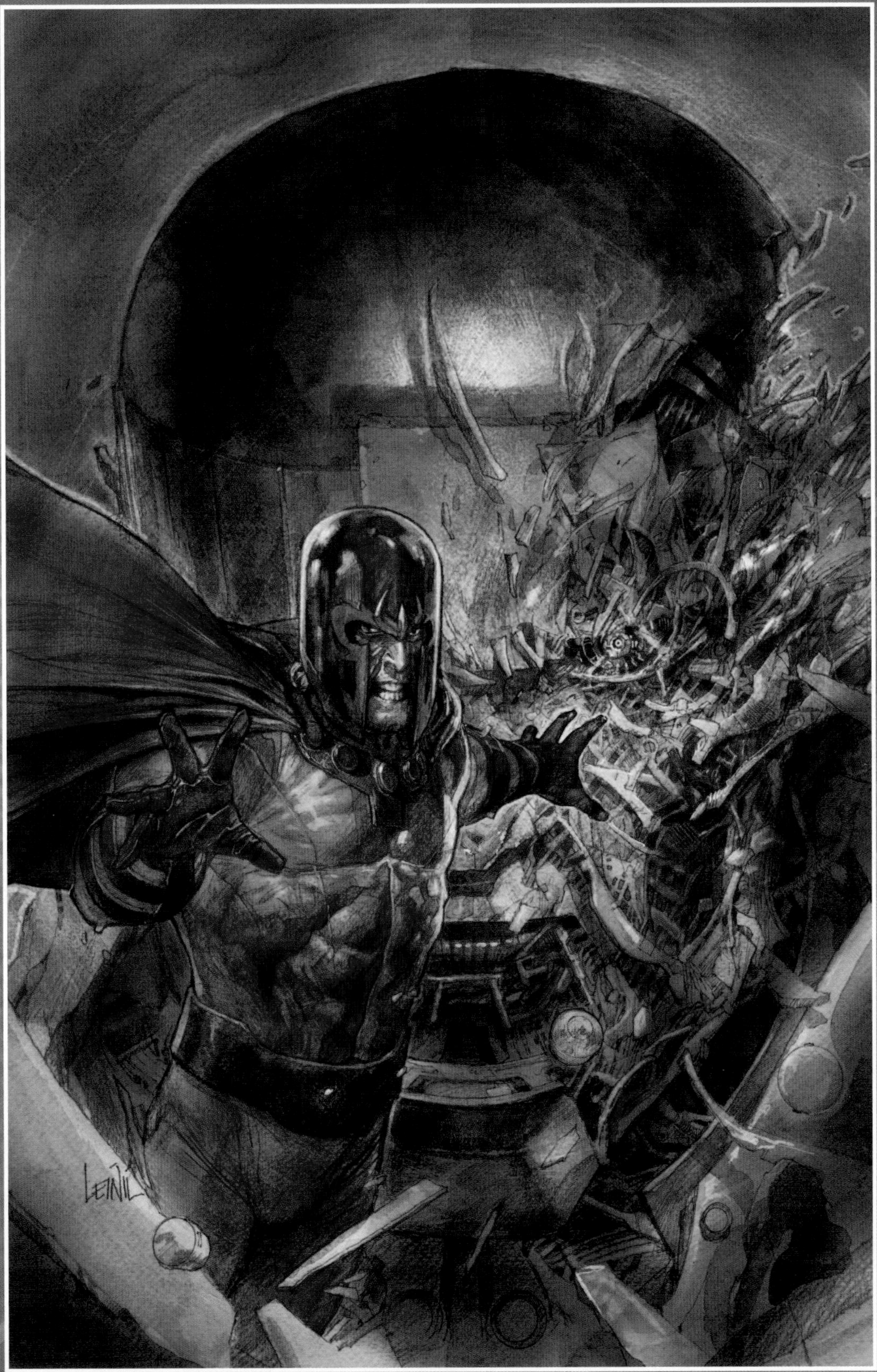
LEINIL

#239

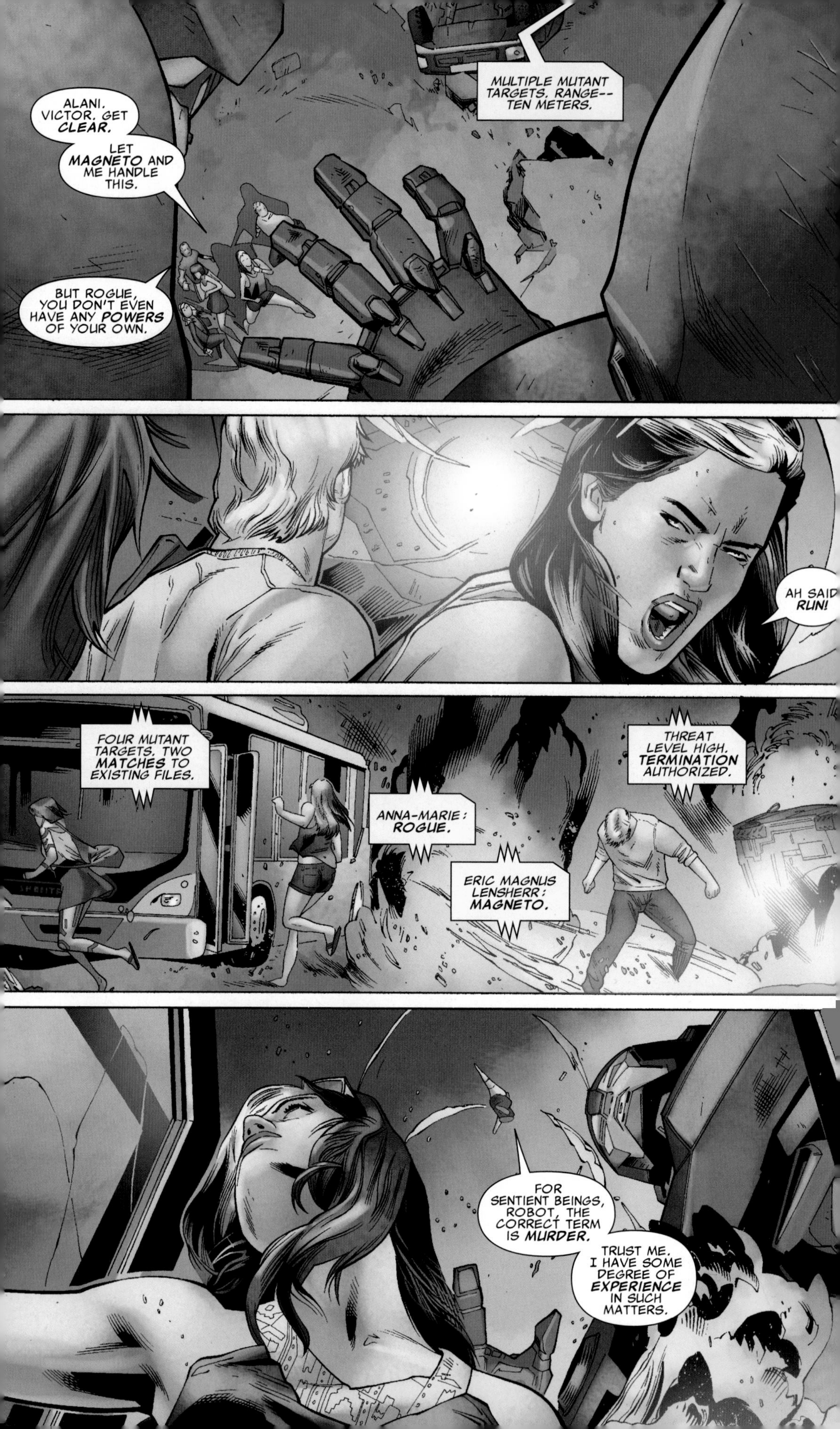
MULTIPLE MUTANT TARGETS. RANGE-- TEN METERS.
ALANI. VICTOR. GET CLEAR.
LET MAGNETO AND ME HANDLE THIS.
BUT ROGUE, YOU DON'T EVEN HAVE ANY POWERS OF YOUR OWN.
AH SAID RUN!
FOUR MUTANT TARGETS. TWO MATCHES TO EXISTING FILES.
ANNA-MARIE: ROGUE.
ERIC MAGNUS LENSHERR: MAGNETO.
THREAT LEVEL HIGH. TERMINATION AUTHORIZED.
FOR SENTIENT BEINGS, ROBOT, THE CORRECT TERM IS MURDER.
TRUST ME. I HAVE SOME DEGREE OF EXPERIENCE IN SUCH MATTERS.

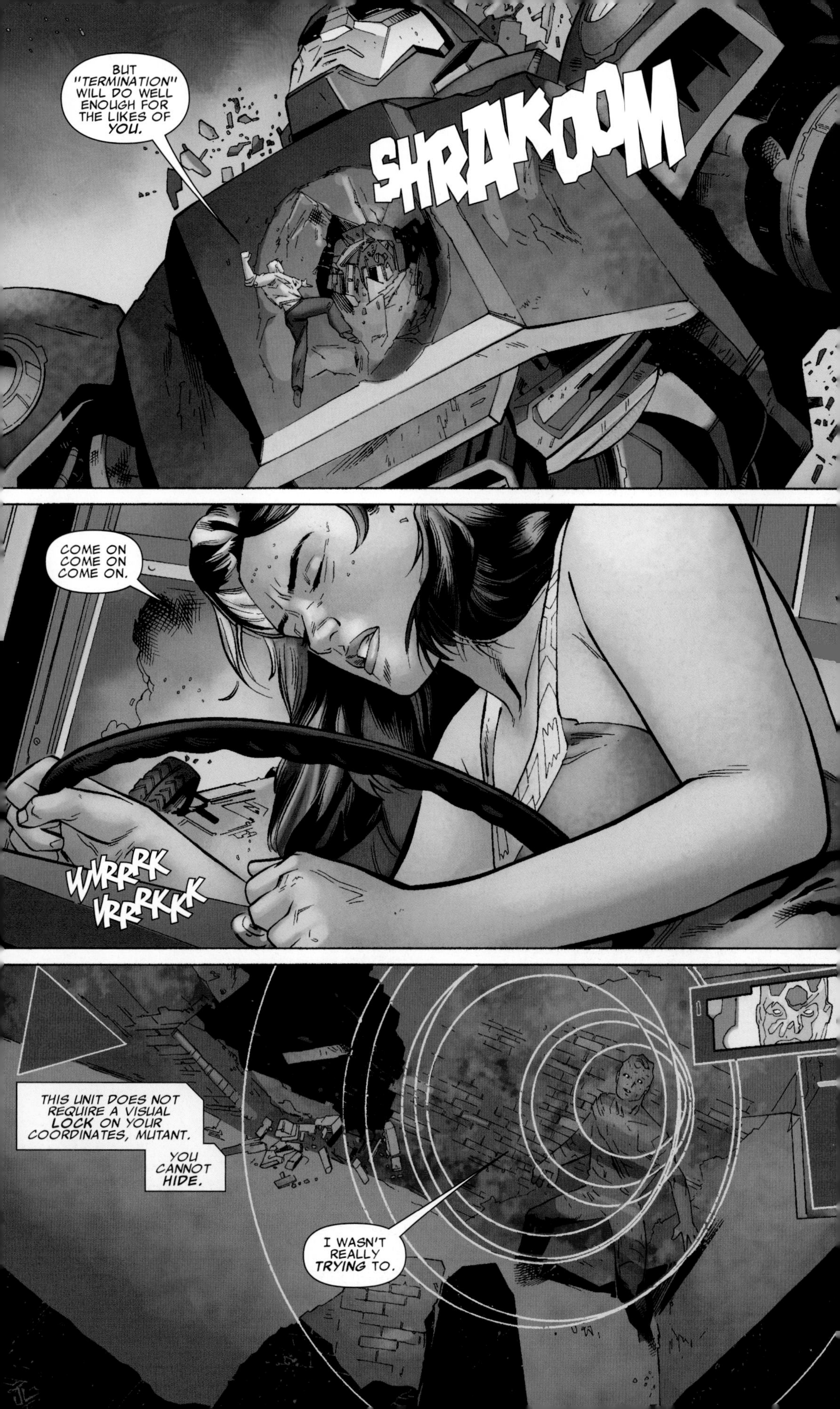

BUT "TERMINATION" WILL DO WELL ENOUGH FOR THE LIKES OF YOU.
SHRAKOOM
COME ON COME ON COME ON.
WVRRRK VRRRKKK
THIS UNIT DOES NOT REQUIRE A VISUAL LOCK ON YOUR COORDINATES, MUTANT.
YOU CANNOT HIDE.
I WASN'T REALLY TRYING TO.

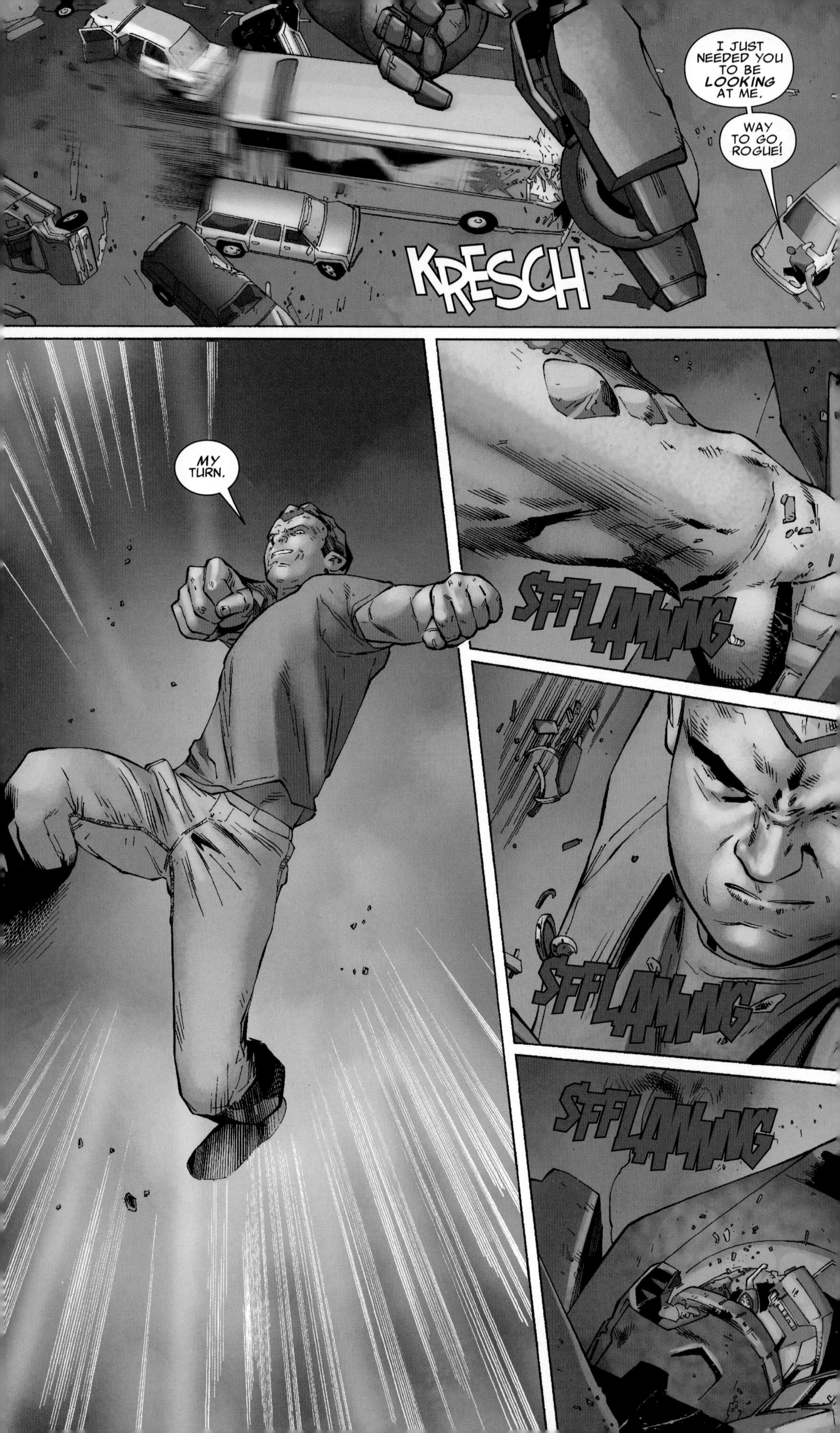
I JUST NEEDED YOU TO BE LOOKING AT ME.
WAY TO GO, ROGUE!
KRESCH
MY TURN.
SFFLAMMNG
SFFLAMMNG
SFFLAMMNG

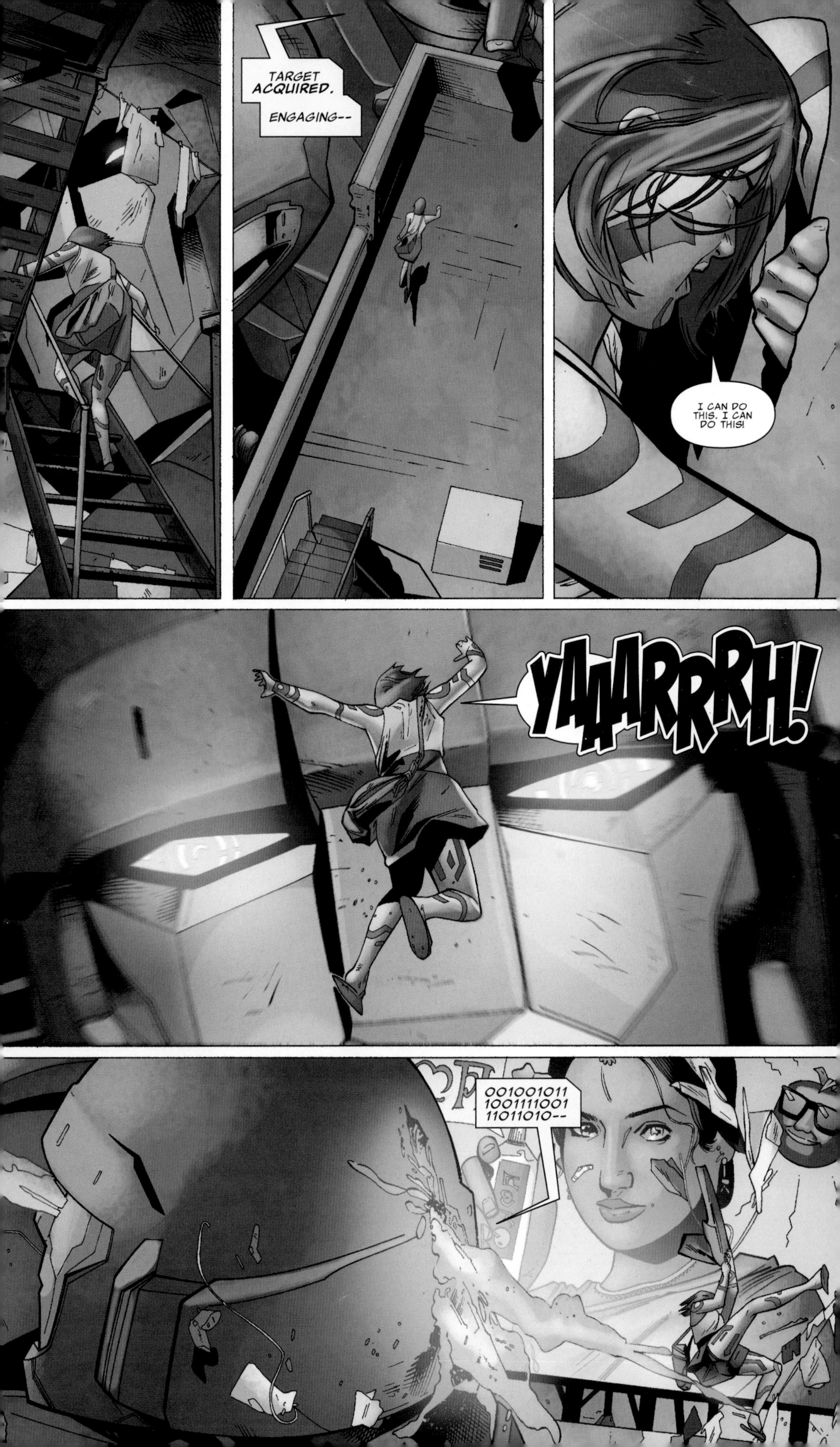
TARGET ACQUIRED.
ENGAGING--
I CAN DO THIS. I CAN DO THIS!
YAAARRRH!
001001011 1001111001 11011010--

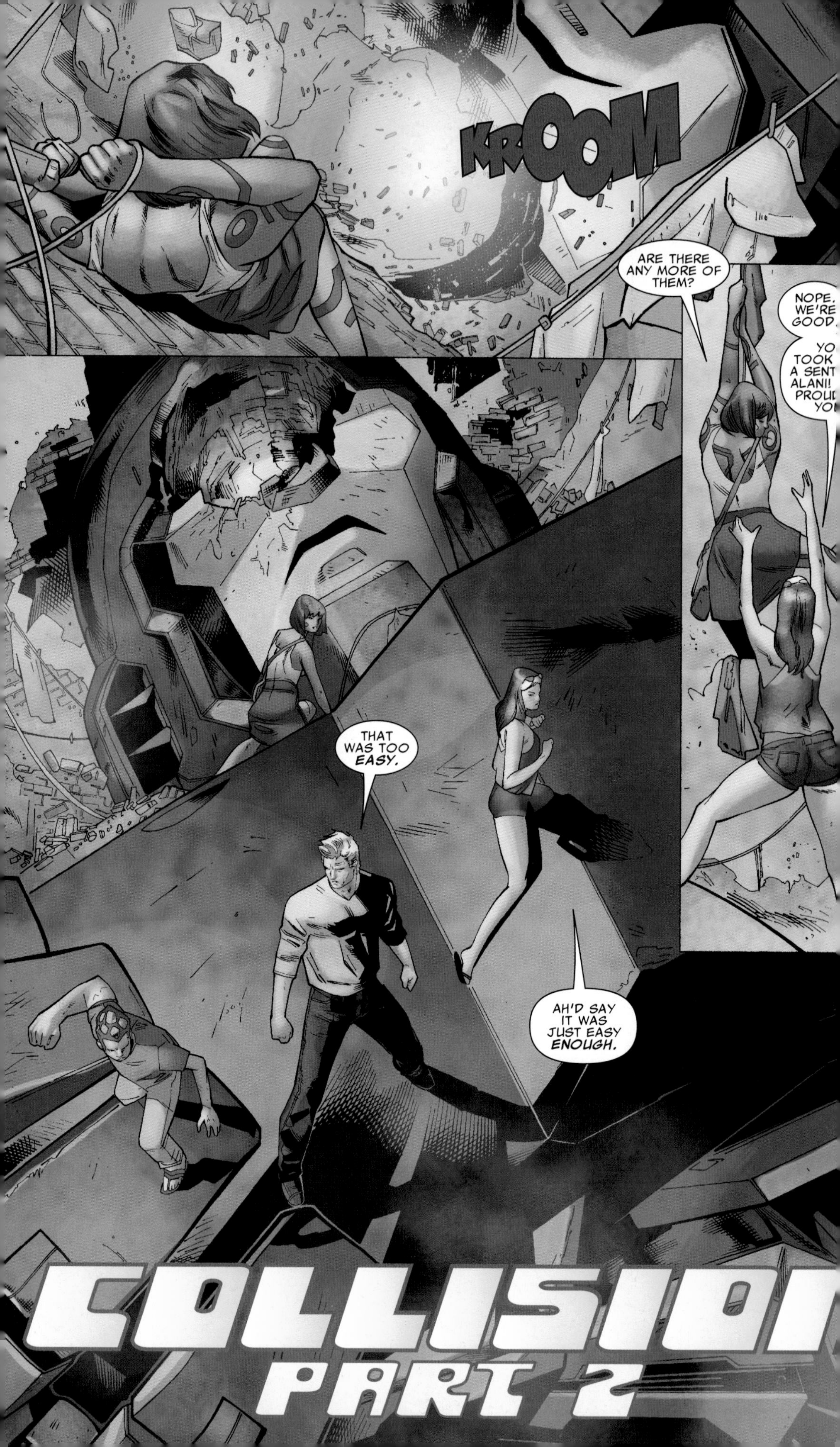
KROOM
ARE THERE ANY MORE OF THEM?
NOPE. WE'RE GOOD.
YO TOOK A SENT ALANI! PROUD YO
THAT WAS TOO EASY.
AH'D SAY IT WAS JUST EASY ENOUGH.
COLLISION
PART 2

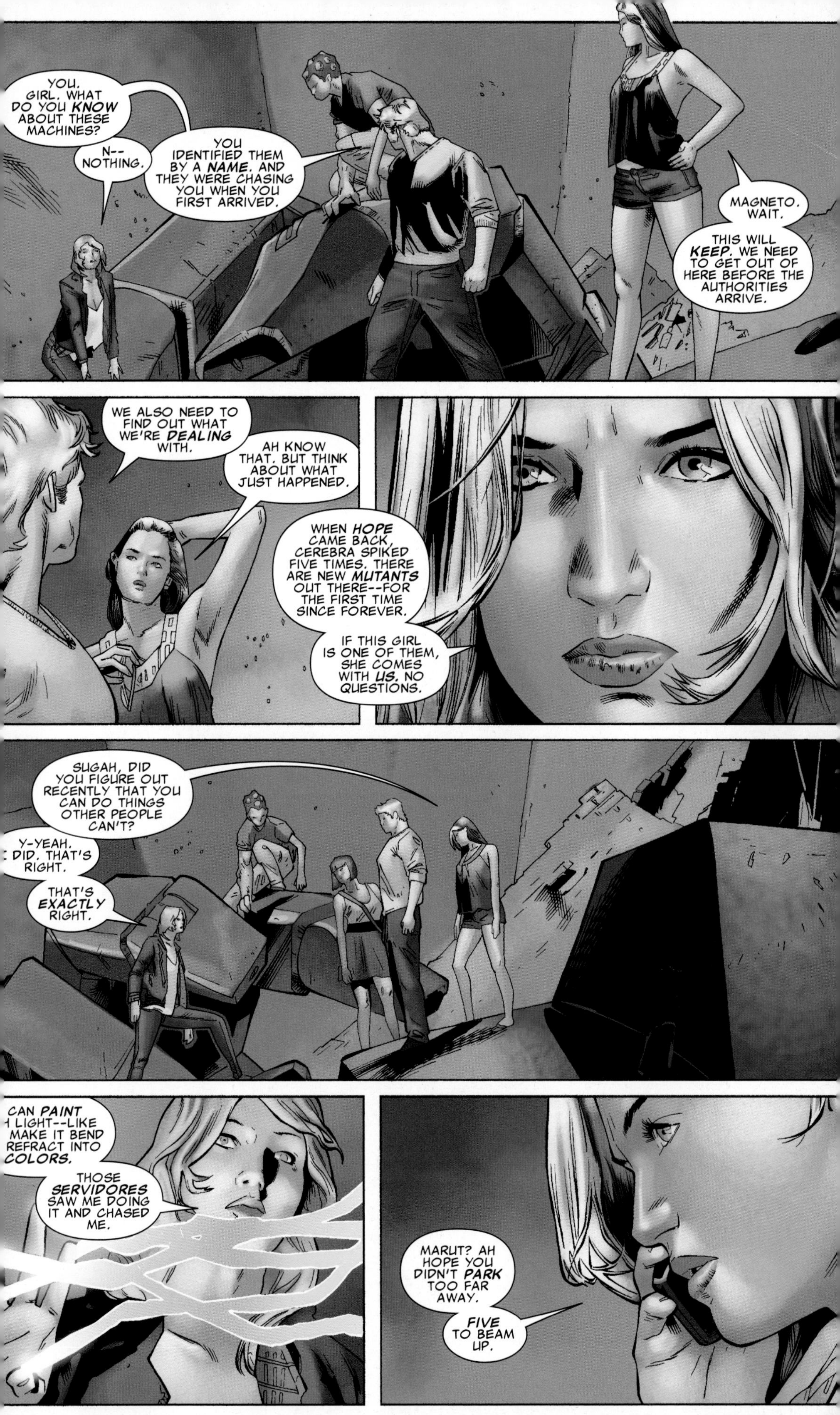
YOU. GIRL. WHAT DO YOU KNOW ABOUT THESE MACHINES?
N-- NOTHING.
YOU IDENTIFIED THEM BY A NAME. AND THEY WERE CHASING YOU WHEN YOU FIRST ARRIVED.
MAGNETO. WAIT.
THIS WILL KEEP. WE NEED TO GET OUT OF HERE BEFORE THE AUTHORITIES ARRIVE.
WE ALSO NEED TO FIND OUT WHAT WE'RE DEALING WITH.
AH KNOW THAT. BUT THINK ABOUT WHAT JUST HAPPENED.
WHEN HOPE CAME BACK, CEREBRA SPIKED FIVE TIMES. THERE ARE NEW MUTANTS OUT THERE--FOR THE FIRST TIME SINCE FOREVER.
IF THIS GIRL IS ONE OF THEM, SHE COMES WITH US. NO QUESTIONS.
SUGAH, DID YOU FIGURE OUT RECENTLY THAT YOU CAN DO THINGS OTHER PEOPLE CAN'T?
Y-YEAH. DID. THAT'S RIGHT.
THAT'S EXACTLY RIGHT.
CAN PAINT LIGHT--LIKE MAKE IT BEND REFRACT INTO COLORS.
THOSE SERVIDORES SAW ME DOING IT AND CHASED ME.
MARUT? AH HOPE YOU DIDN'T PARK TOO FAR AWAY.
FIVE TO BEAM UP.

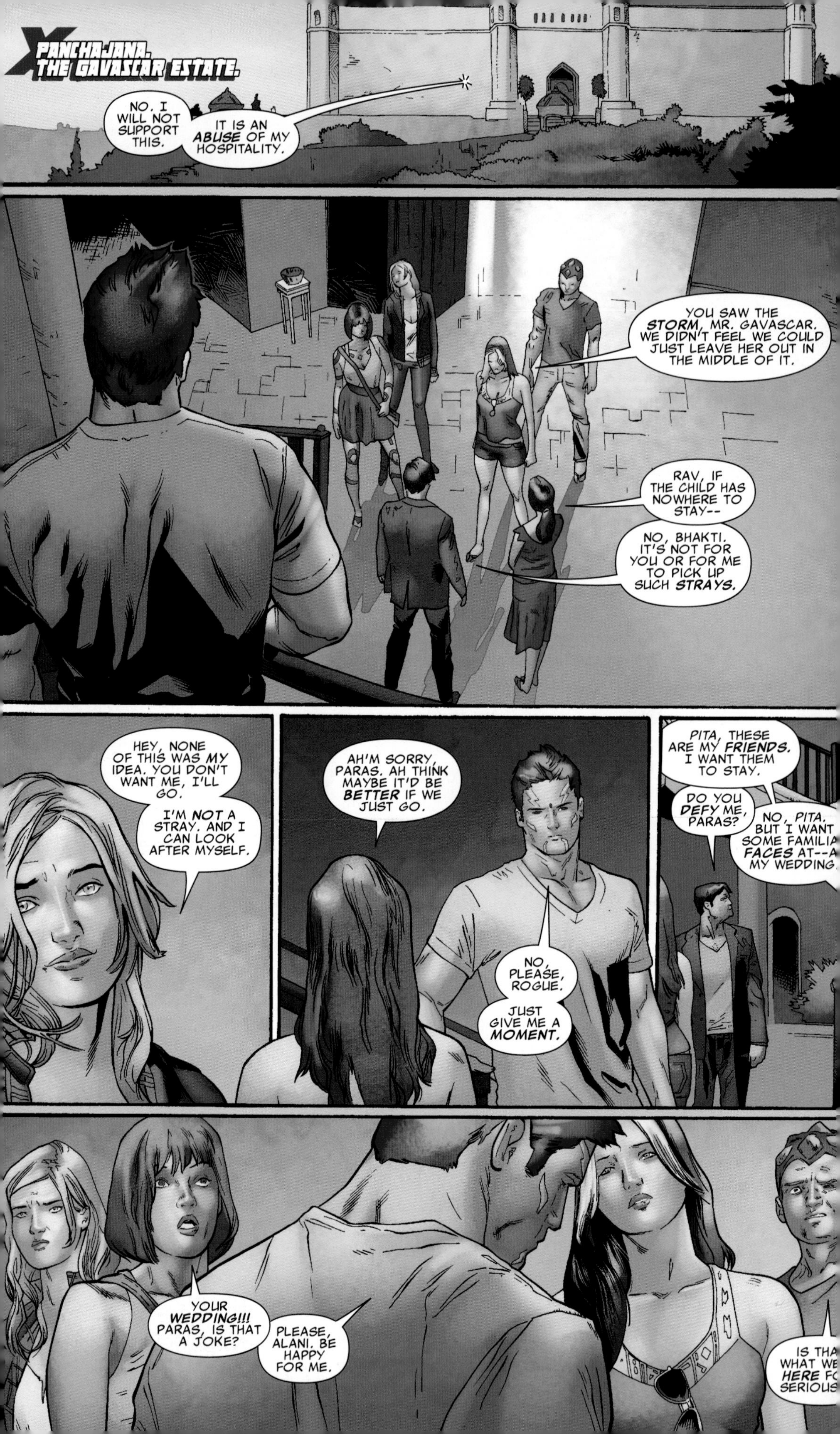
PANCHAJANA.
THE GAVASCAR ESTATE.
NO, I WILL NOT SUPPORT THIS.
IT IS AN ABUSE OF MY HOSPITALITY.
YOU SAW THE STORM, MR. GAVASCAR. WE DIDN'T FEEL WE COULD JUST LEAVE HER OUT IN THE MIDDLE OF IT.
RAV, IF THE CHILD HAS NOWHERE TO STAY--
NO, BHAKTI. IT'S NOT FOR YOU OR FOR ME TO PICK UP SUCH STRAYS.
HEY, NONE OF THIS WAS MY IDEA. YOU DON'T WANT ME, I'LL GO.
I'M NOT A STRAY. AND I CAN LOOK AFTER MYSELF.
AH'M SORRY, PARAS. AH THINK MAYBE IT'D BE BETTER IF WE JUST GO.
NO, PLEASE, ROGUE.
JUST GIVE ME A MOMENT.
PITA, THESE ARE MY FRIENDS. I WANT THEM TO STAY.
DO YOU DEFY ME, PARAS?
NO, PITA. BUT I WANT SOME FAMILIA FACES AT--A MY WEDDING.
YOUR WEDDING!!! PARAS, IS THAT A JOKE?
PLEASE, ALANI. BE HAPPY FOR ME.
IS THA WHAT WE HERE FO SERIOUS

UNTIL SUNDAY, THEN, NO LONGER. PARAS, YOUR **BRIDE** AND HER CHAPERONE ARRIVE THIS AFTERNOON, AHEAD OF THE REST OF THE WEDDING PARTY.

YOU WILL COME TO THE **SAFFRON ROOM** AT THREE O'CLOCK TO MEET HER. BE PROMPT.

YES, PITA.

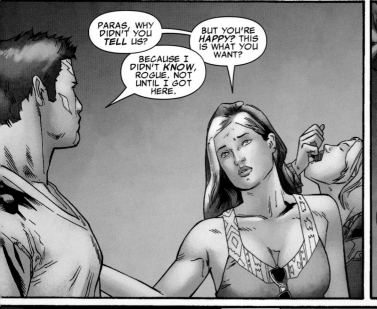

PARAS, WHY DIDN'T YOU **TELL** US?

BUT YOU'RE **HAPPY?** THIS IS WHAT YOU WANT?

BECAUSE I DIDN'T **KNOW**, ROGUE, NOT UNTIL I GOT HERE.

MY BROTHER'S **ENGAGEMENT** HAS TO BE FULFILLED.

WHAT SORT OF PERSON WOULD I BE IF I **SHRANK** FROM THAT?

BUT PARAS, DO YOU **LOVE** HER?

I'VE NEVER **SEEN** HER, ALANI. YOU HEARD. I'LL MEET HER THIS AFTERNOON.

THAT'S **CRAZY** TALK, MAN. IF I KNOW ANYTHING, IT'S THAT YOU CAN'T FORCE SOMETHING LIKE **LOVE** INTO A SHAPE THAT SOMEONE ELSE SAYS IS RIGHT.

HEY!

YOU GOT ANY MORE OF THESE **GULABJAMAN** THINGS? THERE'S NO **WAY** I'M GONNA MAKE IT ALL THE WAY TO DINNERTIME.

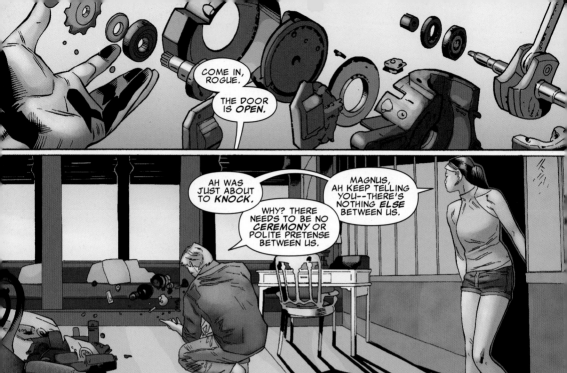

COME IN, ROGUE.

THE DOOR IS OPEN.

AH WAS JUST ABOUT TO KNOCK.

WHY? THERE NEEDS TO BE NO CEREMONY OR POLITE PRETENSE BETWEEN US.

MAGNUS, AH KEEP TELLING YOU--THERE'S NOTHING ELSE BETWEEN US.

THOSE SENTINELS FELL TO A SINGLE ASSAULT BECAUSE THEY'D BEEN STRUCTURALLY WEAKENED BY EXTREME AND CORROSIVE ENERGIES.

THE SAME ENERGIES NOW WASHING OVER THE CITY OF MUMBAI.

THE STORMS?

A STORM IS A NATURAL PHENOMENON. THESE ARE NOT.

FOR ONE THING, SOME OF THE ENERGIES IMPEDE THE FREQUENCIES OF HUMAN THOUGHT, INDUCING COMA.

THAT'S WHAT HAPPENED TO INDRA'S BROTHER.

AND TO THOSE OTHERS WE SAW, WHO FELL WHEN THE STORM HIT.

OH, AND I SPOKE TO EMMA, TOO.

AS SOON AS SHE CAN SPARE THE TIME FROM RECONSTRUCTION, SHE'LL CARRY OUT FULL CEREBRA SCA OF THE SUB-CONTINENT...

IF YOUR NEW FRIEND A MUTANT, WE KNOW IT SOO ENOUGH.

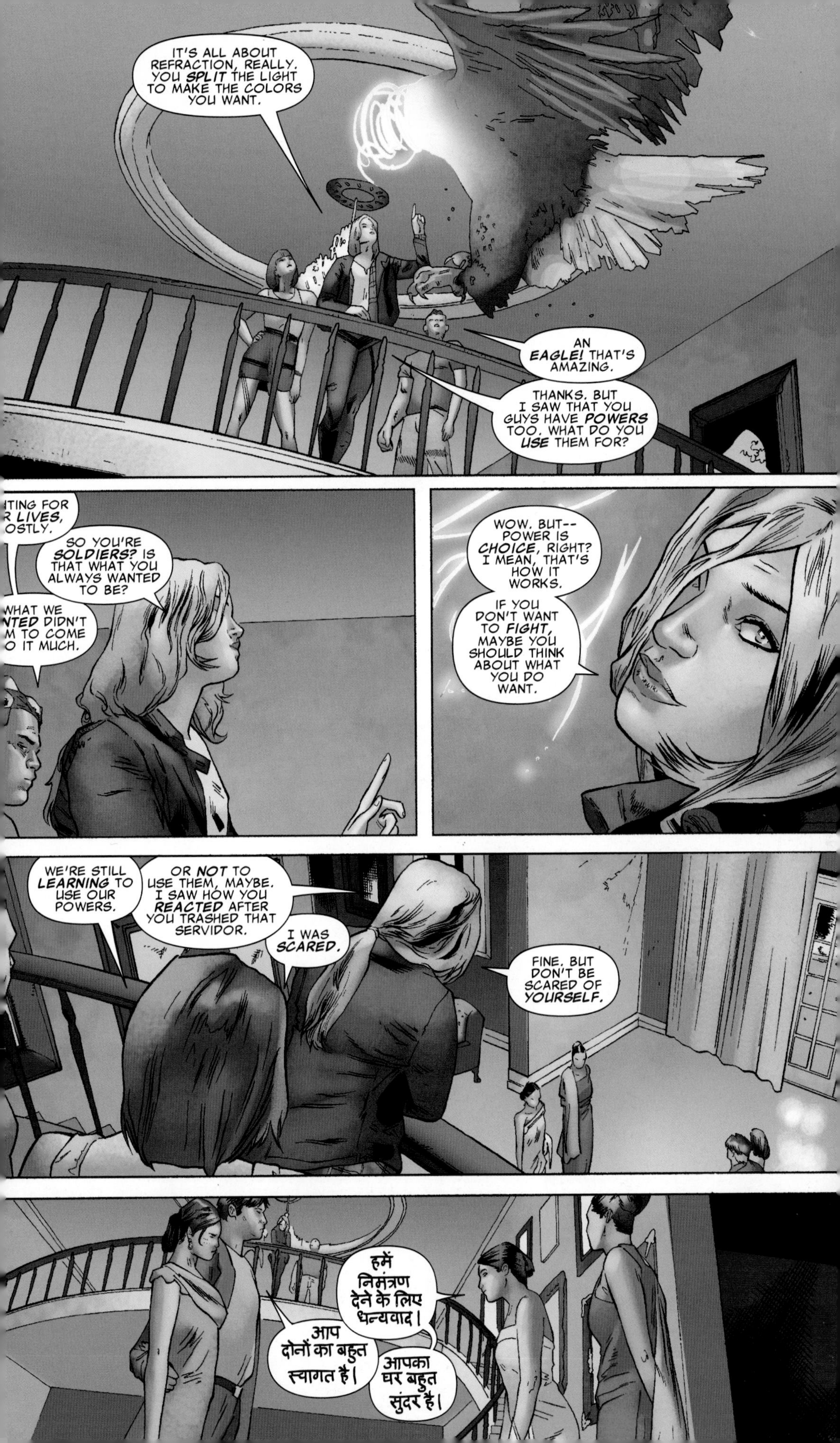
IT'S ALL ABOUT REFRACTION, REALLY. YOU SPLIT THE LIGHT TO MAKE THE COLORS YOU WANT.
AN EAGLE! THAT'S AMAZING.
THANKS. BUT I SAW THAT YOU GUYS HAVE POWERS TOO. WHAT DO YOU USE THEM FOR?
TING FOR R LIVES, OSTLY.
SO YOU'RE SOLDIERS? IS THAT WHAT YOU ALWAYS WANTED TO BE?
WHAT WE NTED DIDN'T M TO COME O IT MUCH.
WOW. BUT-- POWER IS CHOICE, RIGHT? I MEAN, THAT'S HOW IT WORKS.
IF YOU DON'T WANT TO FIGHT, MAYBE YOU SHOULD THINK ABOUT WHAT YOU DO WANT.
WE'RE STILL LEARNING TO USE OUR POWERS.
OR NOT TO USE THEM, MAYBE. I SAW HOW YOU REACTED AFTER YOU TRASHED THAT SERVIDOR.
I WAS SCARED.
FINE. BUT DON'T BE SCARED OF YOURSELF.
हमें निमंत्रण देने के लिए धन्यवाद।
आप दोनों का बहुत स्वागत है।
आपका घर बहुत सुंदर है।

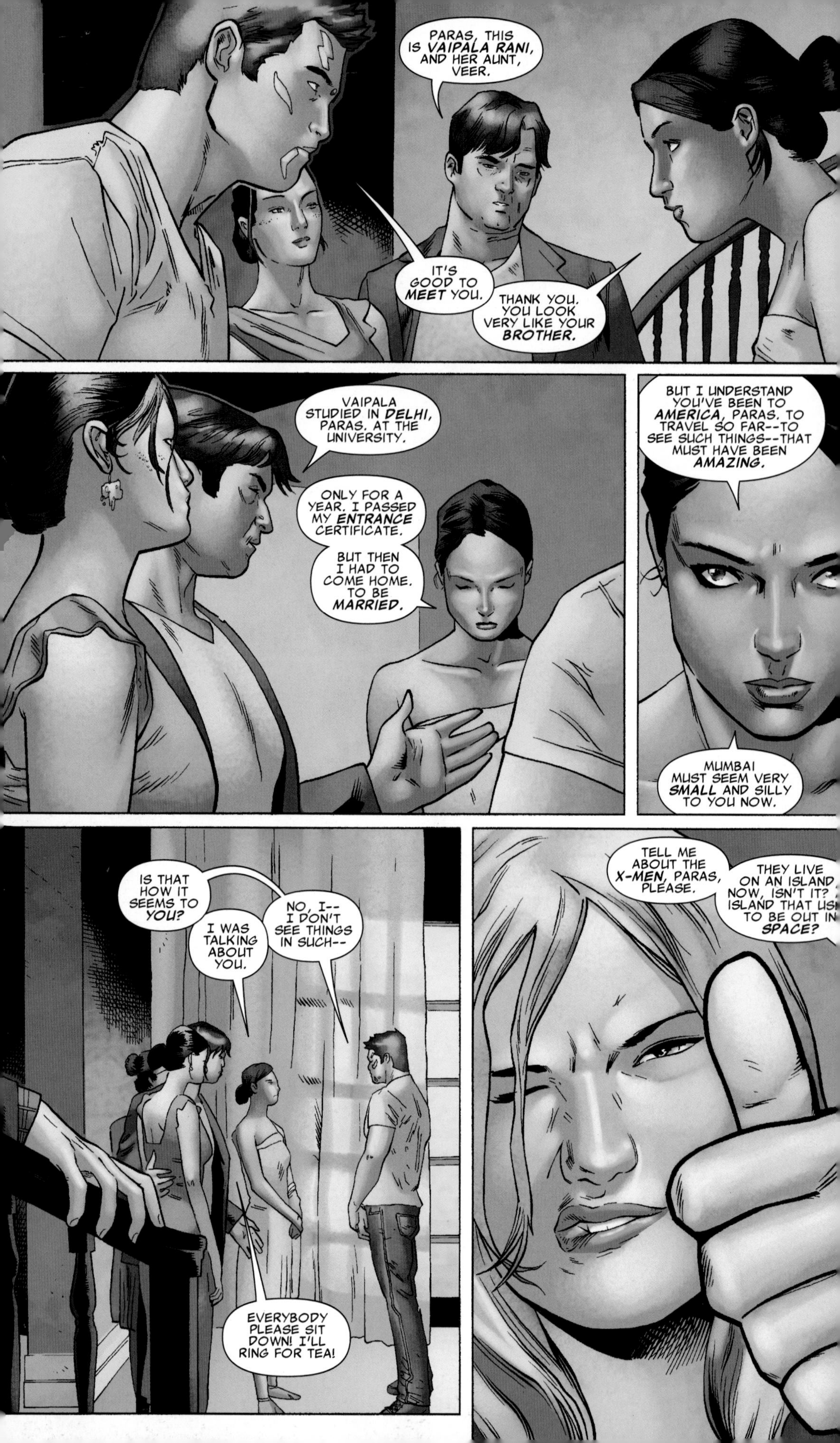
PARAS, THIS IS VAIPALA RANI, AND HER AUNT, VEER.
IT'S GOOD TO MEET YOU.
THANK YOU. YOU LOOK VERY LIKE YOUR BROTHER.
VAIPALA STUDIED IN DELHI, PARAS. AT THE UNIVERSITY.
ONLY FOR A YEAR. I PASSED MY ENTRANCE CERTIFICATE.
BUT THEN I HAD TO COME HOME. TO BE MARRIED.
BUT I UNDERSTAND YOU'VE BEEN TO AMERICA, PARAS. TO TRAVEL SO FAR--TO SEE SUCH THINGS--THAT MUST HAVE BEEN AMAZING.
MUMBAI MUST SEEM VERY SMALL AND SILLY TO YOU NOW.
IS THAT HOW IT SEEMS TO YOU?
I WAS TALKING ABOUT YOU.
NO, I-- I DON'T SEE THINGS IN SUCH--
EVERYBODY PLEASE SIT DOWN! I'LL RING FOR TEA!
TELL ME ABOUT THE X-MEN, PARAS, PLEASE.
THEY LIVE ON AN ISLAND NOW, ISN'T IT? ISLAND THAT US TO BE OUT IN SPACE?

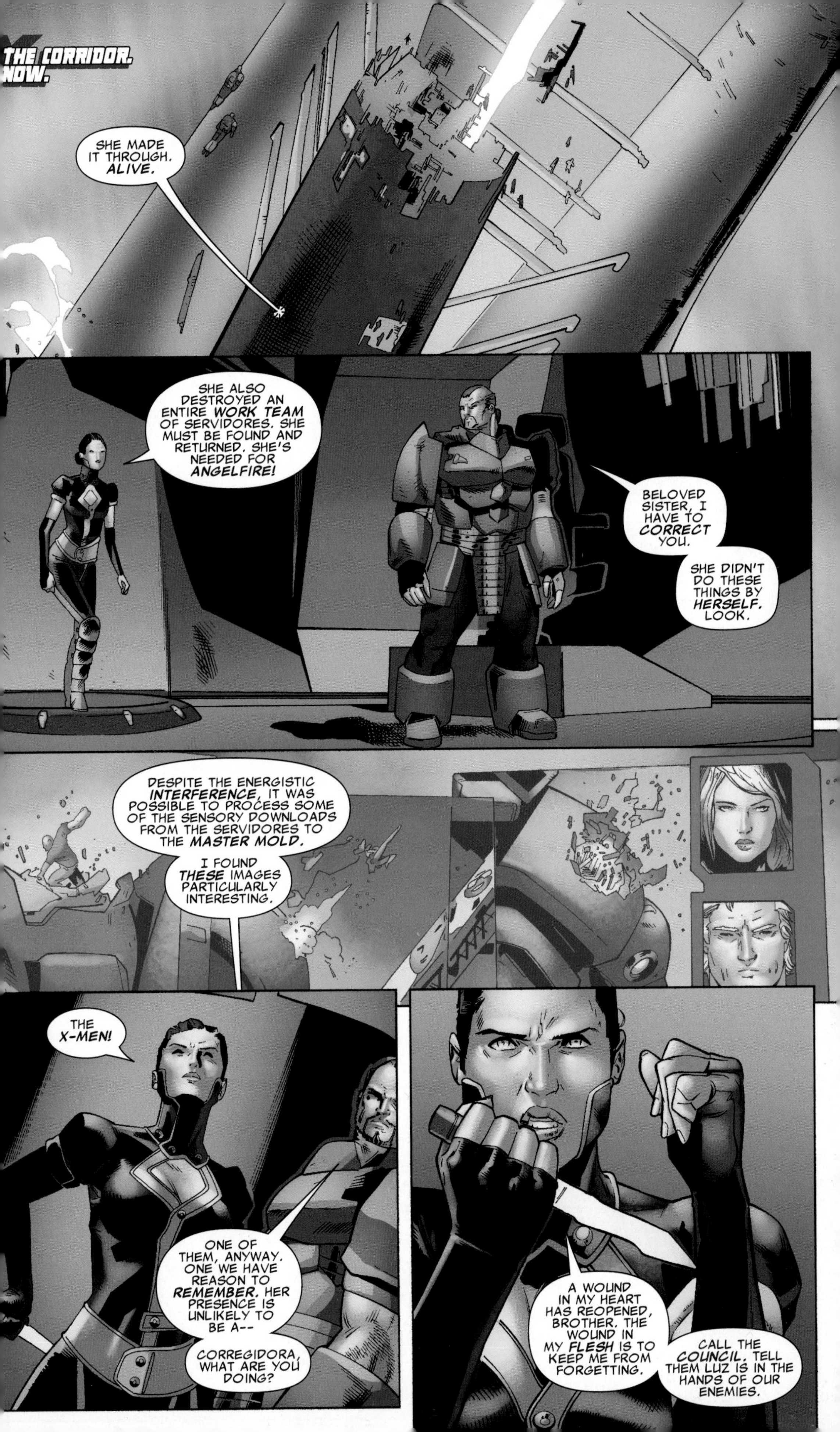
THE CORRIDOR. NOW.
SHE MADE IT THROUGH. ALIVE.
SHE ALSO DESTROYED AN ENTIRE WORK TEAM OF SERVIDORES. SHE MUST BE FOUND AND RETURNED. SHE'S NEEDED FOR ANGELFIRE!
BELOVED SISTER, I HAVE TO CORRECT YOU.
SHE DIDN'T DO THESE THINGS BY HERSELF. LOOK.
DESPITE THE ENERGISTIC INTERFERENCE, IT WAS POSSIBLE TO PROCESS SOME OF THE SENSORY DOWNLOADS FROM THE SERVIDORES TO THE MASTER MOLD.
I FOUND THESE IMAGES PARTICULARLY INTERESTING.
THE X-MEN!
ONE OF THEM, ANYWAY. ONE WE HAVE REASON TO REMEMBER. HER PRESENCE IS UNLIKELY TO BE A--
CORREGIDORA, WHAT ARE YOU DOING?
A WOUND IN MY HEART HAS REOPENED, BROTHER. THE WOUND IN MY FLESH IS TO KEEP ME FROM FORGETTING.
CALL THE COUNCIL. TELL THEM LUZ IS IN THE HANDS OF OUR ENEMIES.

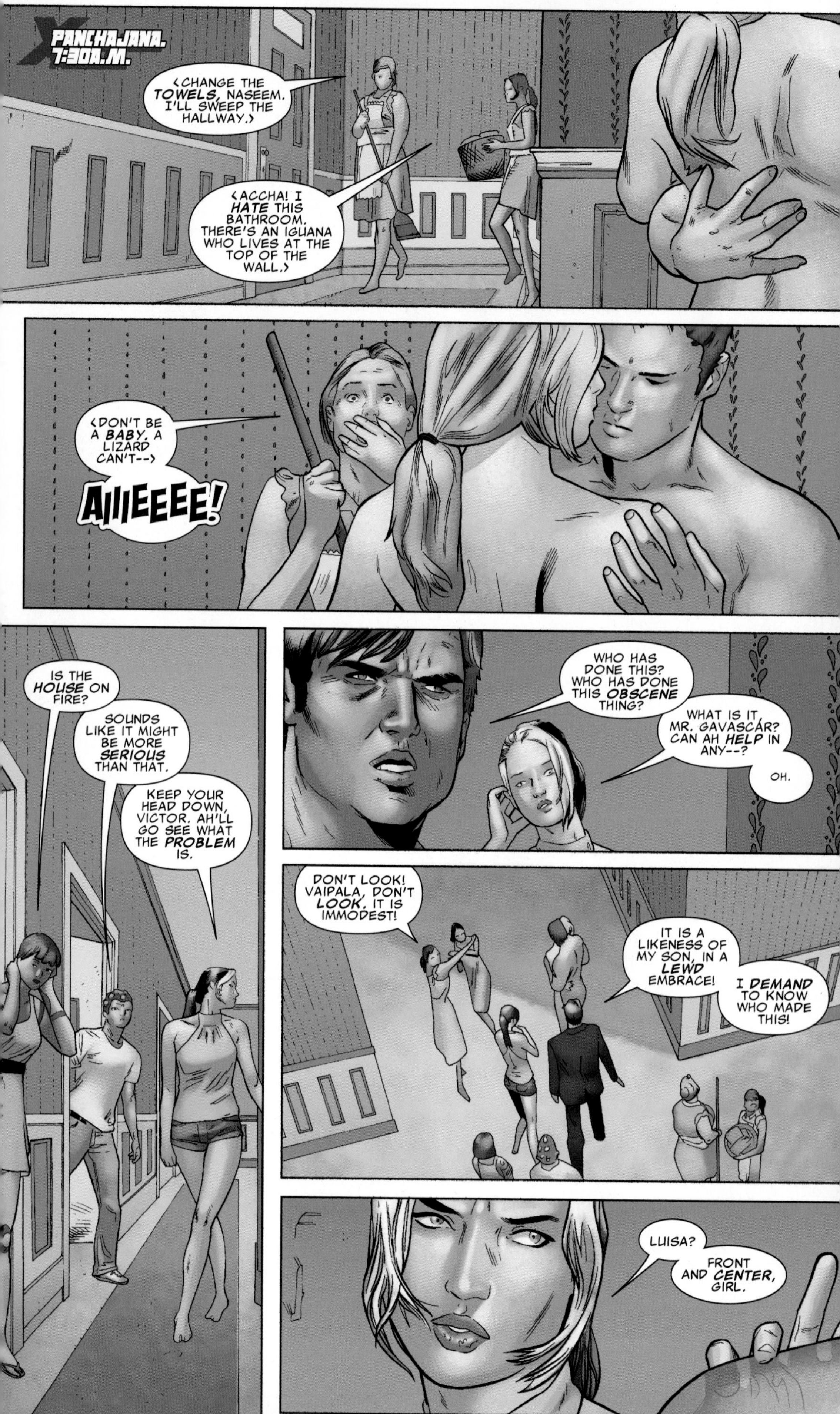
PANCHAJANA. 7:30A.M.
‹CHANGE THE TOWELS, NASEEM. I'LL SWEEP THE HALLWAY.›
‹ACCHA! I HATE THIS BATHROOM. THERE'S AN IGUANA WHO LIVES AT THE TOP OF THE WALL.›
‹DON'T BE A BABY. A LIZARD CAN'T--›
AIIIEEEE!
IS THE HOUSE ON FIRE?
SOUNDS LIKE IT MIGHT BE MORE SERIOUS THAN THAT.
KEEP YOUR HEAD DOWN, VICTOR. AH'LL GO SEE WHAT THE PROBLEM IS.
WHO HAS DONE THIS? WHO HAS DONE THIS OBSCENE THING?
WHAT IS IT, MR. GAVASCÁR? CAN AH HELP IN ANY--?
OH.
DON'T LOOK! VAIPALA, DON'T LOOK. IT IS IMMODEST!
IT IS A LIKENESS OF MY SON, IN A LEWD EMBRACE!
I DEMAND TO KNOW WHO MADE THIS!
LUISA?
FRONT AND CENTER, GIRL.

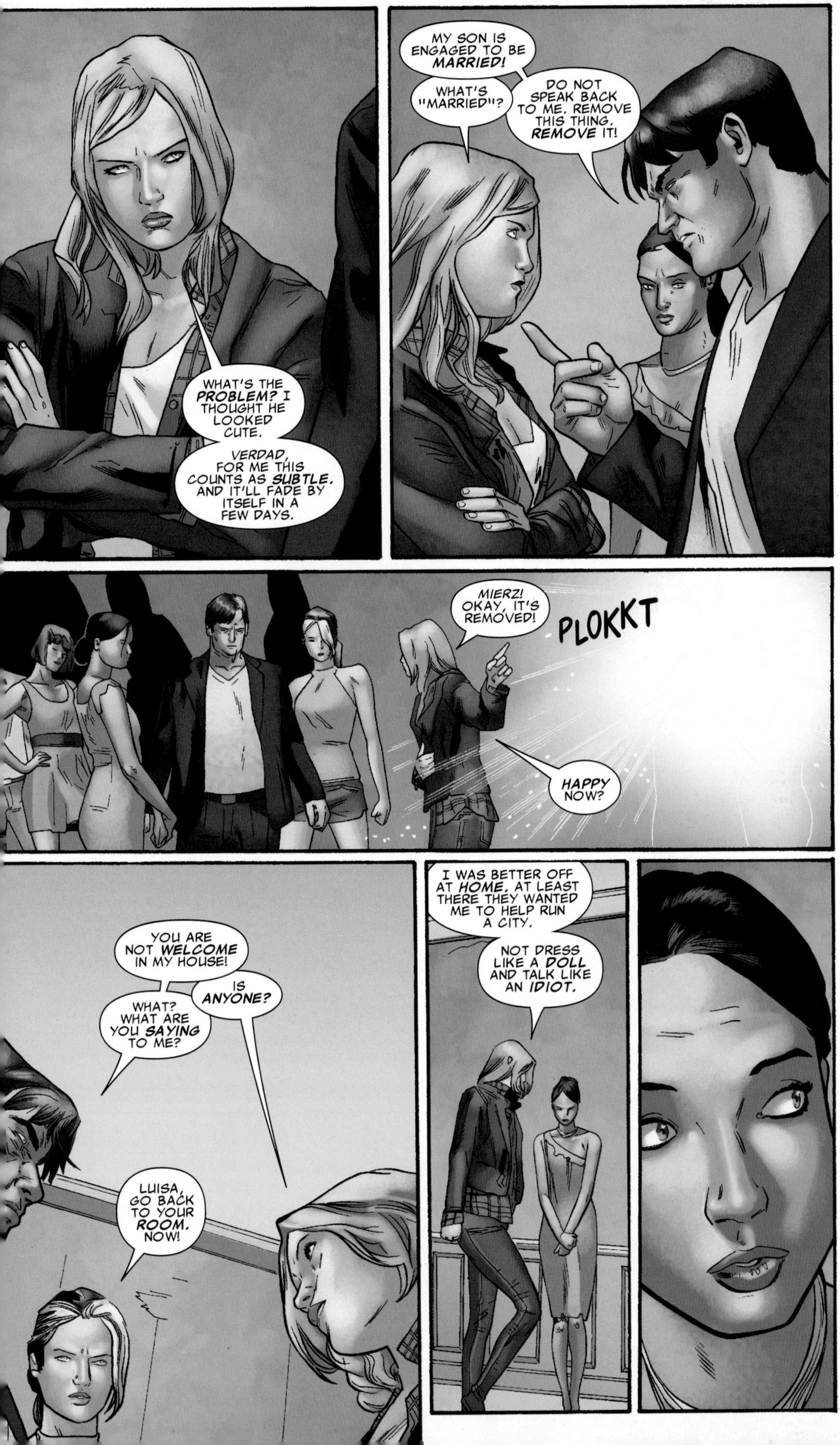
WHAT'S THE PROBLEM? I THOUGHT HE LOOKED CUTE.
VERDAD, FOR ME THIS COUNTS AS SUBTLE. AND IT'LL FADE BY ITSELF IN A FEW DAYS.
MY SON IS ENGAGED TO BE MARRIED!
WHAT'S "MARRIED"?
DO NOT SPEAK BACK TO ME. REMOVE THIS THING. REMOVE IT!
MIERZ! OKAY, IT'S REMOVED!
PLOKKT
HAPPY NOW?
YOU ARE NOT WELCOME IN MY HOUSE!
IS ANYONE?
WHAT? WHAT ARE YOU SAYING TO ME?
LUISA, GO BACK TO YOUR ROOM. NOW!
I WAS BETTER OFF AT HOME. AT LEAST THERE THEY WANTED ME TO HELP RUN A CITY.
NOT DRESS LIKE A DOLL AND TALK LIKE AN IDIOT.

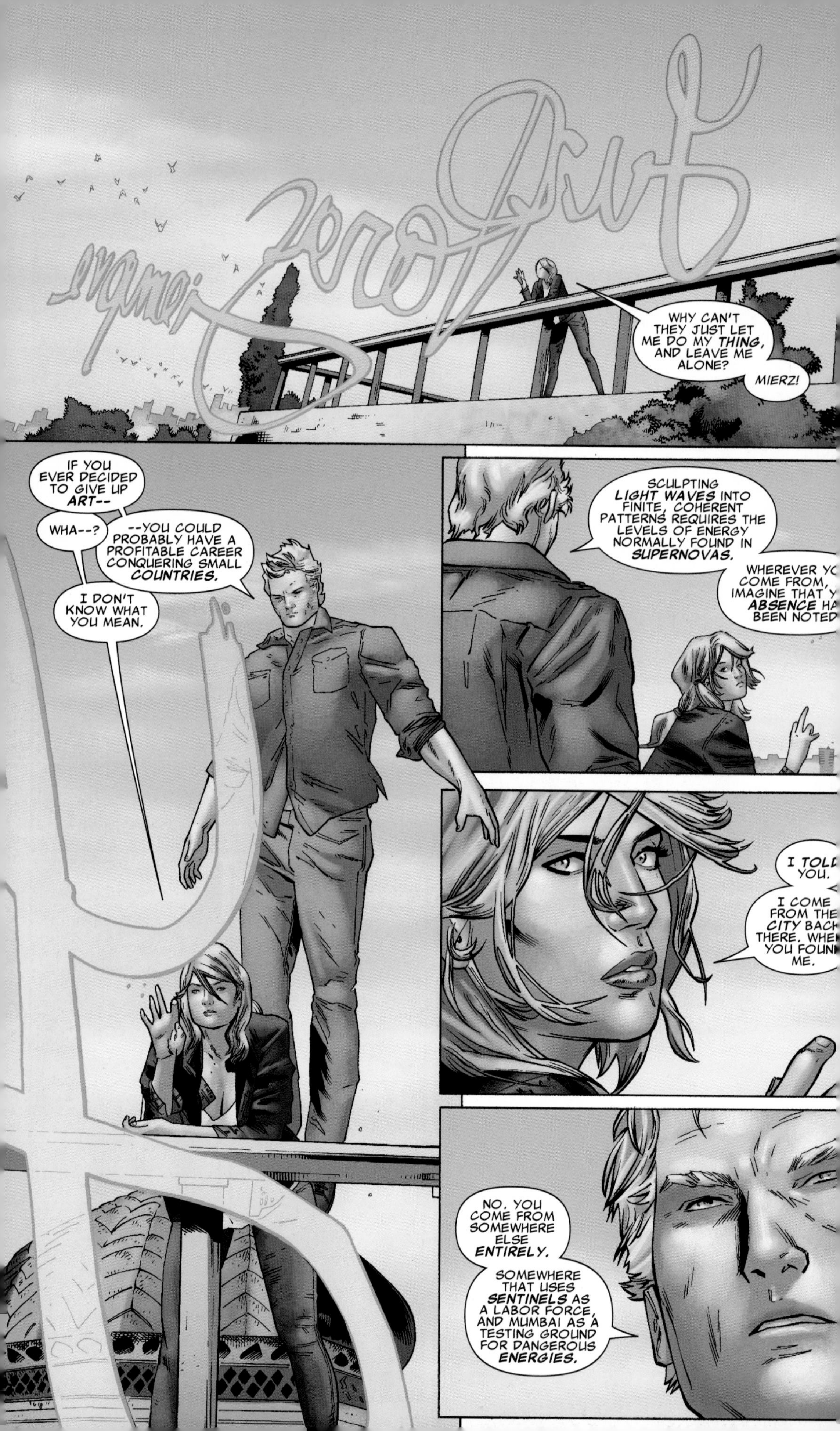

WHY CAN'T THEY JUST LET ME DO MY THING, AND LEAVE ME ALONE?
MIERZ!
IF YOU EVER DECIDED TO GIVE UP ART--
WHA--?
--YOU COULD PROBABLY HAVE A PROFITABLE CAREER CONQUERING SMALL COUNTRIES.
I DON'T KNOW WHAT YOU MEAN.
SCULPTING LIGHT WAVES INTO FINITE, COHERENT PATTERNS REQUIRES THE LEVELS OF ENERGY NORMALLY FOUND IN SUPERNOVAS.
WHEREVER YO COME FROM, IMAGINE THAT Y ABSENCE HA BEEN NOTED
I TOLD YOU.
I COME FROM THE CITY BACK THERE. WHE YOU FOUN ME.
NO. YOU COME FROM SOMEWHERE ELSE ENTIRELY.
SOMEWHERE THAT USES SENTINELS AS A LABOR FORCE, AND MUMBAI AS A TESTING GROUND FOR DANGEROUS ENERGIES.

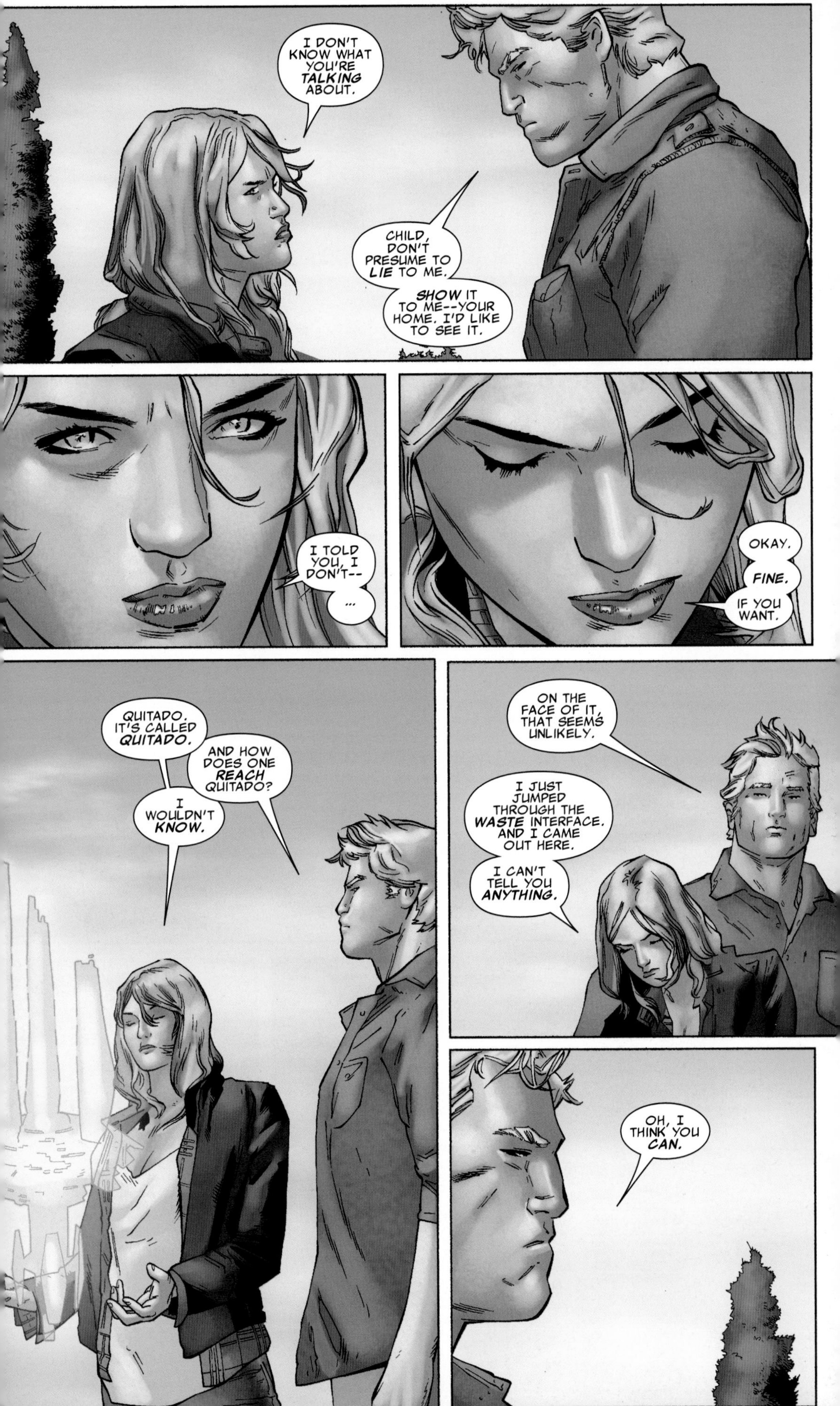
I DON'T KNOW WHAT YOU'RE TALKING ABOUT.
CHILD, DON'T PRESUME TO LIE TO ME.
SHOW IT TO ME--YOUR HOME. I'D LIKE TO SEE IT.
I TOLD YOU, I DON'T--
...
OKAY.
FINE.
IF YOU WANT.
QUITADO. IT'S CALLED QUITADO.
AND HOW DOES ONE REACH QUITADO?
I WOULDN'T KNOW.
ON THE FACE OF IT, THAT SEEMS UNLIKELY.
I JUST JUMPED THROUGH THE WASTE INTERFACE. AND I CAME OUT HERE.
I CAN'T TELL YOU ANYTHING.
OH, I THINK YOU CAN.

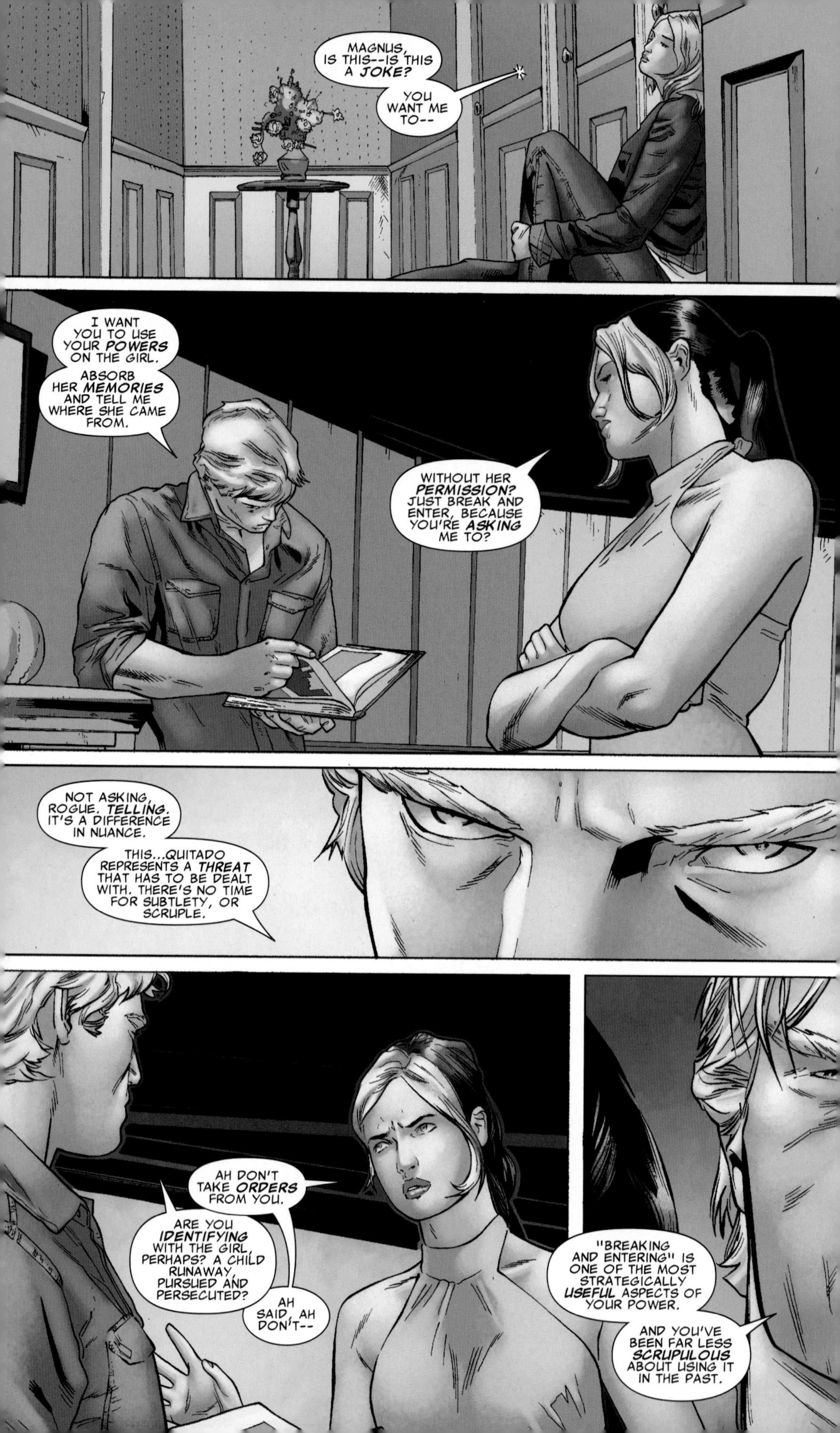
MAGNUS, IS THIS--IS THIS A JOKE?
YOU WANT ME TO--
I WANT YOU TO USE YOUR POWERS ON THE GIRL.
ABSORB HER MEMORIES AND TELL ME WHERE SHE CAME FROM.
WITHOUT HER PERMISSION? JUST BREAK AND ENTER, BECAUSE YOU'RE ASKING ME TO?
NOT ASKING, ROGUE. TELLING. IT'S A DIFFERENCE IN NUANCE.
THIS...QUITADO REPRESENTS A THREAT THAT HAS TO BE DEALT WITH. THERE'S NO TIME FOR SUBTLETY, OR SCRUPLE.
AH DON'T TAKE ORDERS FROM YOU.
ARE YOU IDENTIFYING WITH THE GIRL, PERHAPS? A CHILD RUNAWAY, PURSUED AND PERSECUTED?
AH SAID, AH DON'T--
"BREAKING AND ENTERING" IS ONE OF THE MOST STRATEGICALLY USEFUL ASPECTS OF YOUR POWER.
AND YOU'VE BEEN FAR LESS SCRUPULOUS ABOUT USING IT IN THE PAST.

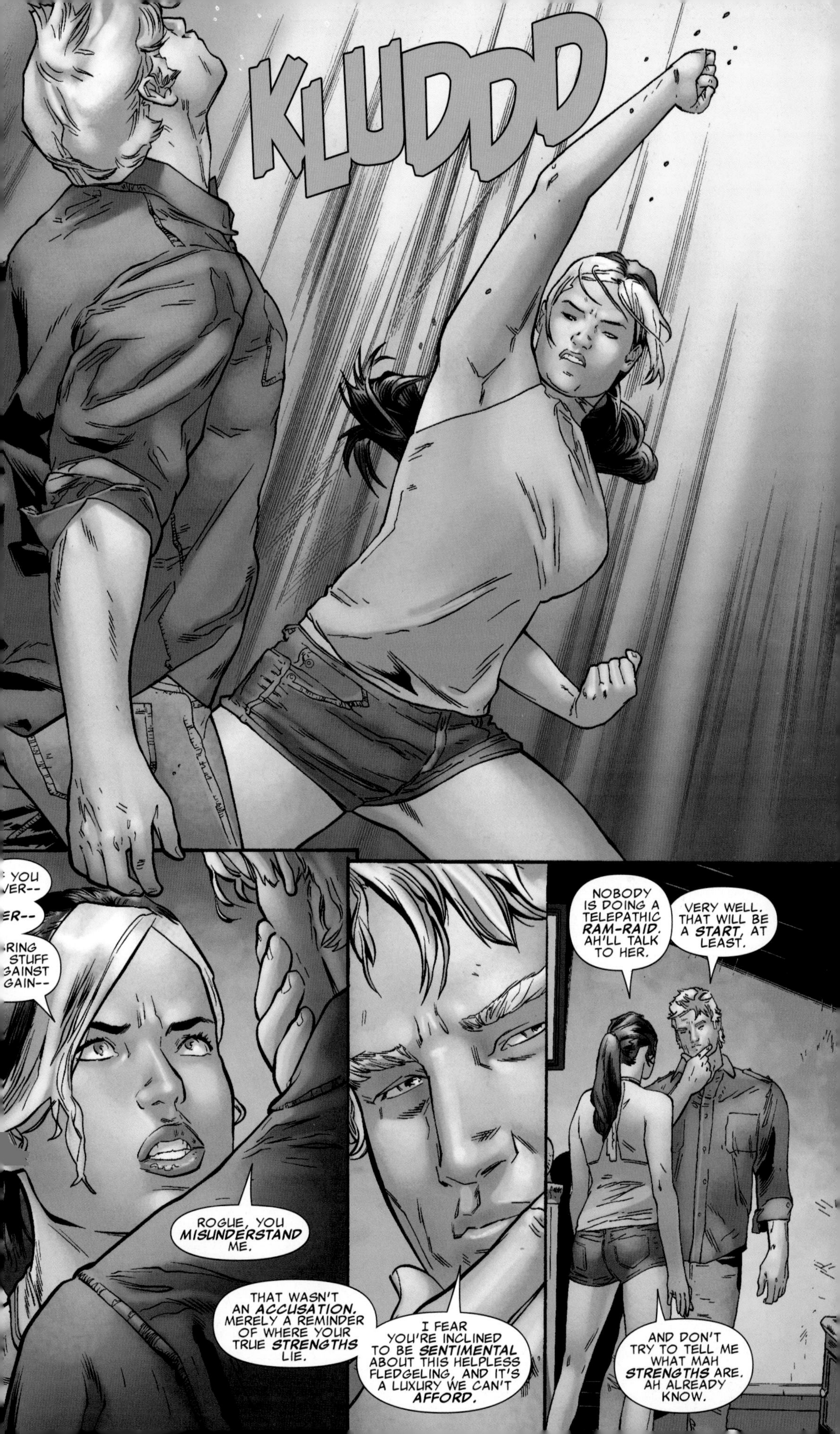
KLUDDD
ROGUE, YOU MISUNDERSTAND ME.
THAT WASN'T AN ACCUSATION. MERELY A REMINDER OF WHERE YOUR TRUE STRENGTHS LIE.
I FEAR YOU'RE INCLINED TO BE SENTIMENTAL ABOUT THIS HELPLESS FLEDGELING, AND IT'S A LUXURY WE CAN'T AFFORD.
NOBODY IS DOING A TELEPATHIC RAM-RAID. AH'LL TALK TO HER.
VERY WELL. THAT WILL BE A START, AT LEAST.
AND DON'T TRY TO TELL ME WHAT MAH STRENGTHS ARE. AH ALREADY KNOW.

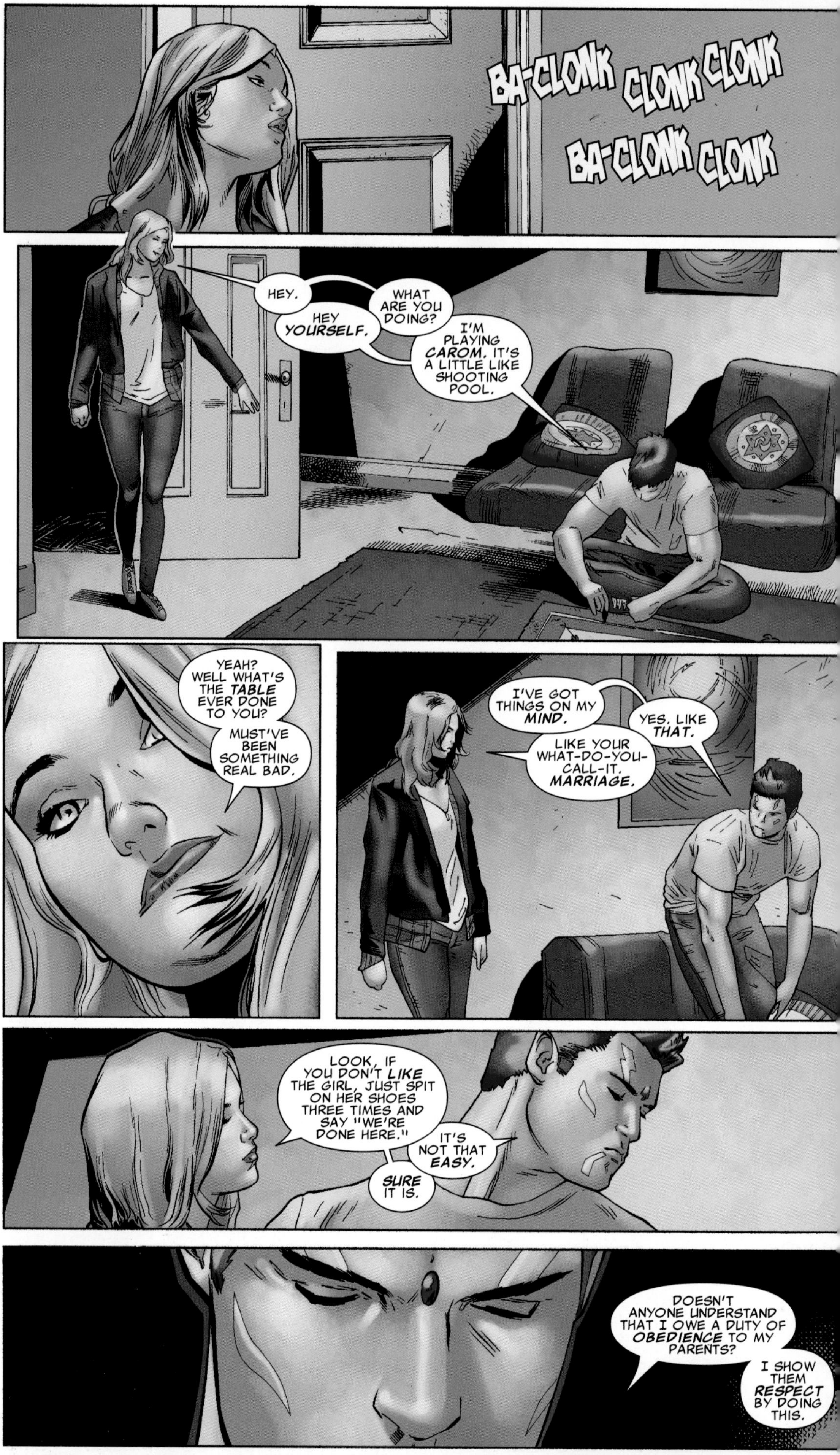
BA-CLONK CLONK CLONK
BA-CLONK CLONK
HEY.
HEY YOURSELF.
WHAT ARE YOU DOING?
I'M PLAYING CAROM. IT'S A LITTLE LIKE SHOOTING POOL.
YEAH? WELL WHAT'S THE TABLE EVER DONE TO YOU?
MUST'VE BEEN SOMETHING REAL BAD.
I'VE GOT THINGS ON MY MIND.
YES. LIKE THAT.
LIKE YOUR WHAT-DO-YOU-CALL-IT. MARRIAGE.
LOOK, IF YOU DON'T LIKE THE GIRL, JUST SPIT ON HER SHOES THREE TIMES AND SAY "WE'RE DONE HERE."
IT'S NOT THAT EASY.
SURE IT IS.
DOESN'T ANYONE UNDERSTAND THAT I OWE A DUTY OF OBEDIENCE TO MY PARENTS?
I SHOW THEM RESPECT BY DOING THIS.

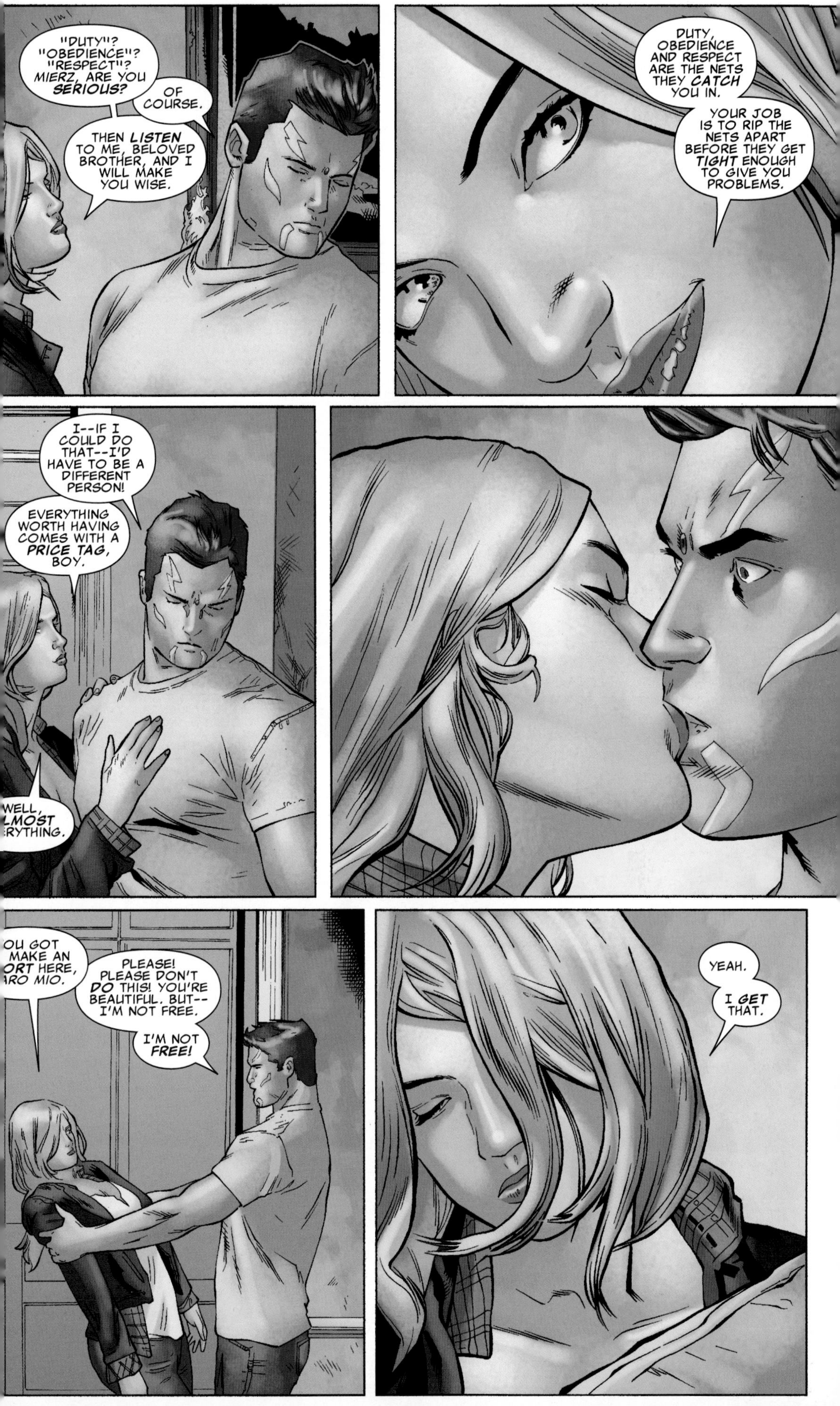
"DUTY"? "OBEDIENCE"? "RESPECT"? MIERZ, ARE YOU SERIOUS?
OF COURSE.
THEN LISTEN TO ME, BELOVED BROTHER, AND I WILL MAKE YOU WISE.
DUTY, OBEDIENCE AND RESPECT ARE THE NETS THEY CATCH YOU IN.
YOUR JOB IS TO RIP THE NETS APART BEFORE THEY GET TIGHT ENOUGH TO GIVE YOU PROBLEMS.
I--IF I COULD DO THAT--I'D HAVE TO BE A DIFFERENT PERSON!
EVERYTHING WORTH HAVING COMES WITH A PRICE TAG, BOY.
WELL, LMOST RYTHING.
OU GOT MAKE AN ORT HERE, ARO MIO.
PLEASE! PLEASE DON'T DO THIS! YOU'RE BEAUTIFUL. BUT-- I'M NOT FREE.
I'M NOT FREE!
YEAH.
I GET THAT.

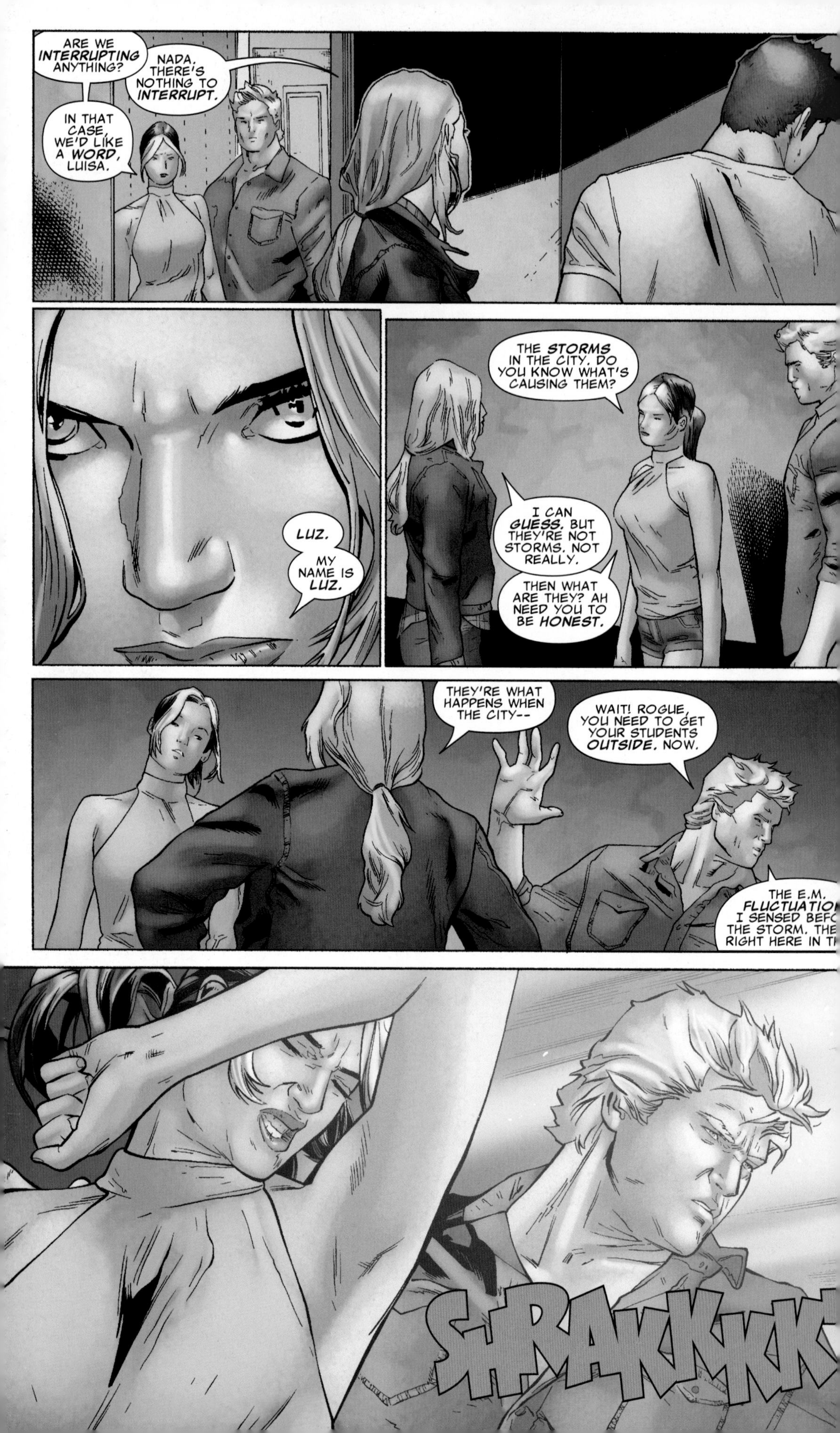
ARE WE INTERRUPTING ANYTHING?
NADA. THERE'S NOTHING TO INTERRUPT.
IN THAT CASE, WE'D LIKE A WORD, LUISA.
LUZ. MY NAME IS LUZ.
THE STORMS IN THE CITY. DO YOU KNOW WHAT'S CAUSING THEM?
I CAN GUESS. BUT THEY'RE NOT STORMS. NOT REALLY.
THEN WHAT ARE THEY? AH NEED YOU TO BE HONEST.
THEY'RE WHAT HAPPENS WHEN THE CITY--
WAIT! ROGUE, YOU NEED TO GET YOUR STUDENTS OUTSIDE. NOW.
SHRAKKKK

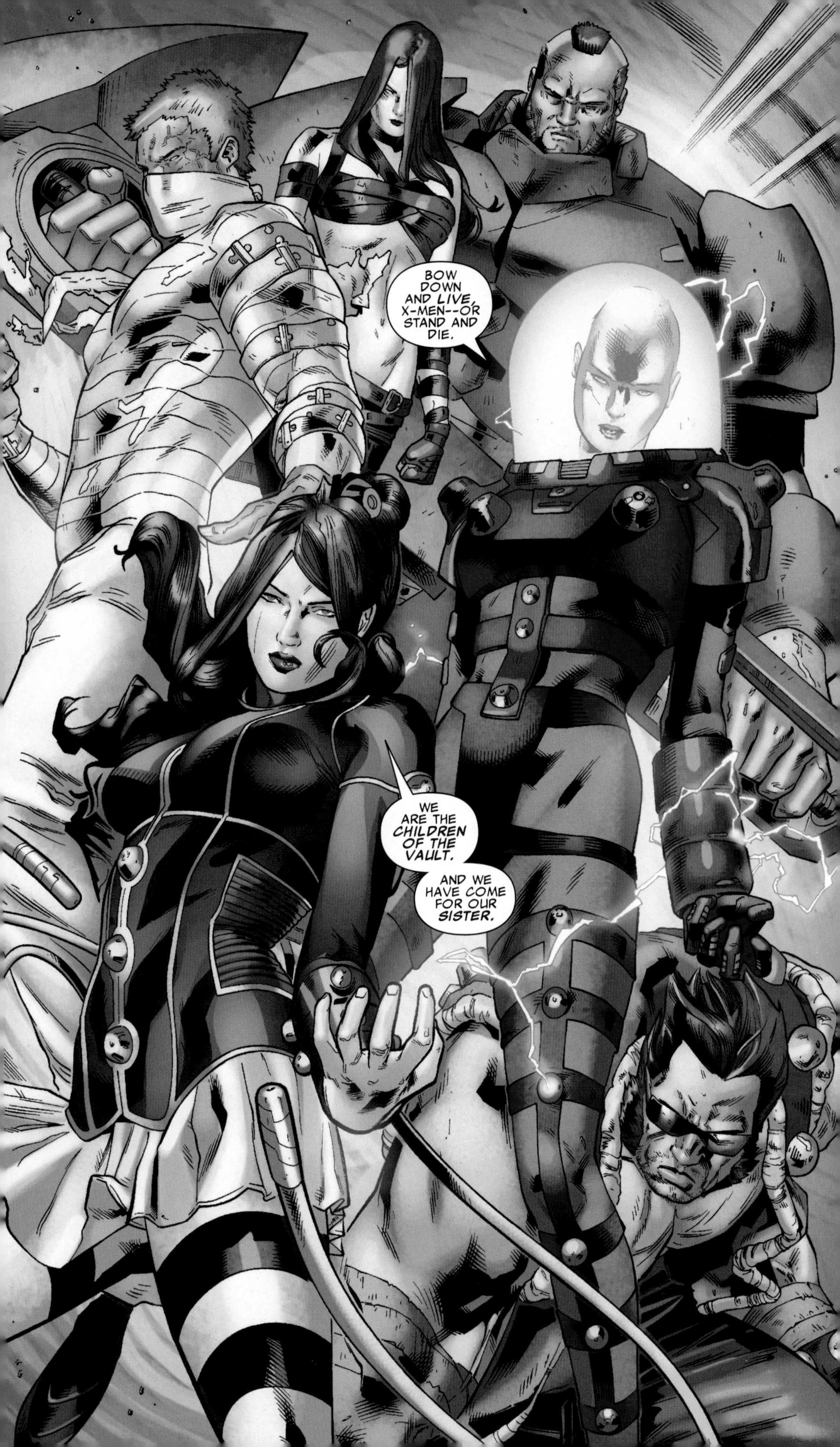
BOW DOWN AND LIVE, X-MEN--OR STAND AND DIE.
WE ARE THE CHILDREN OF THE VAULT.
AND WE HAVE COME FOR OUR SISTER.

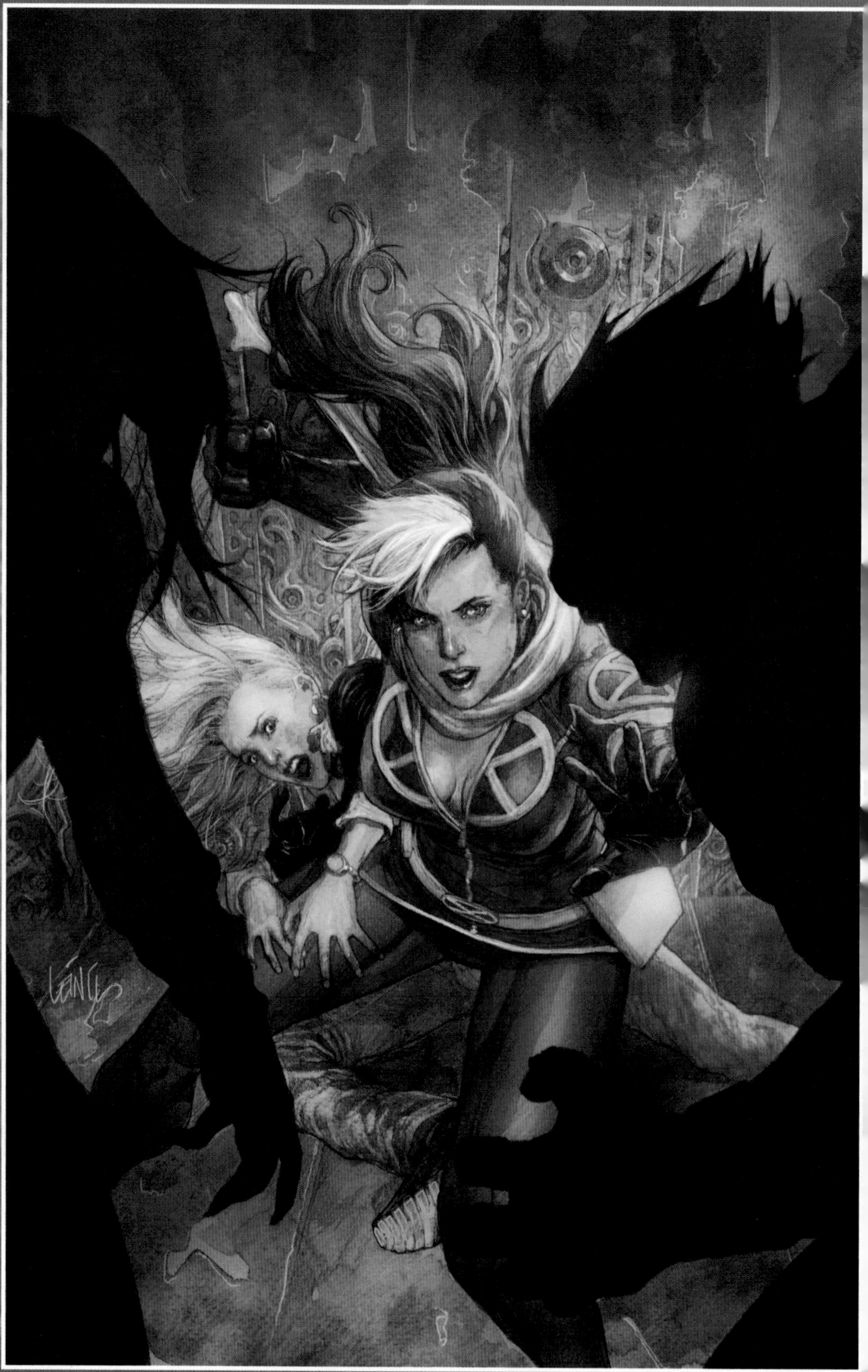

#240

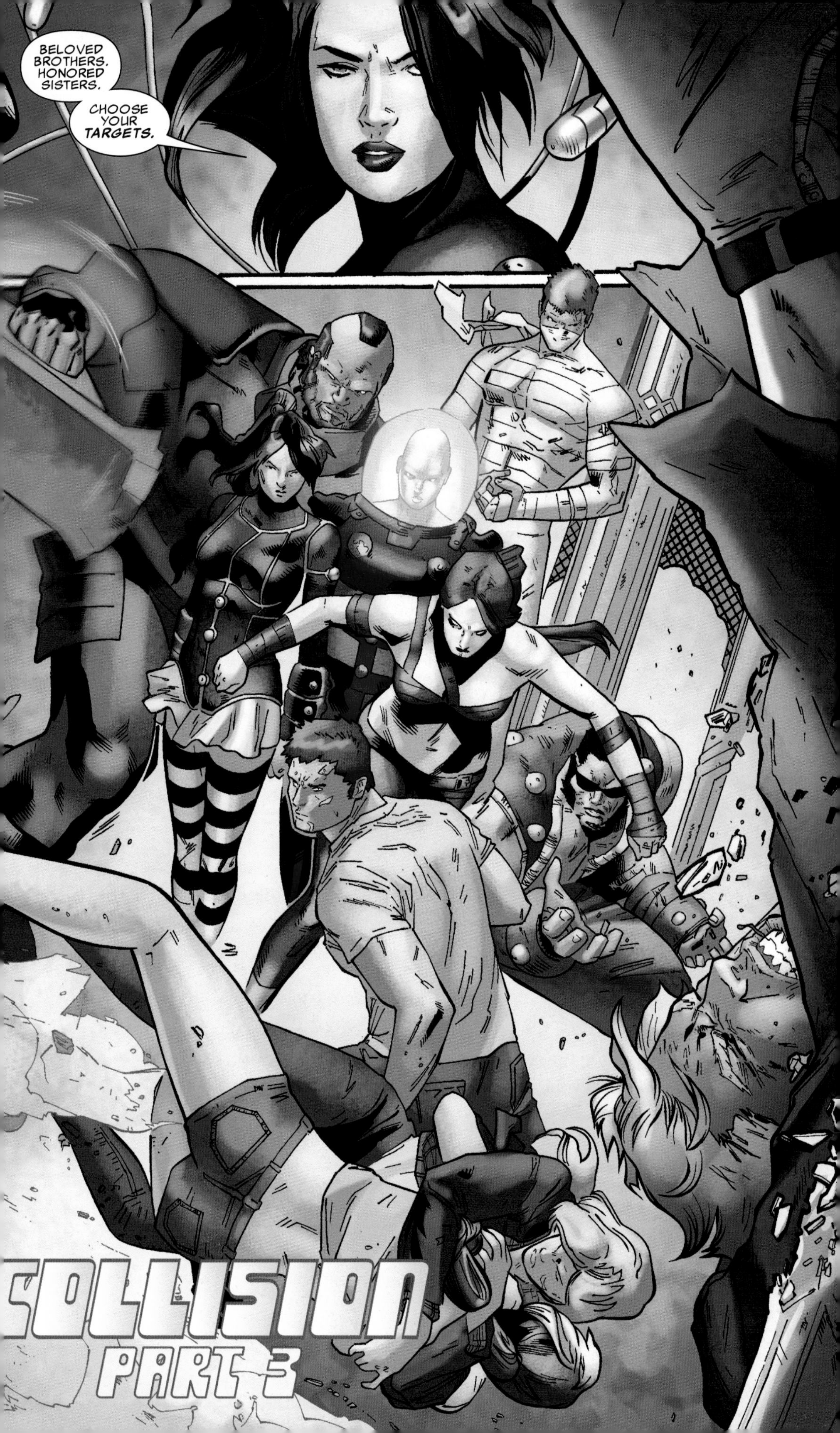
BELOVED BROTHERS. HONORED SISTERS.
CHOOSE YOUR TARGETS.
COLLISION
PART 3

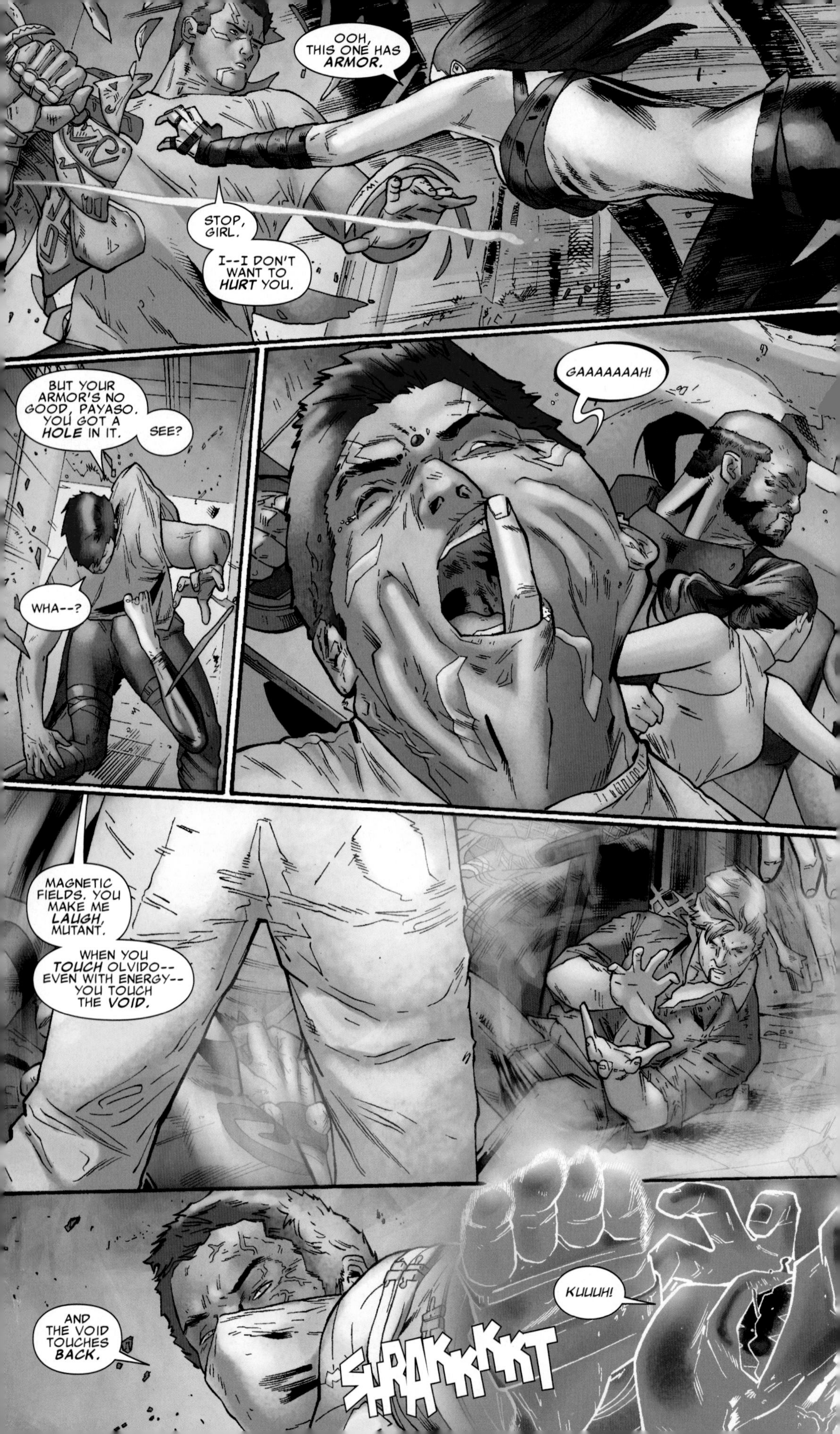
OOH, THIS ONE HAS ARMOR.
STOP, GIRL.
I--I DON'T WANT TO HURT YOU.
BUT YOUR ARMOR'S NO GOOD, PAYASO. YOU GOT A HOLE IN IT.
SEE?
WHA--?
GAAAAAAAH!
MAGNETIC FIELDS. YOU MAKE ME LAUGH, MUTANT.
WHEN YOU TOUCH OLVIDO-- EVEN WITH ENERGY-- YOU TOUCH THE VOID.
AND THE VOID TOUCHES BACK.
KUUUH!
SHRAKKKKT

OH, MIERZ!

MIERZ AL CIELO!

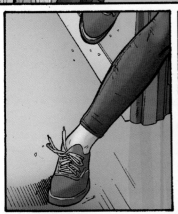

WH-WHAT'S *HAPPENING?* WHAT IS THIS *NOISE?*

SHUT UP, DOLL GIRL. JUST...HIDE UNDER THE *BED* OR SOMETHING.

AND YOU MIGHT ACTUALLY *SURVIVE* THIS.

TELL ME WHAT'S HAPPENING.

MY PEOPLE-- THEY'VE *COME* FOR ME.

OH MIERZ, THEY'RE *GOING* TO TAKE ME BACK. AND THEY'LL *KILL* ANYONE WHO TRIES TO STOP THEM!

BUT...YOU HAVE POWERS, YES? YOU MUST *USE* THEM, THEN.

YOU HAVE TO DO WHAT YOU *CAN* TO *STOP* THIS.

...

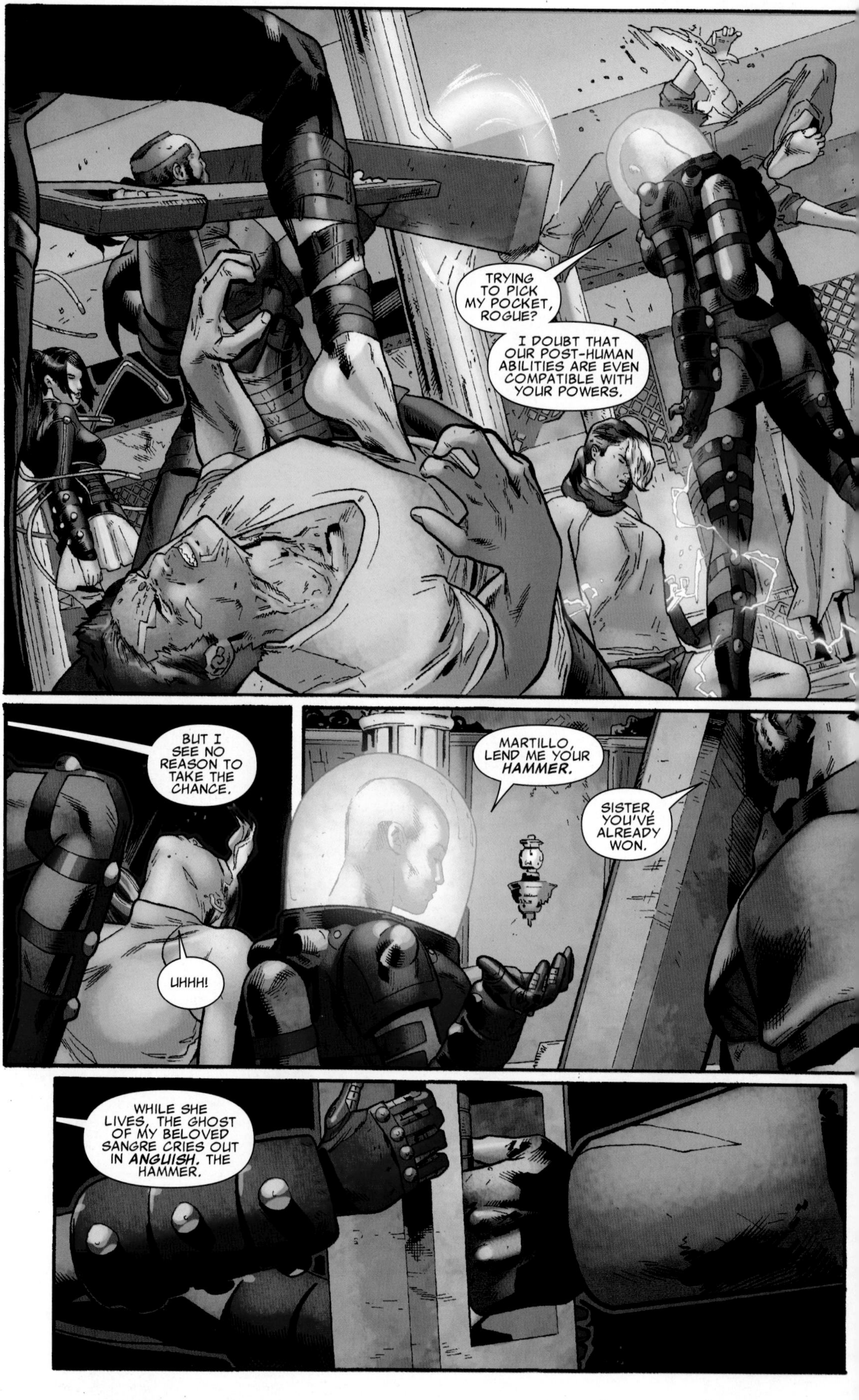
TRYING TO PICK MY POCKET, ROGUE?
I DOUBT THAT OUR POST-HUMAN ABILITIES ARE EVEN COMPATIBLE WITH YOUR POWERS.
BUT I SEE NO REASON TO TAKE THE CHANCE.
UHHH!
MARTILLO, LEND ME YOUR HAMMER.
SISTER, YOU'VE ALREADY WON.
WHILE SHE LIVES, THE GHOST OF MY BELOVED SANGRE CRIES OUT IN ANGUISH. THE HAMMER.

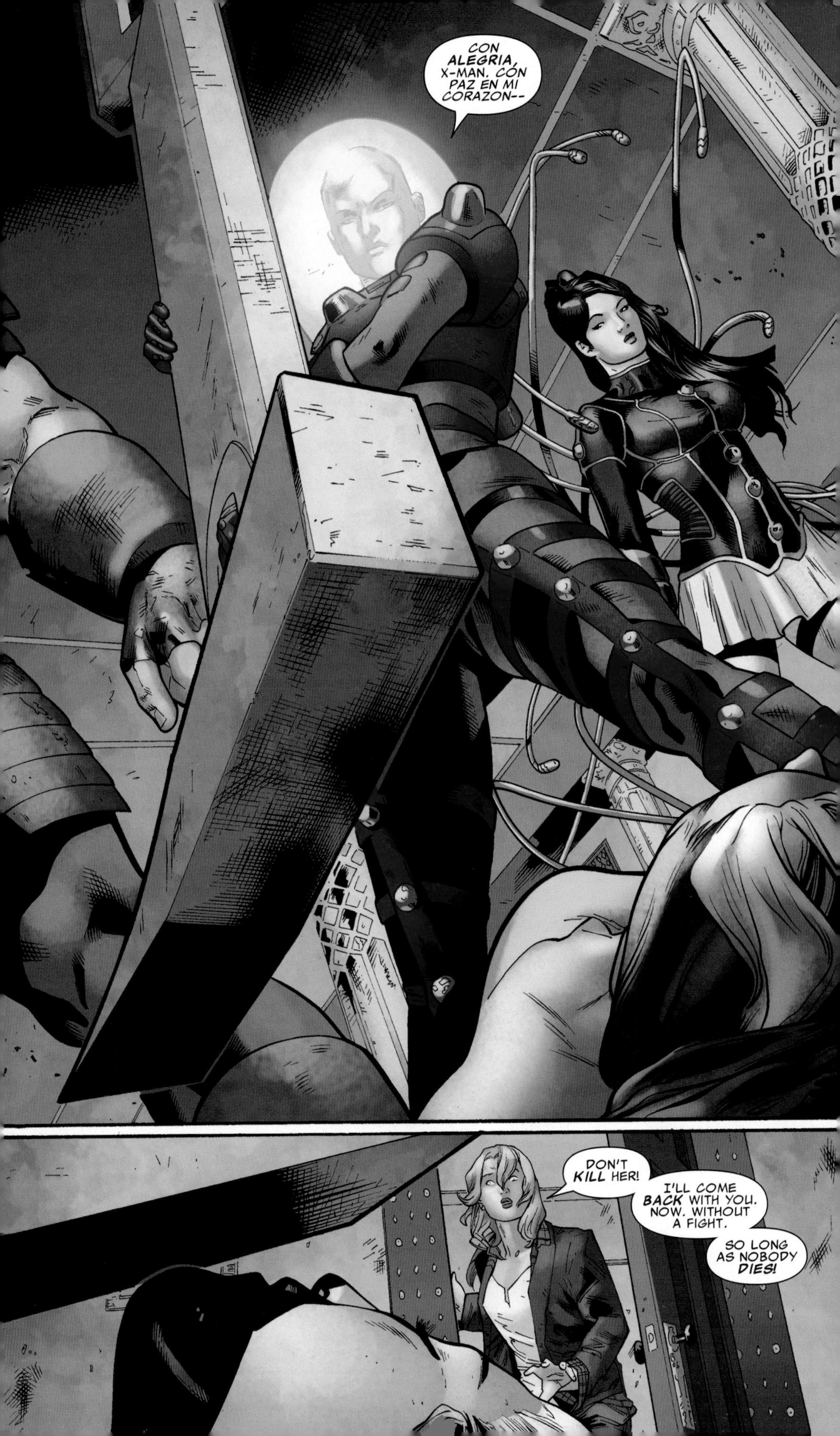
CON ALEGRIA, X-MAN. CON PAZ EN MI CORAZON--
DON'T KILL HER!
I'LL COME BACK WITH YOU. NOW. WITHOUT A FIGHT.
SO LONG AS NOBODY DIES!

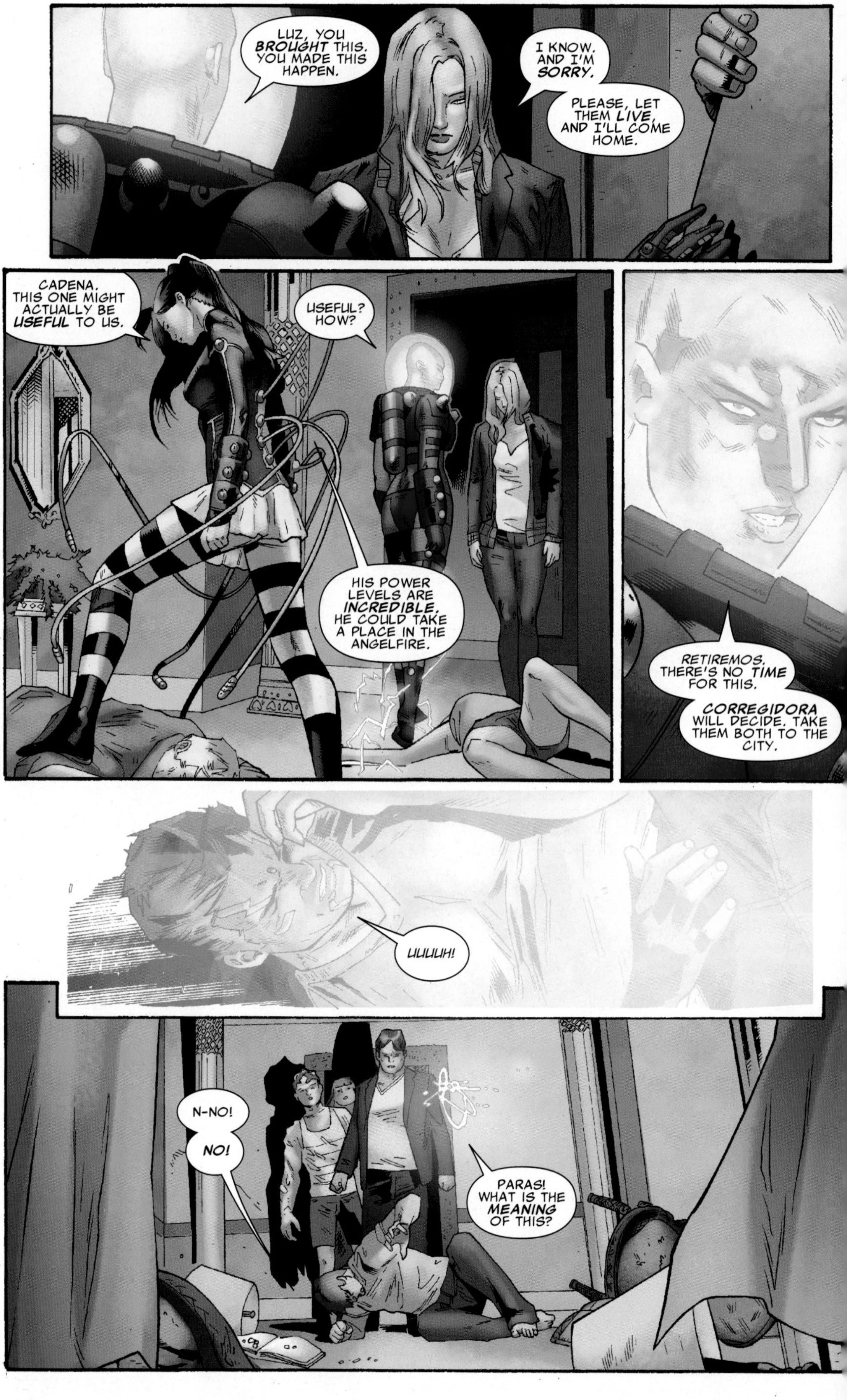
LUZ, YOU BROUGHT THIS. YOU MADE THIS HAPPEN.
I KNOW. AND I'M SORRY.
PLEASE, LET THEM LIVE, AND I'LL COME HOME.
CADENA. THIS ONE MIGHT ACTUALLY BE USEFUL TO US.
USEFUL? HOW?
HIS POWER LEVELS ARE INCREDIBLE. HE COULD TAKE A PLACE IN THE ANGELFIRE.
RETIREMOS. THERE'S NO TIME FOR THIS.
CORREGIDORA WILL DECIDE. TAKE THEM BOTH TO THE CITY.
UUUUH!
N-NO!
NO!
PARAS! WHAT IS THE MEANING OF THIS?

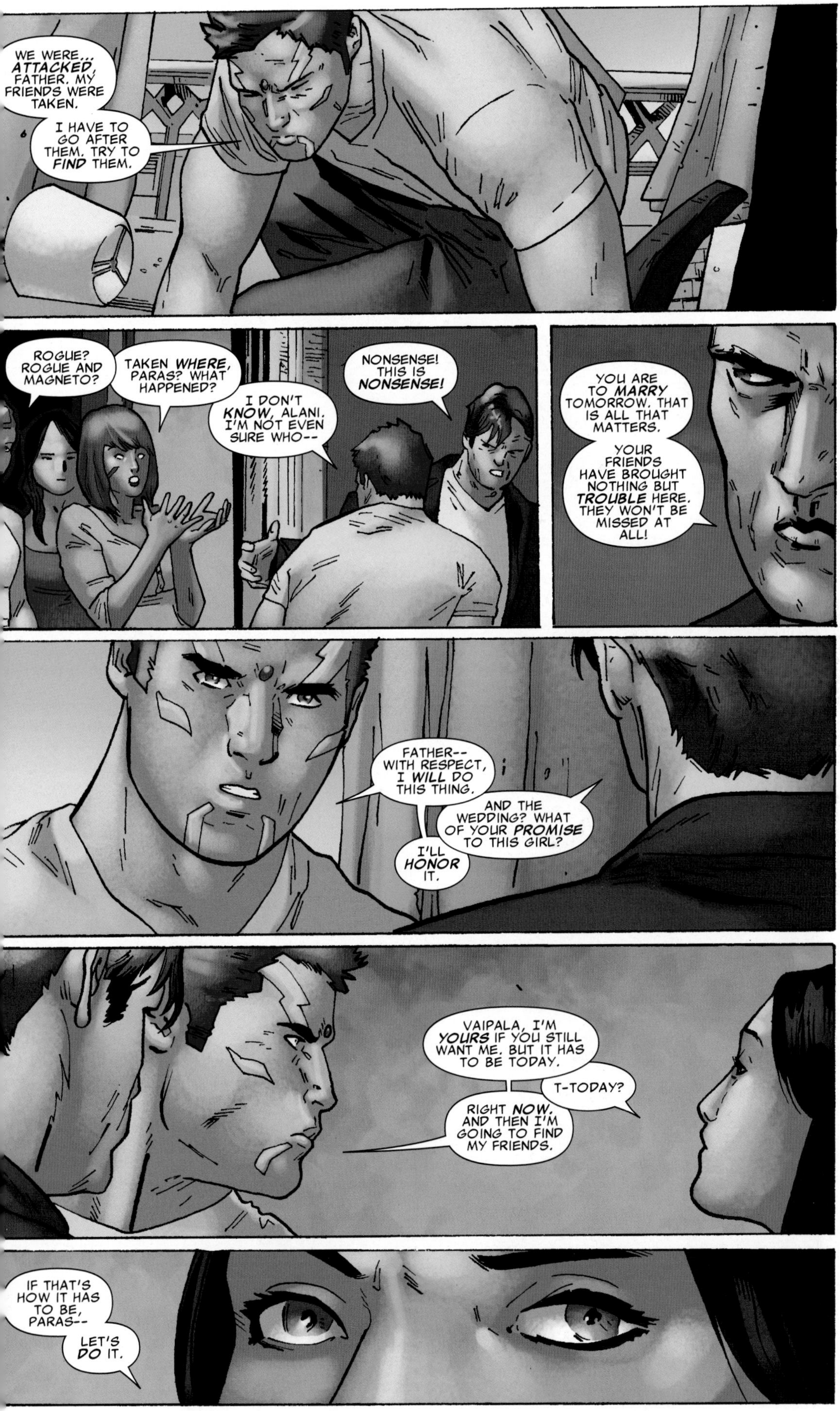

WE WERE... ATTACKED, FATHER. MY FRIENDS WERE TAKEN.
I HAVE TO GO AFTER THEM. TRY TO FIND THEM.
ROGUE? ROGUE AND MAGNETO?
TAKEN WHERE, PARAS? WHAT HAPPENED?
I DON'T KNOW, ALANI. I'M NOT EVEN SURE WHO--
NONSENSE! THIS IS NONSENSE!
YOU ARE TO MARRY TOMORROW. THAT IS ALL THAT MATTERS.
YOUR FRIENDS HAVE BROUGHT NOTHING BUT TROUBLE HERE. THEY WON'T BE MISSED AT ALL!
FATHER-- WITH RESPECT, I WILL DO THIS THING.
AND THE WEDDING? WHAT OF YOUR PROMISE TO THIS GIRL?
I'LL HONOR IT.
VAIPALA, I'M YOURS IF YOU STILL WANT ME. BUT IT HAS TO BE TODAY.
T-TODAY?
RIGHT NOW, AND THEN I'M GOING TO FIND MY FRIENDS.
IF THAT'S HOW IT HAS TO BE, PARAS--
LET'S DO IT.

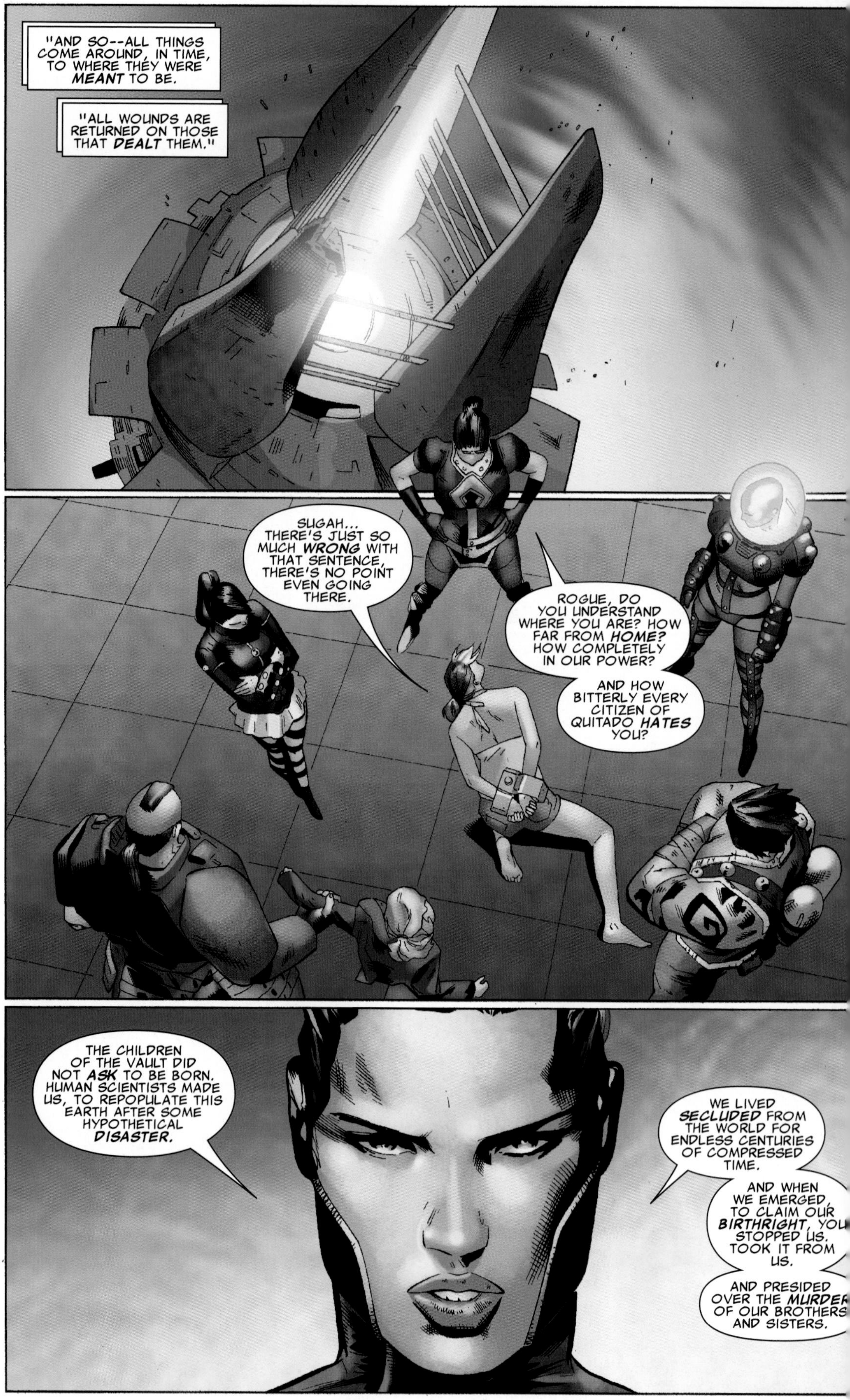
"AND SO--ALL THINGS COME AROUND, IN TIME, TO WHERE THEY WERE MEANT TO BE.
"ALL WOUNDS ARE RETURNED ON THOSE THAT DEALT THEM."
SUGAH... THERE'S JUST SO MUCH WRONG WITH THAT SENTENCE, THERE'S NO POINT EVEN GOING THERE.
ROGUE, DO YOU UNDERSTAND WHERE YOU ARE? HOW FAR FROM HOME? HOW COMPLETELY IN OUR POWER?
AND HOW BITTERLY EVERY CITIZEN OF QUITADO HATES YOU?
THE CHILDREN OF THE VAULT DID NOT ASK TO BE BORN. HUMAN SCIENTISTS MADE US, TO REPOPULATE THIS EARTH AFTER SOME HYPOTHETICAL DISASTER.
WE LIVED SECLUDED FROM THE WORLD FOR ENDLESS CENTURIES OF COMPRESSED TIME.
AND WHEN WE EMERGED, TO CLAIM OUR BIRTHRIGHT, YOU STOPPED US. TOOK IT FROM US.
AND PRESIDED OVER THE MURDER OF OUR BROTHERS AND SISTERS.

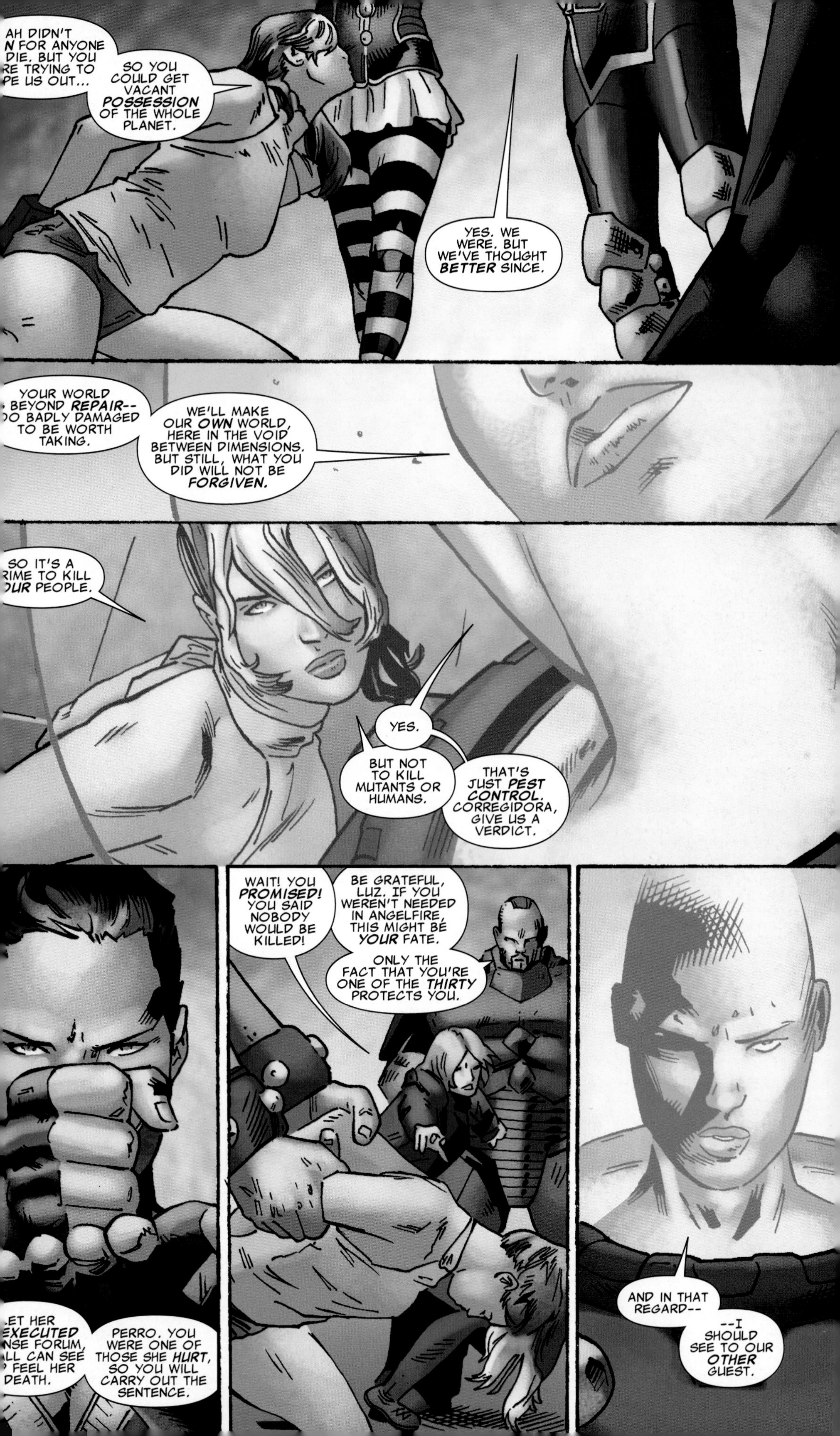

AH DIDN'T
N FOR ANYONE
DIE. BUT YOU
RE TRYING TO
PE US OUT...
SO YOU COULD GET VACANT POSSESSION OF THE WHOLE PLANET.
YES. WE WERE. BUT WE'VE THOUGHT BETTER SINCE.
YOUR WORLD
BEYOND REPAIR--
OO BADLY DAMAGED TO BE WORTH TAKING.
WE'LL MAKE OUR OWN WORLD, HERE IN THE VOID BETWEEN DIMENSIONS. BUT STILL, WHAT YOU DID WILL NOT BE FORGIVEN.
SO IT'S A
RIME TO KILL
OUR PEOPLE.
YES.
BUT NOT TO KILL MUTANTS OR HUMANS.
THAT'S JUST PEST CONTROL. CORREGIDORA, GIVE US A VERDICT.
ET HER
EXECUTED
NSE FORUM,
LL CAN SEE
FEEL HER
DEATH.
PERRO. YOU WERE ONE OF THOSE SHE HURT, SO YOU WILL CARRY OUT THE SENTENCE.
WAIT! YOU PROMISED! YOU SAID NOBODY WOULD BE KILLED!
BE GRATEFUL, LUZ. IF YOU WEREN'T NEEDED IN ANGELFIRE, THIS MIGHT BE YOUR FATE.
ONLY THE FACT THAT YOU'RE ONE OF THE THIRTY PROTECTS YOU.
AND IN THAT REGARD--
--I SHOULD SEE TO OUR OTHER GUEST.

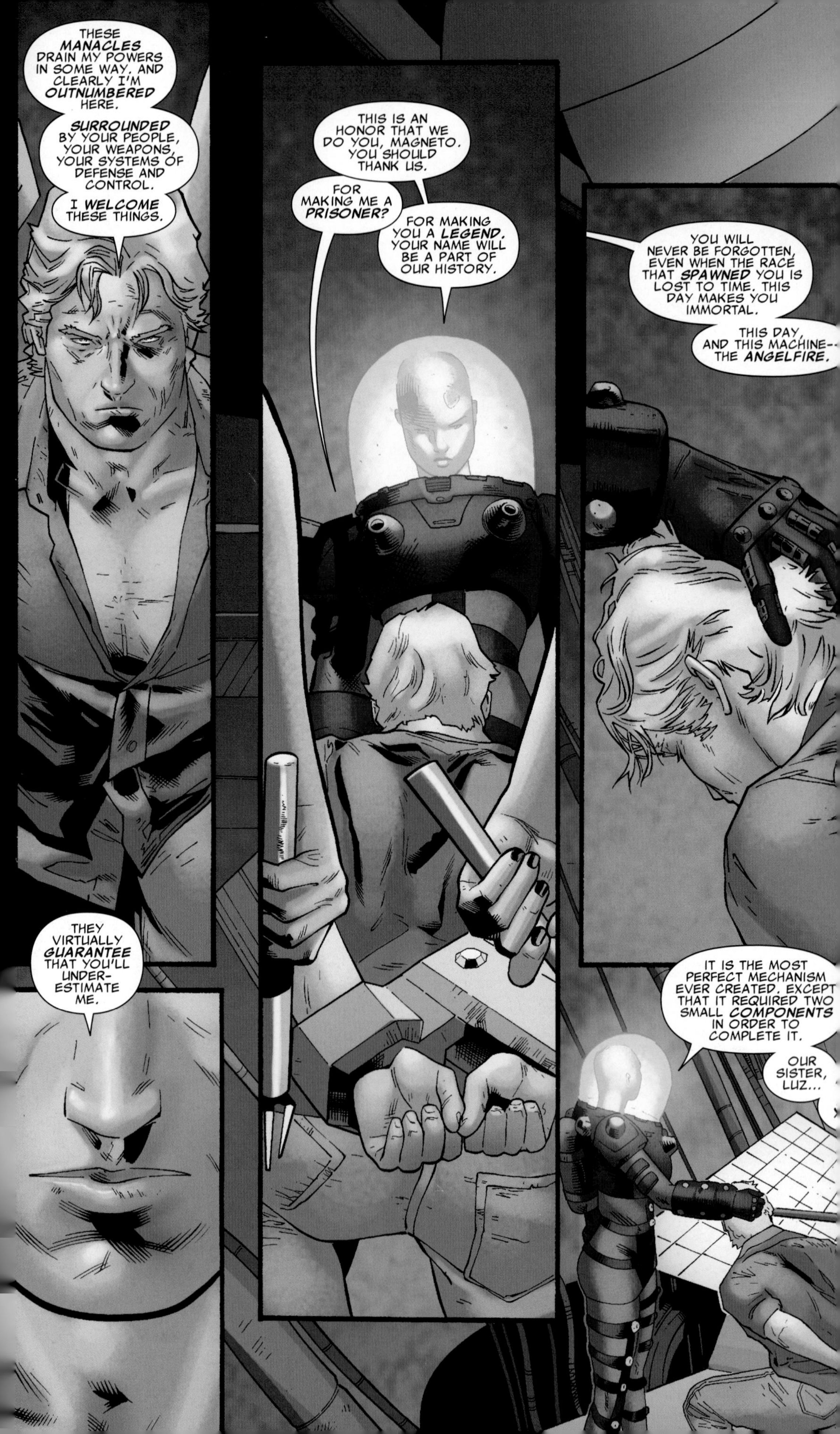
THESE MANACLES DRAIN MY POWERS IN SOME WAY, AND CLEARLY I'M OUTNUMBERED HERE.
SURROUNDED BY YOUR PEOPLE, YOUR WEAPONS, YOUR SYSTEMS OF DEFENSE AND CONTROL.
I WELCOME THESE THINGS.
THEY VIRTUALLY GUARANTEE THAT YOU'LL UNDER-ESTIMATE ME.
THIS IS AN HONOR THAT WE DO YOU, MAGNETO. YOU SHOULD THANK US.
FOR MAKING ME A PRISONER?
FOR MAKING YOU A LEGEND. YOUR NAME WILL BE A PART OF OUR HISTORY.
YOU WILL NEVER BE FORGOTTEN, EVEN WHEN THE RACE THAT SPAWNED YOU IS LOST TO TIME. THIS DAY MAKES YOU IMMORTAL.
THIS DAY, AND THIS MACHINE-- THE ANGELFIRE.
IT IS THE MOST PERFECT MECHANISM EVER CREATED. EXCEPT THAT IT REQUIRED TWO SMALL COMPONENTS IN ORDER TO COMPLETE IT.
OUR SISTER, LUZ...

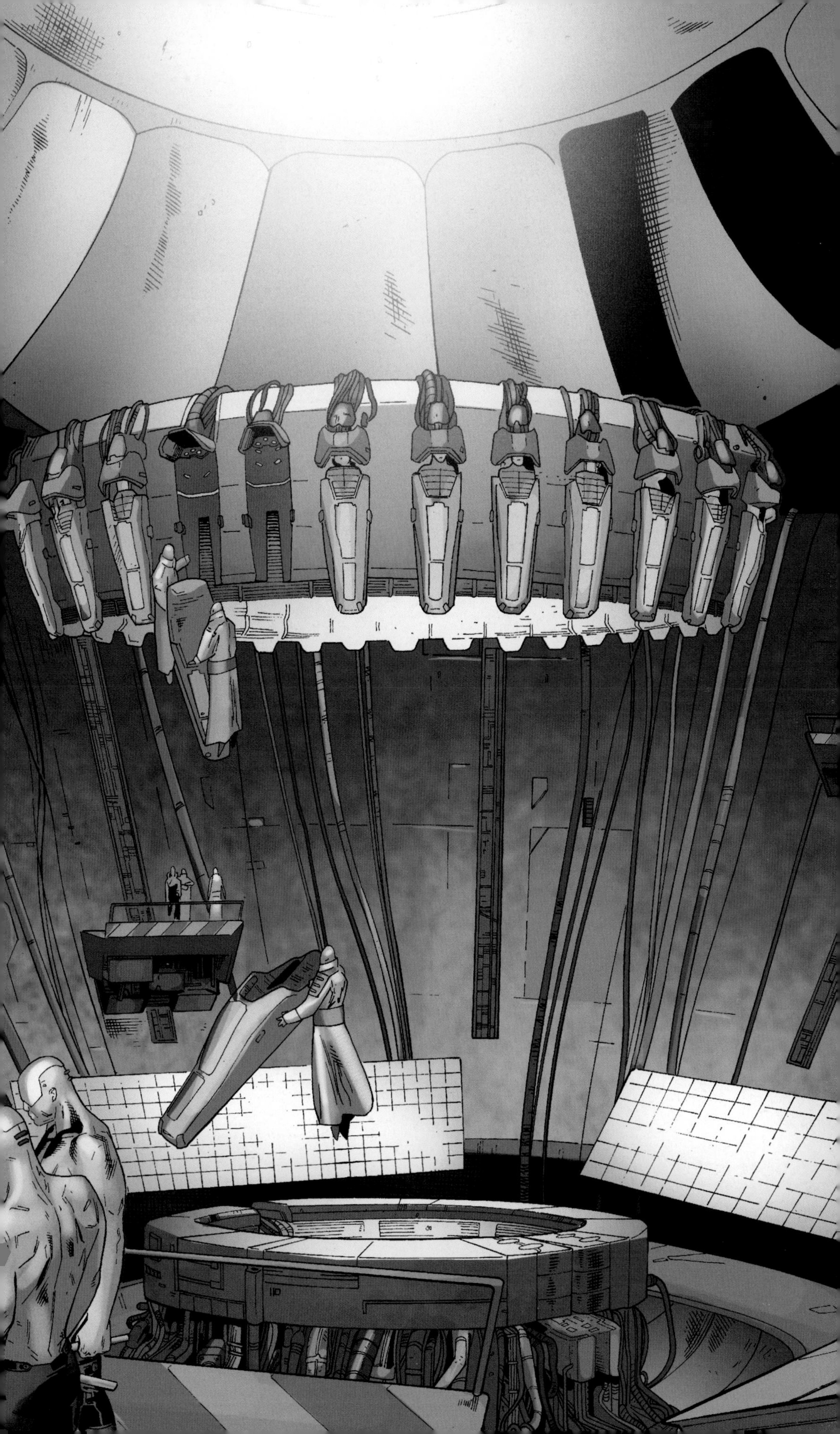

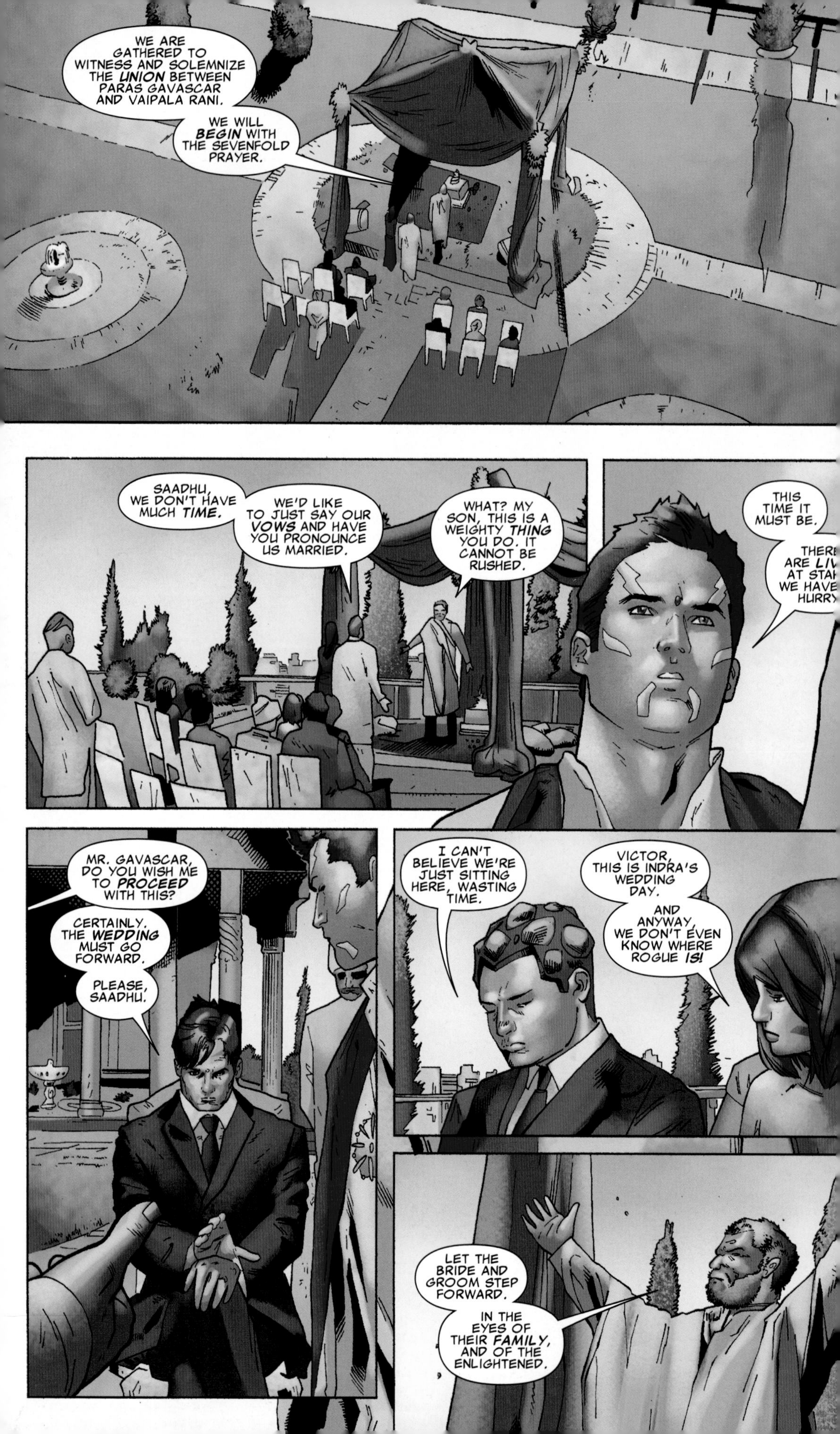
WE ARE GATHERED TO WITNESS AND SOLEMNIZE THE UNION BETWEEN PARAS GAVASCAR AND VAIPALA RANI.
WE WILL BEGIN WITH THE SEVENFOLD PRAYER.
SAADHU, WE DON'T HAVE MUCH TIME.
WE'D LIKE TO JUST SAY OUR VOWS AND HAVE YOU PRONOUNCE US MARRIED.
WHAT? MY SON, THIS IS A WEIGHTY THING YOU DO. IT CANNOT BE RUSHED.
THIS TIME IT MUST BE.
THERE ARE LIV AT STAK WE HAVE HURRY
MR. GAVASCAR, DO YOU WISH ME TO PROCEED WITH THIS?
CERTAINLY. THE WEDDING MUST GO FORWARD.
PLEASE, SAADHU.
I CAN'T BELIEVE WE'RE JUST SITTING HERE, WASTING TIME.
VICTOR, THIS IS INDRA'S WEDDING DAY.
AND ANYWAY, WE DON'T EVEN KNOW WHERE ROGUE IS!
LET THE BRIDE AND GROOM STEP FORWARD.
IN THE EYES OF THEIR FAMILY, AND OF THE ENLIGHTENED.

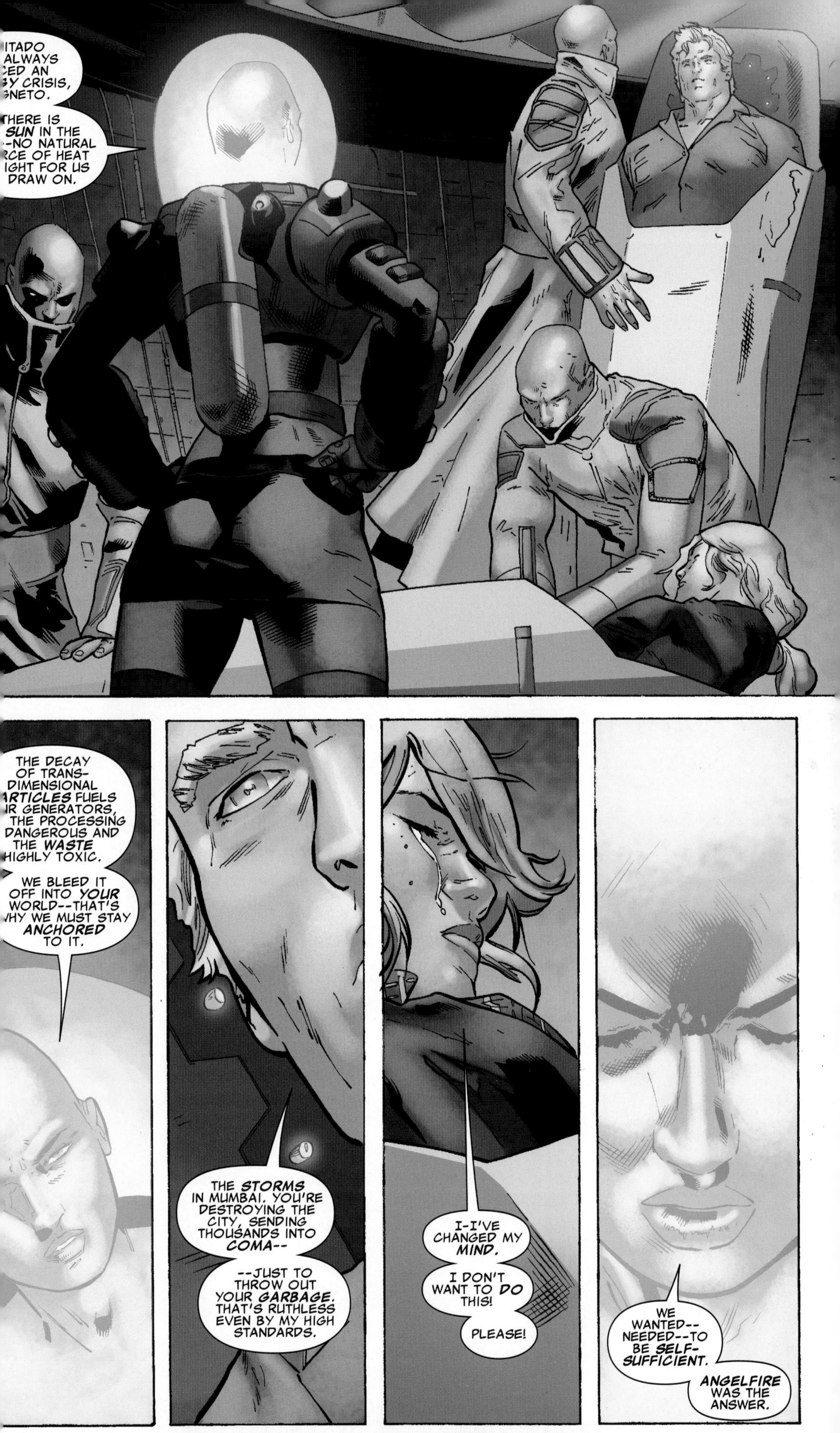
ITADO ALWAYS CED AN GY CRISIS, GNETO.
THERE IS SUN IN THE -NO NATURAL RCE OF HEAT IGHT FOR US DRAW ON.
THE DECAY OF TRANS-DIMENSIONAL ARTICLES FUELS R GENERATORS, THE PROCESSING DANGEROUS AND THE WASTE HIGHLY TOXIC.
WE BLEED IT OFF INTO YOUR WORLD--THAT'S HY WE MUST STAY ANCHORED TO IT.
THE STORMS IN MUMBAI. YOU'RE DESTROYING THE CITY, SENDING THOUSANDS INTO COMA--
--JUST TO THROW OUT YOUR GARBAGE. THAT'S RUTHLESS EVEN BY MY HIGH STANDARDS.
I-I'VE CHANGED MY MIND.
I DON'T WANT TO DO THIS!
PLEASE!
WE WANTED--NEEDED--TO BE SELF-SUFFICIENT.
ANGELFIRE WAS THE ANSWER.

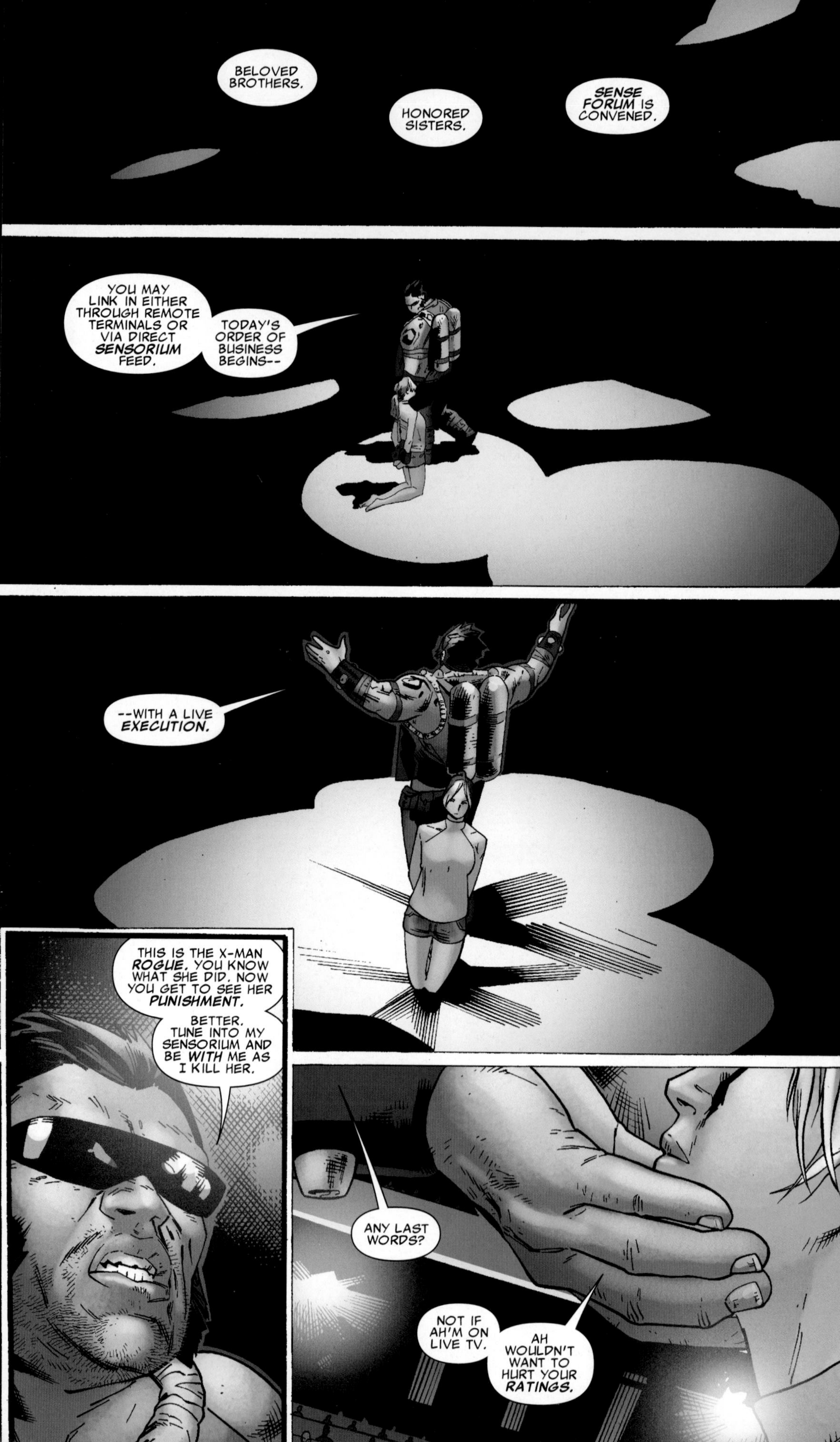
BELOVED BROTHERS.
HONORED SISTERS.
SENSE FORUM IS CONVENED.
YOU MAY LINK IN EITHER THROUGH REMOTE TERMINALS OR VIA DIRECT SENSORIUM FEED.
TODAY'S ORDER OF BUSINESS BEGINS--
--WITH A LIVE EXECUTION.
THIS IS THE X-MAN ROGUE. YOU KNOW WHAT SHE DID. NOW YOU GET TO SEE HER PUNISHMENT.
BETTER. TUNE INTO MY SENSORIUM AND BE WITH ME AS I KILL HER.
ANY LAST WORDS?
NOT IF AH'M ON LIVE TV.
AH WOULDN'T WANT TO HURT YOUR RATINGS.

MANY OF OUR NUMBER HAVE POWERS THAT INVOLVE *ENERGY.* THEY PRODUCE HEAT, ELECTRICITY, RADIATION, OR--LIKE OUR DEAR LUZ--LIGHT.

WHAT, WE WONDERED, IF A *DEVICE* COULD BE BUILT THAT DREW ON ALL THESE POWERS?

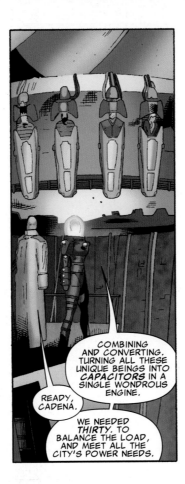

READY, CADENA.

COMBINING AND CONVERTING. TURNING ALL THESE UNIQUE BEINGS INTO *CAPACITORS* IN A SINGLE WONDROUS ENGINE.

WE NEEDED *THIRTY.* TO BALANCE THE LOAD, AND MEET ALL THE CITY'S POWER NEEDS.

SIMULTANEOUS *BIO-FEEDBACK* WOULD REPAIR THE BODY CELLS OF OUR VOLUNTEERS. PREVENT ALL DAMAGE, ALL *AGING.* THEY'D LIVE FOREVER, BARRING ACCIDENTS.

BUT WE ONLY HAD TWENTY-NINE.

UNTIL WE FOUND *YOU.*

THIS *RICE,* FOR PLENTY.

THIS *COIN,* FOR *WEALTH.*

YOUR GARMENTS BOUND, AS YOUR *SOULS* ARE BOUND.

WALK FOUR TIMES AROUND THE *PHERE* FIRE.

AND BECOME AS YOU ARE *MEANT* TO BE.

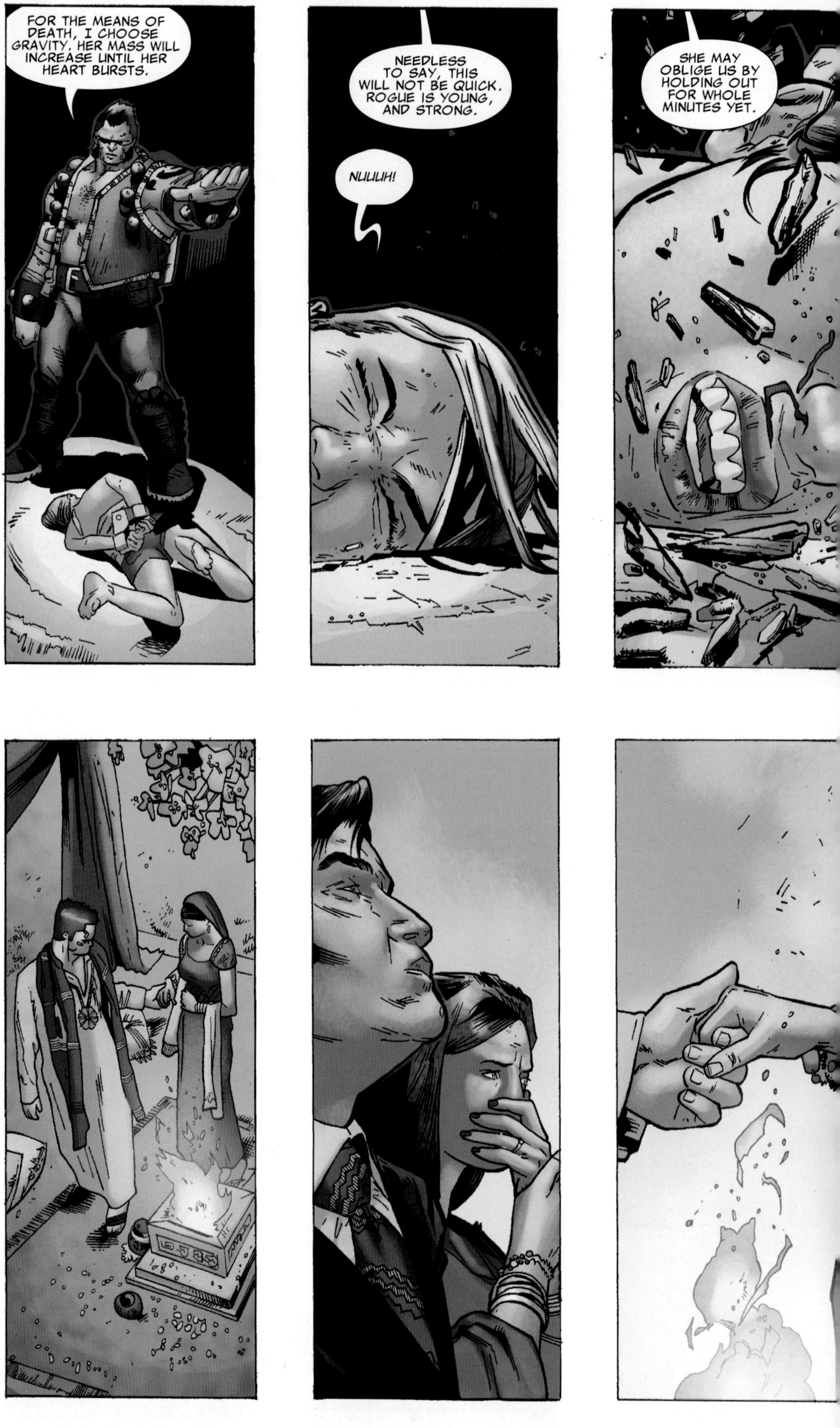
FOR THE MEANS OF DEATH, I CHOOSE GRAVITY. HER MASS WILL INCREASE UNTIL HER HEART BURSTS.
NEEDLESS TO SAY, THIS WILL NOT BE QUICK. ROGUE IS YOUNG, AND STRONG.
NUUUH!
SHE MAY OBLIGE US BY HOLDING OUT FOR WHOLE MINUTES YET.

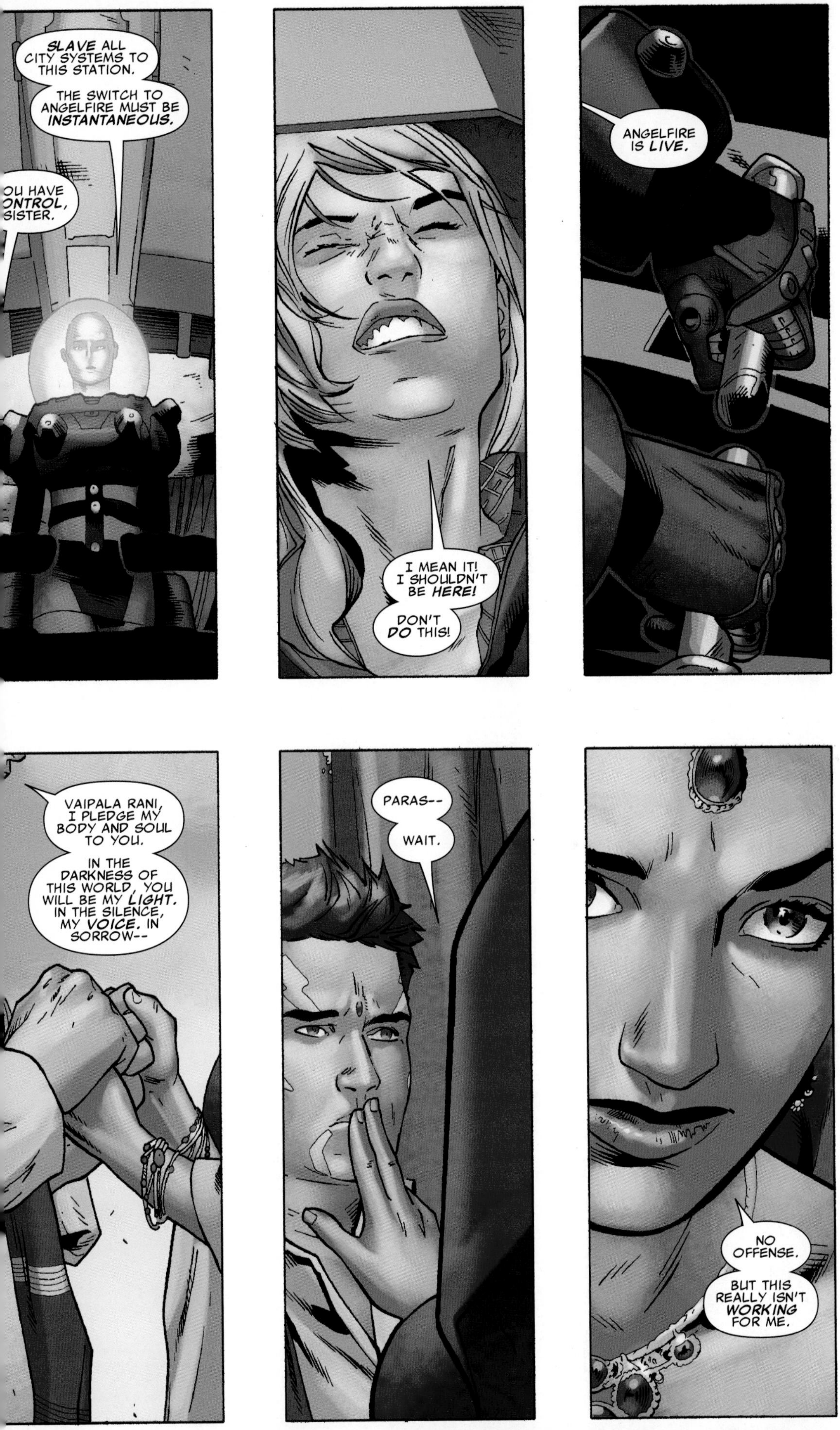

SLAVE ALL CITY SYSTEMS TO THIS STATION.
THE SWITCH TO ANGELFIRE MUST BE INSTANTANEOUS.
OU HAVE ONTROL, SISTER.
I MEAN IT! I SHOULDN'T BE HERE!
DON'T DO THIS!
ANGELFIRE IS LIVE.
VAIPALA RANI, I PLEDGE MY BODY AND SOUL TO YOU.
IN THE DARKNESS OF THIS WORLD, YOU WILL BE MY LIGHT. IN THE SILENCE, MY VOICE. IN SORROW--
PARAS--
WAIT.
NO OFFENSE.
BUT THIS REALLY ISN'T WORKING FOR ME.

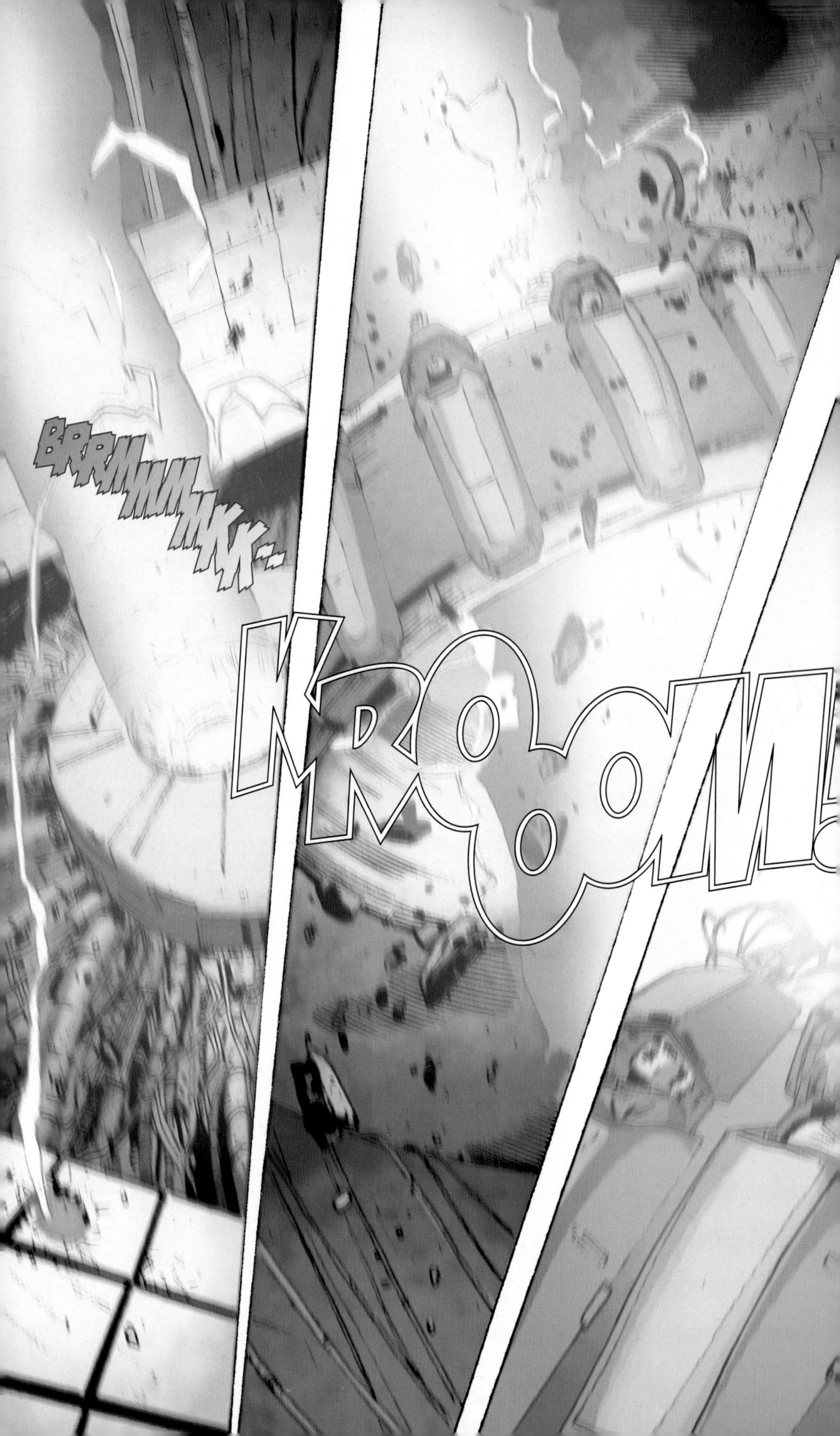
BRRMMMMNK--
KROOOM!

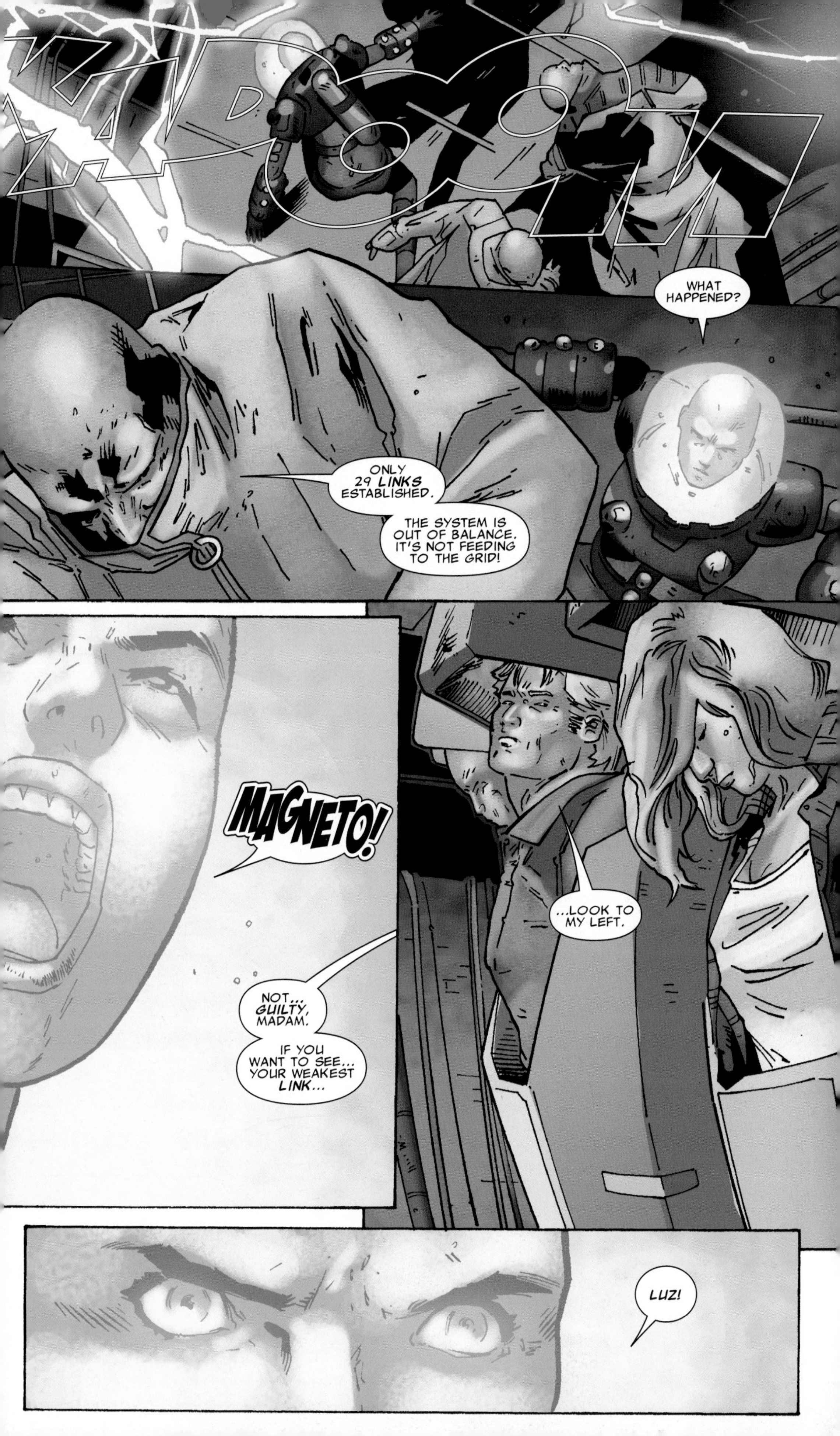
KADOOM
WHAT HAPPENED?
ONLY 29 LINKS ESTABLISHED.
THE SYSTEM IS OUT OF BALANCE. IT'S NOT FEEDING TO THE GRID!
MAGNETO!
...LOOK TO MY LEFT.
NOT... GUILTY, MADAM.
IF YOU WANT TO SEE... YOUR WEAKEST LINK...
LUZ!

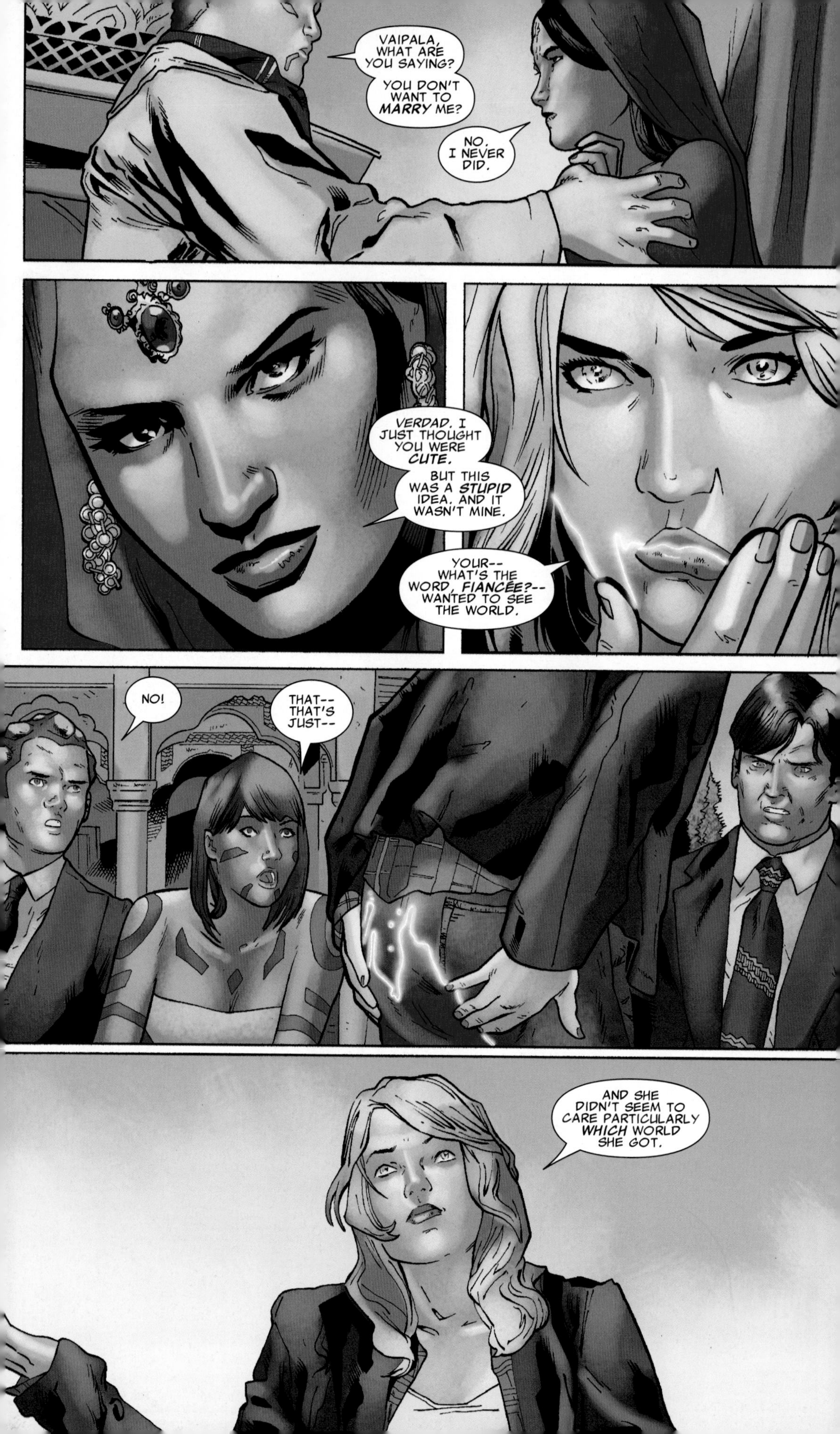
VAIPALA, WHAT ARE YOU SAYING?
YOU DON'T WANT TO MARRY ME?
NO. I NEVER DID.
VERDAD. I JUST THOUGHT YOU WERE CUTE.
BUT THIS WAS A STUPID IDEA. AND IT WASN'T MINE.
YOUR-- WHAT'S THE WORD, FIANCÉE?-- WANTED TO SEE THE WORLD.
NO!
THAT-- THAT'S JUST--
AND SHE DIDN'T SEEM TO CARE PARTICULARLY WHICH WORLD SHE GOT.

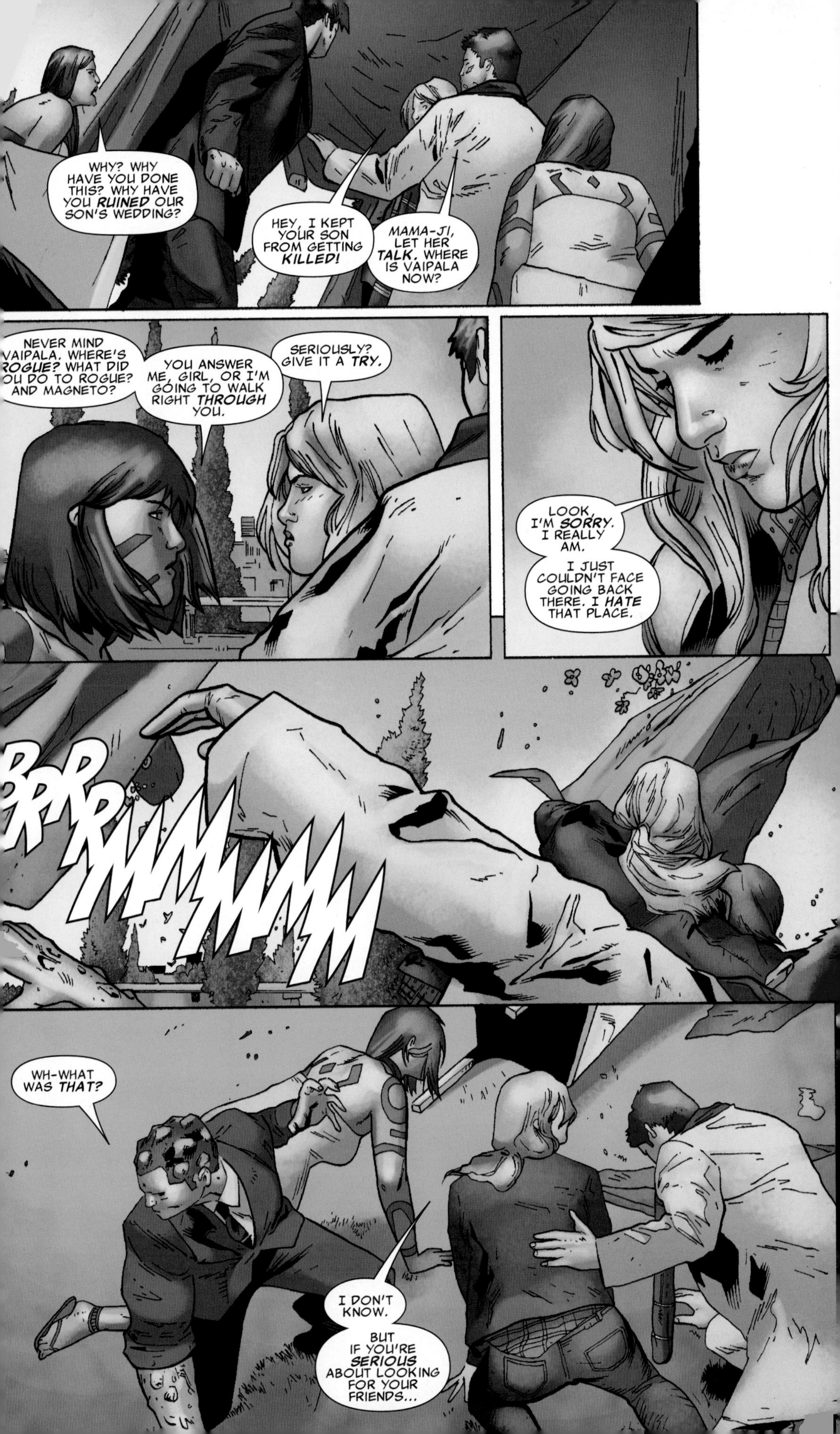
WHY? WHY HAVE YOU DONE THIS? WHY HAVE YOU RUINED OUR SON'S WEDDING?
HEY, I KEPT YOUR SON FROM GETTING KILLED!
MAMA-JI, LET HER TALK. WHERE IS VAIPALA NOW?
NEVER MIND VAIPALA. WHERE'S ROGUE? WHAT DID OU DO TO ROGUE? AND MAGNETO?
YOU ANSWER ME, GIRL, OR I'M GOING TO WALK RIGHT THROUGH YOU.
SERIOUSLY? GIVE IT A TRY.
LOOK, I'M SORRY. I REALLY AM.
I JUST COULDN'T FACE GOING BACK THERE. I HATE THAT PLACE.
BRRRMMMMMMM
WH-WHAT WAS THAT?
I DON'T KNOW.
BUT IF YOU'RE SERIOUS ABOUT LOOKING FOR YOUR FRIENDS...

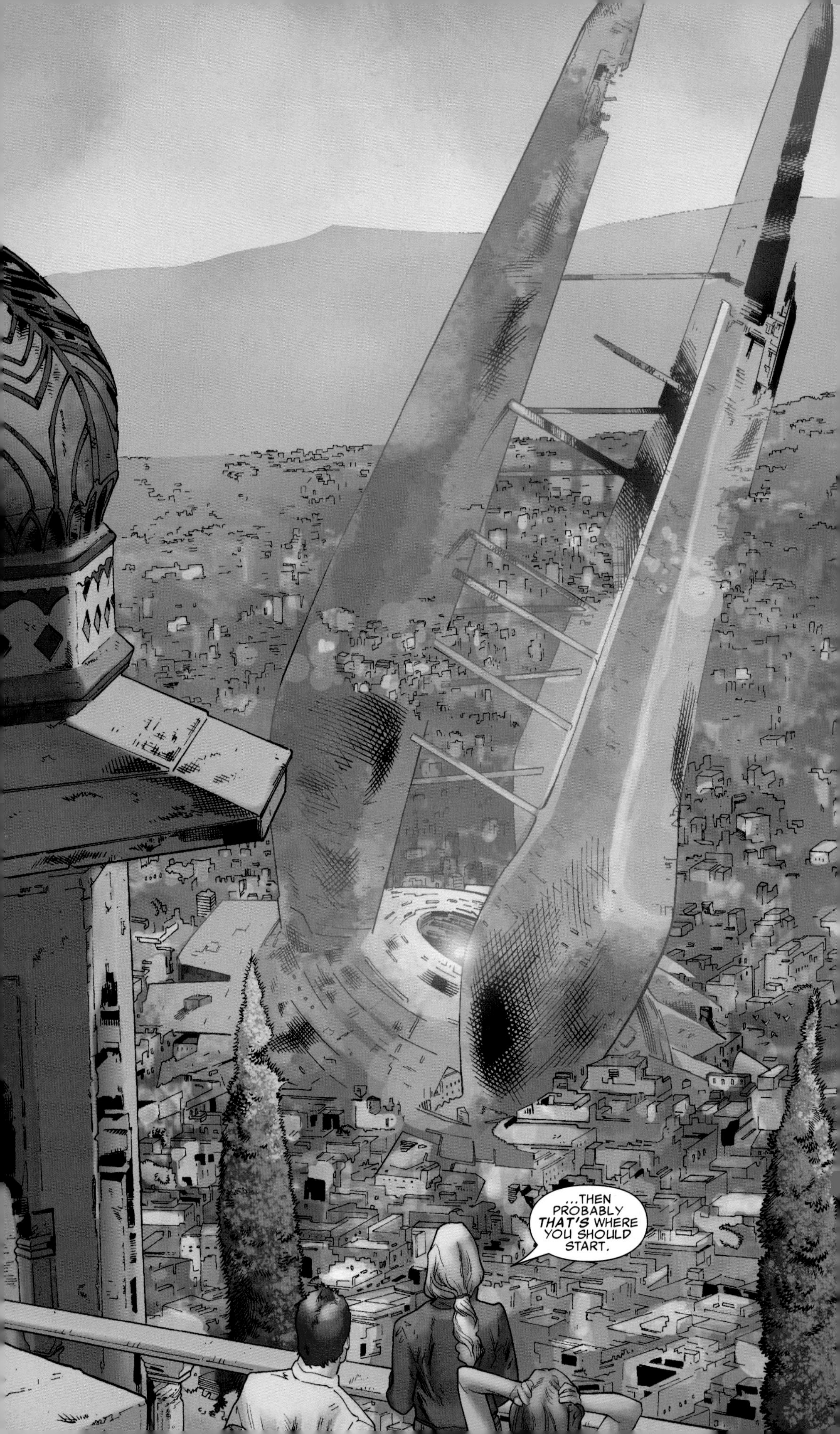
...THEN PROBABLY *THAT'S* WHERE YOU SHOULD START.

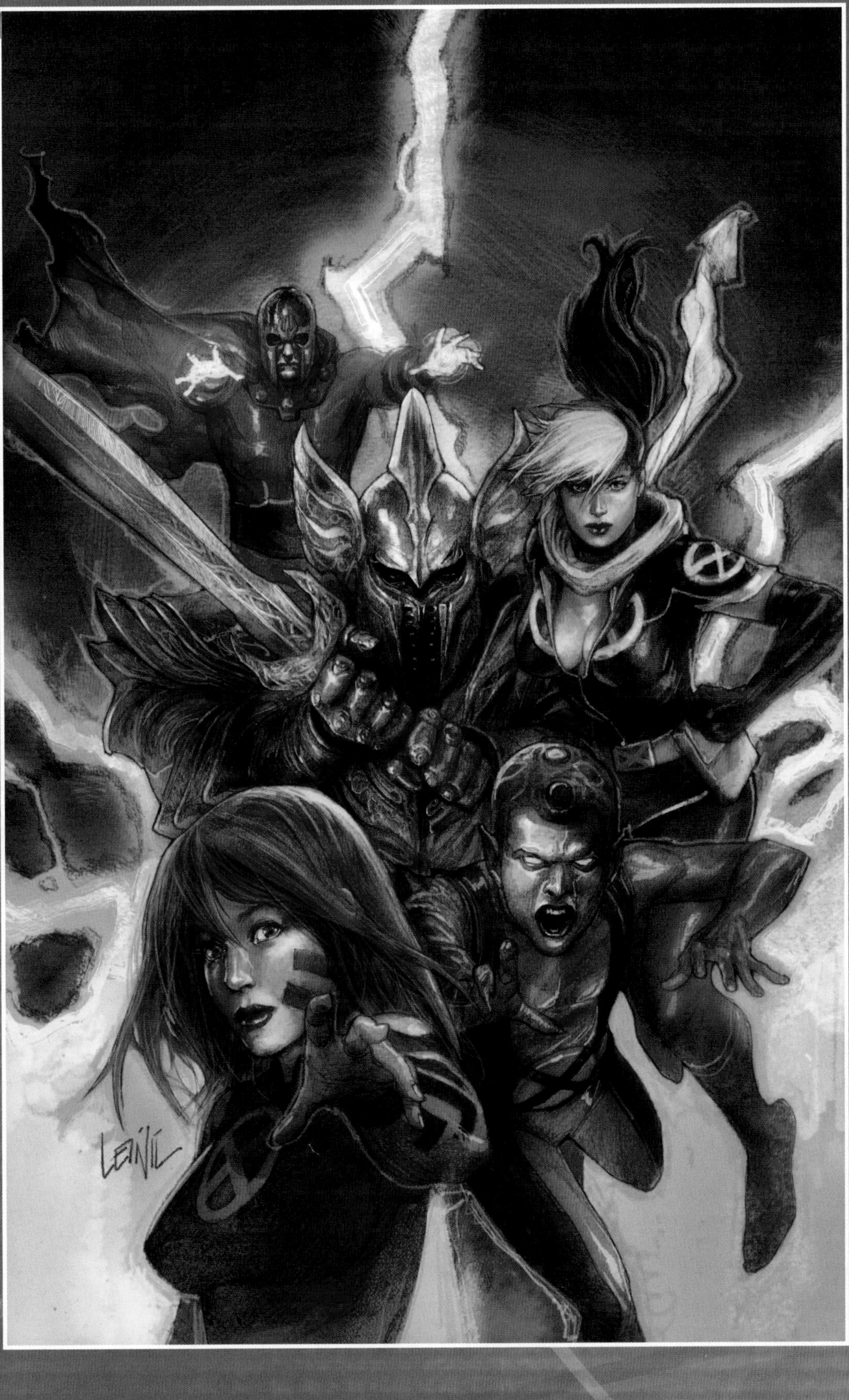
LEINIL

#241

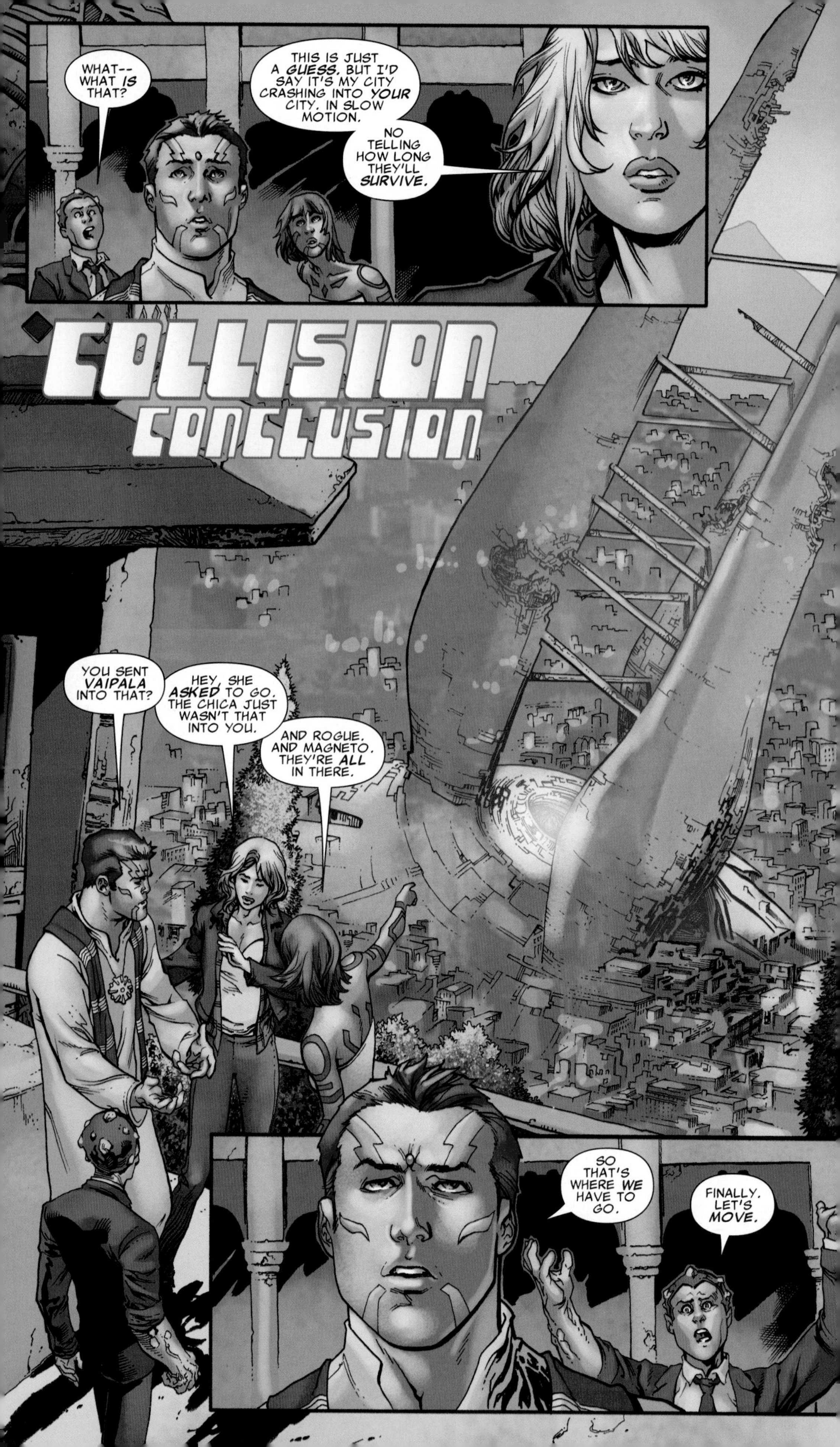

WHAT-- WHAT IS THAT?
THIS IS JUST A GUESS, BUT I'D SAY IT'S MY CITY CRASHING INTO YOUR CITY. IN SLOW MOTION.
NO TELLING HOW LONG THEY'LL SURVIVE.
COLLISION CONCLUSION
YOU SENT VAIPALA INTO THAT?
HEY, SHE ASKED TO GO. THE CHICA JUST WASN'T THAT INTO YOU.
AND ROGUE. AND MAGNETO. THEY'RE ALL IN THERE.
SO THAT'S WHERE WE HAVE TO GO.
FINALLY. LET'S MOVE.

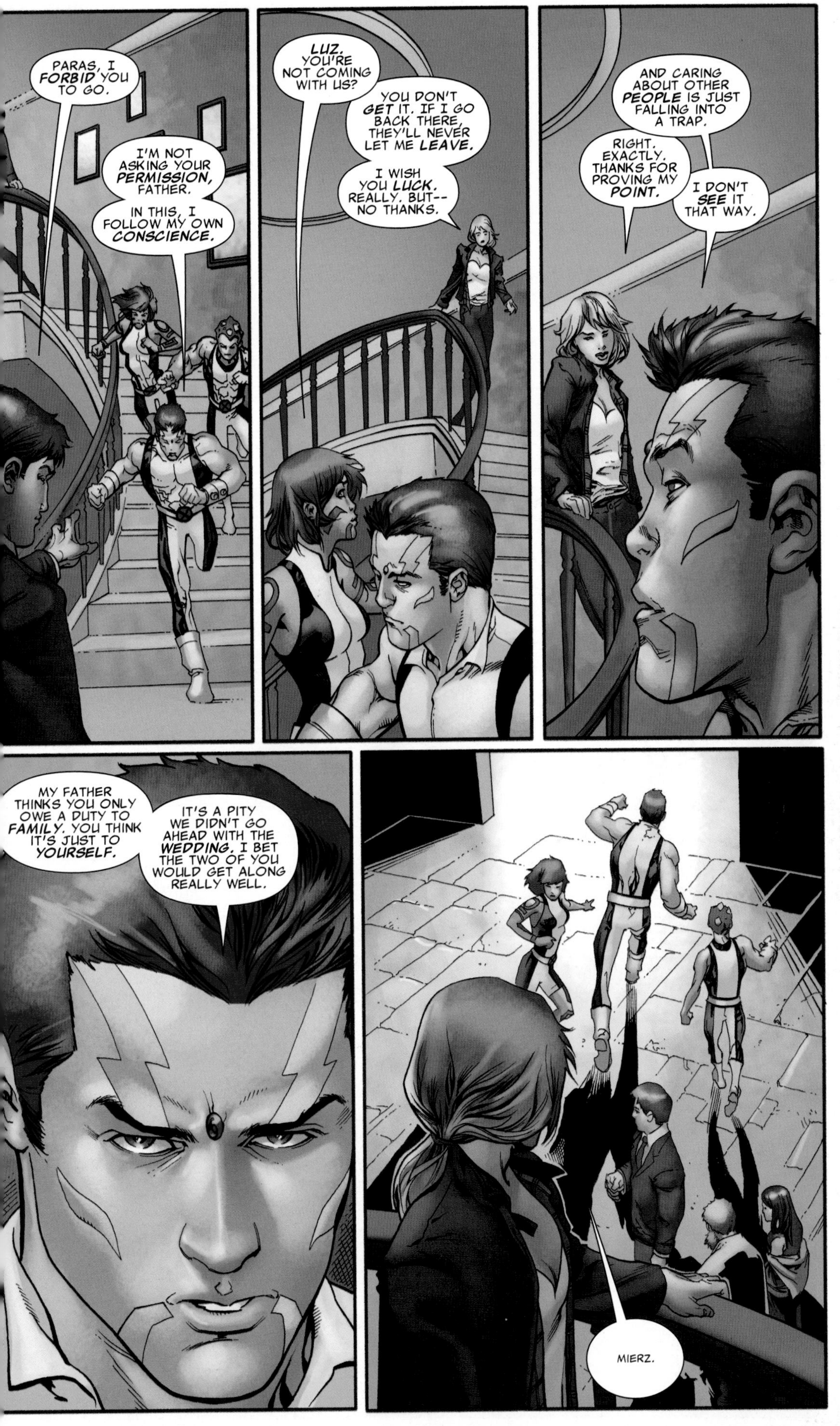

PARAS, I FORBID YOU TO GO.
I'M NOT ASKING YOUR PERMISSION, FATHER.
IN THIS, I FOLLOW MY OWN CONSCIENCE.
LUZ. YOU'RE NOT COMING WITH US?
YOU DON'T GET IT. IF I GO BACK THERE, THEY'LL NEVER LET ME LEAVE.
I WISH YOU LUCK. REALLY. BUT-- NO THANKS.
AND CARING ABOUT OTHER PEOPLE IS JUST FALLING INTO A TRAP.
RIGHT. EXACTLY. THANKS FOR PROVING MY POINT.
I DON'T SEE IT THAT WAY.
MY FATHER THINKS YOU ONLY OWE A DUTY TO FAMILY. YOU THINK IT'S JUST TO YOURSELF.
IT'S A PITY WE DIDN'T GO AHEAD WITH THE WEDDING. I BET THE TWO OF YOU WOULD GET ALONG REALLY WELL.
MIERZ.

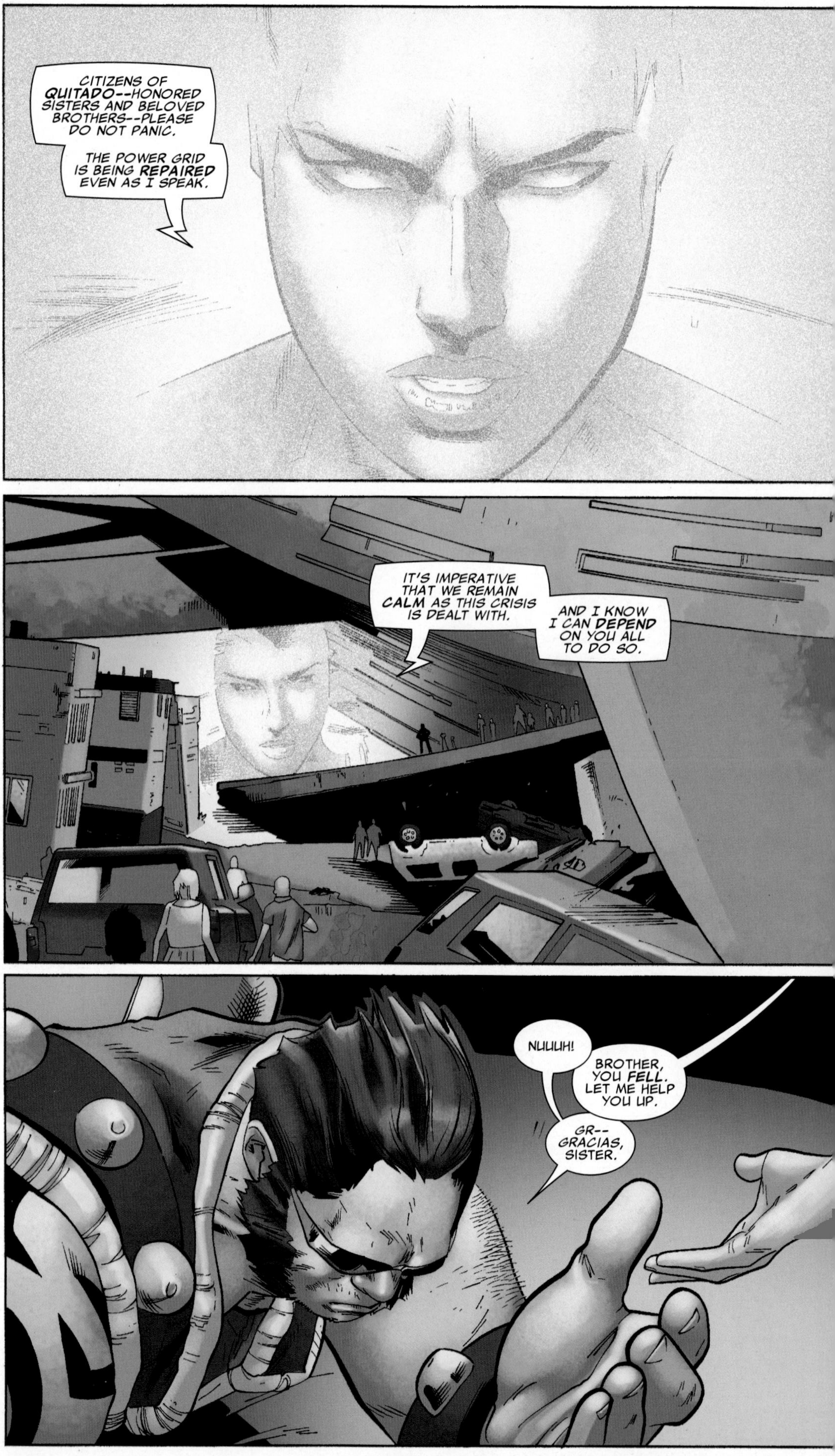
CITIZENS OF QUITADO--HONORED SISTERS AND BELOVED BROTHERS--PLEASE DO NOT PANIC.
THE POWER GRID IS BEING REPAIRED EVEN AS I SPEAK.
IT'S IMPERATIVE THAT WE REMAIN CALM AS THIS CRISIS IS DEALT WITH.
AND I KNOW I CAN DEPEND ON YOU ALL TO DO SO.
NUUUH!
BROTHER, YOU FELL. LET ME HELP YOU UP.
GR-- GRACIAS, SISTER.

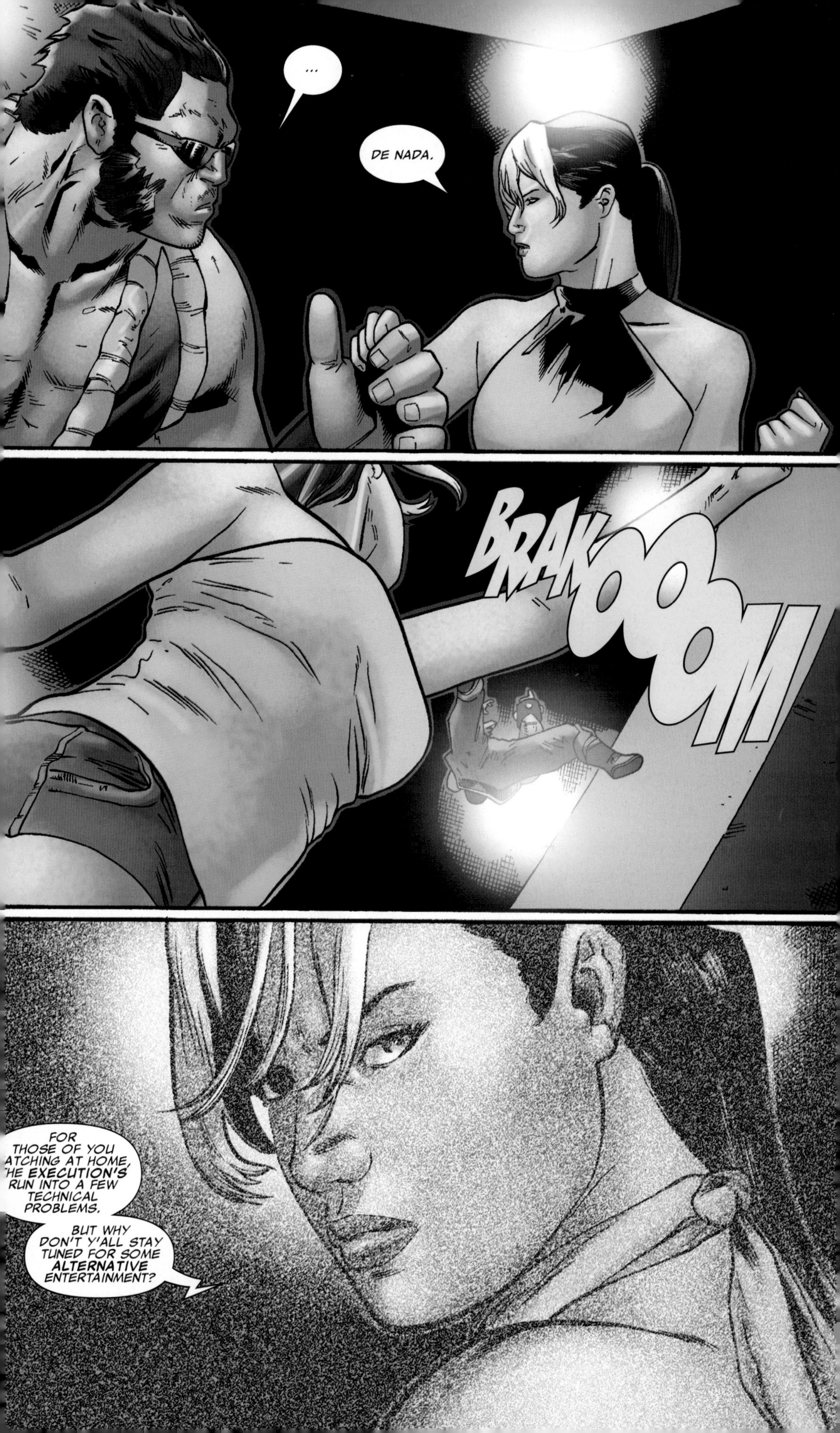
...
DE NADA.
BRAKOOOM
FOR THOSE OF YOU WATCHING AT HOME, THE EXECUTION'S RUN INTO A FEW TECHNICAL PROBLEMS.
BUT WHY DON'T Y'ALL STAY TUNED FOR SOME ALTERNATIVE ENTERTAINMENT?

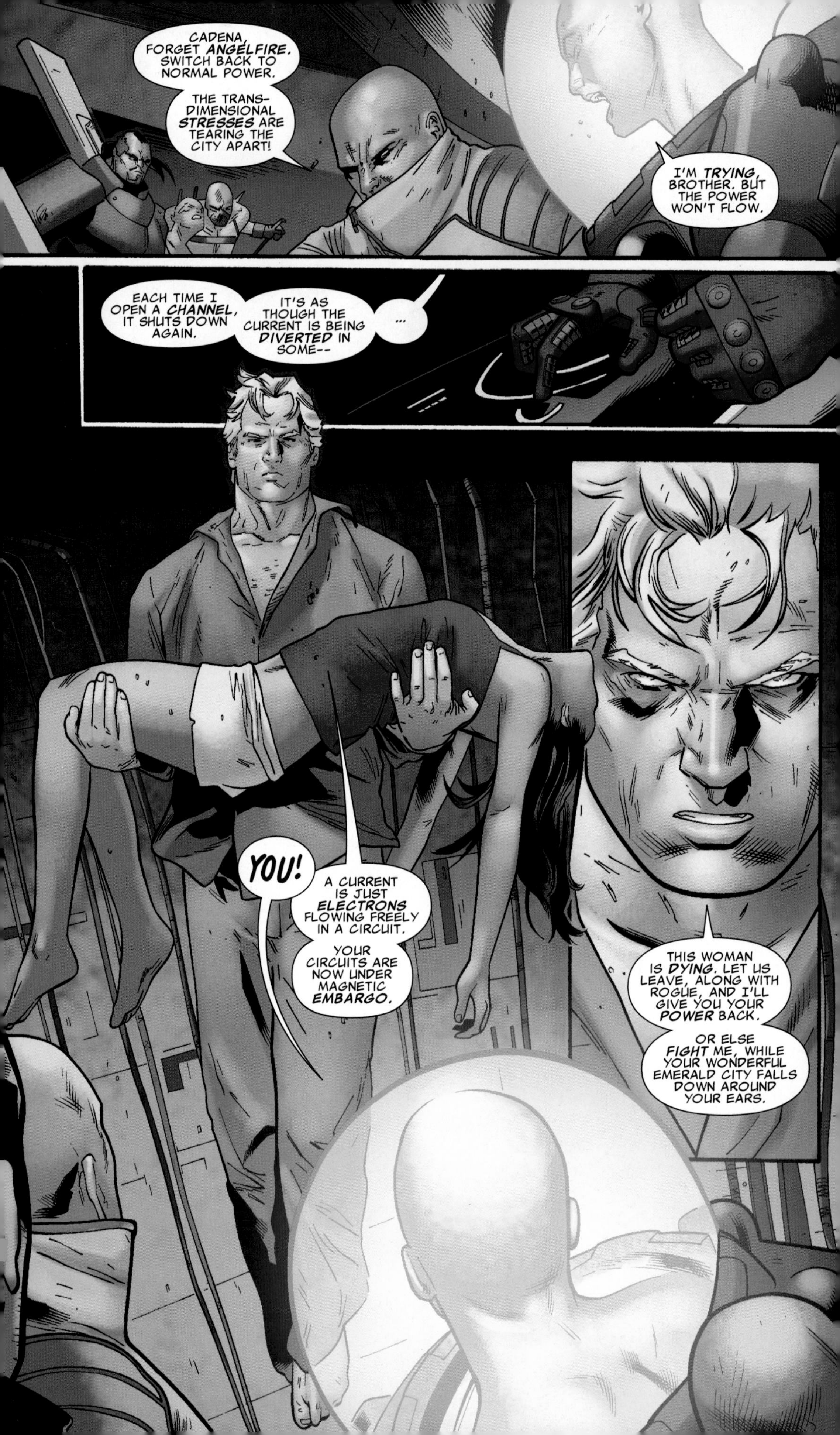
CADENA, FORGET ANGELFIRE. SWITCH BACK TO NORMAL POWER.
THE TRANS-DIMENSIONAL STRESSES ARE TEARING THE CITY APART!
I'M TRYING, BROTHER. BUT THE POWER WON'T FLOW.
EACH TIME I OPEN A CHANNEL, IT SHUTS DOWN AGAIN.
IT'S AS THOUGH THE CURRENT IS BEING DIVERTED IN SOME--
...
YOU!
A CURRENT IS JUST ELECTRONS FLOWING FREELY IN A CIRCUIT.
YOUR CIRCUITS ARE NOW UNDER MAGNETIC EMBARGO.
THIS WOMAN IS DYING. LET US LEAVE, ALONG WITH ROGUE, AND I'LL GIVE YOU YOUR POWER BACK.
OR ELSE FIGHT ME, WHILE YOUR WONDERFUL EMERALD CITY FALLS DOWN AROUND YOUR EARS.

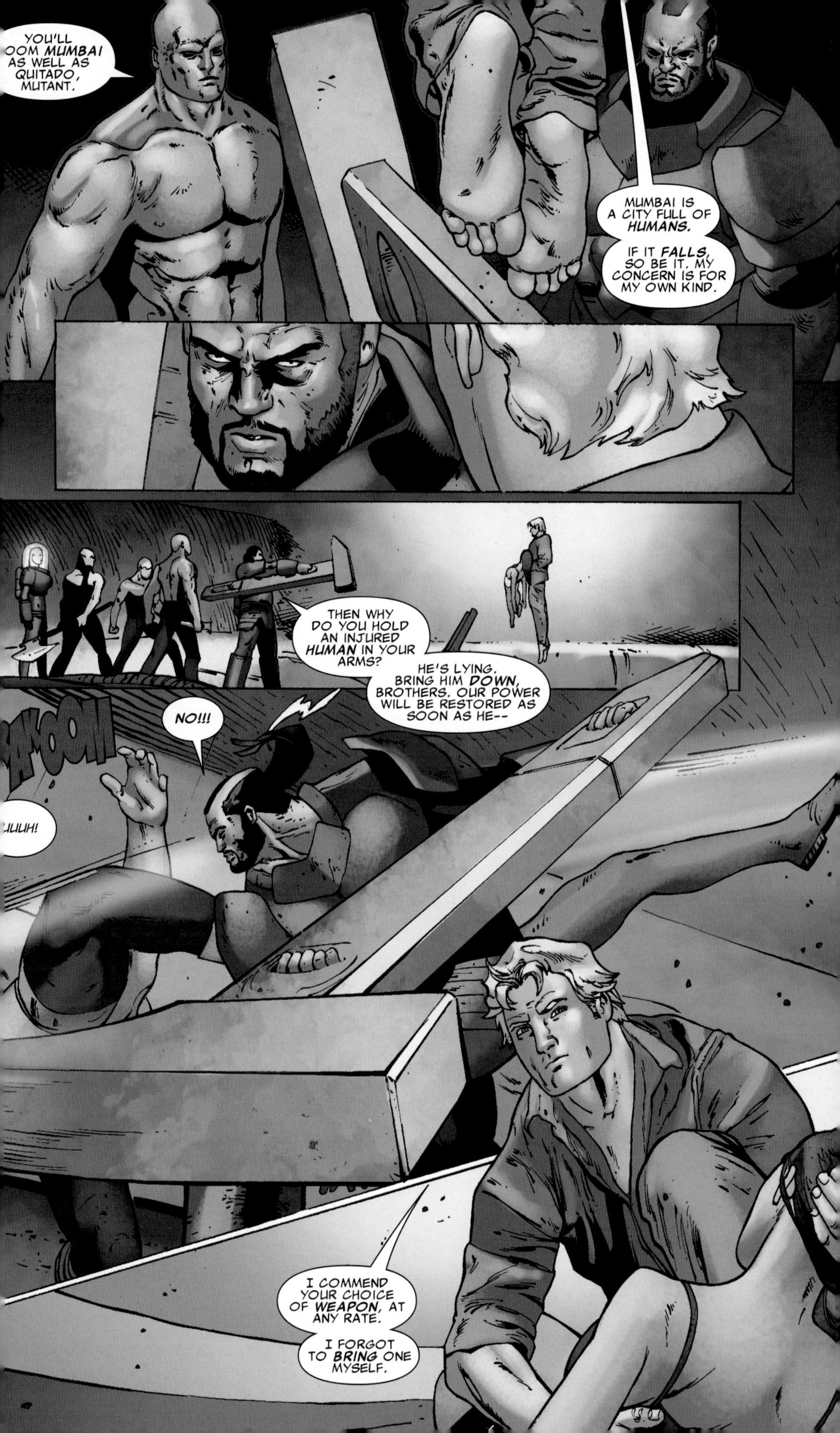

YOU'LL OOM MUMBAI AS WELL AS QUITADO, MUTANT.
MUMBAI IS A CITY FULL OF HUMANS.
IF IT FALLS, SO BE IT. MY CONCERN IS FOR MY OWN KIND.
THEN WHY DO YOU HOLD AN INJURED HUMAN IN YOUR ARMS?
HE'S LYING. BRING HIM DOWN, BROTHERS. OUR POWER WILL BE RESTORED AS SOON AS HE--
NO!!!
UUUH!
I COMMEND YOUR CHOICE OF WEAPON, AT ANY RATE.
I FORGOT TO BRING ONE MYSELF.

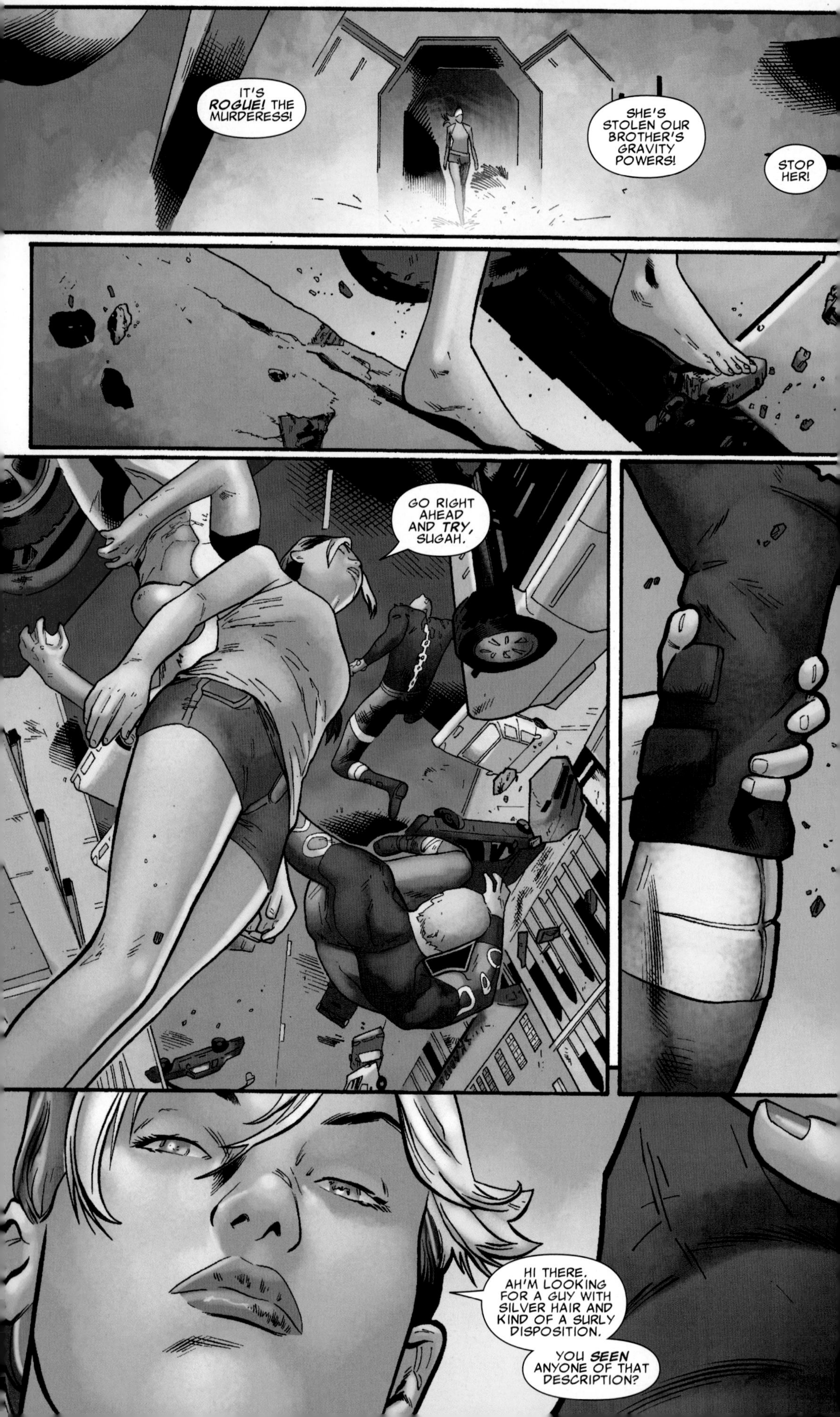
IT'S ROGUE! THE MURDERESS!
SHE'S STOLEN OUR BROTHER'S GRAVITY POWERS!
STOP HER!
GO RIGHT AHEAD AND TRY, SUGAH.
HI THERE. AH'M LOOKING FOR A GUY WITH SILVER HAIR AND KIND OF A SURLY DISPOSITION.
YOU SEEN ANYONE OF THAT DESCRIPTION?

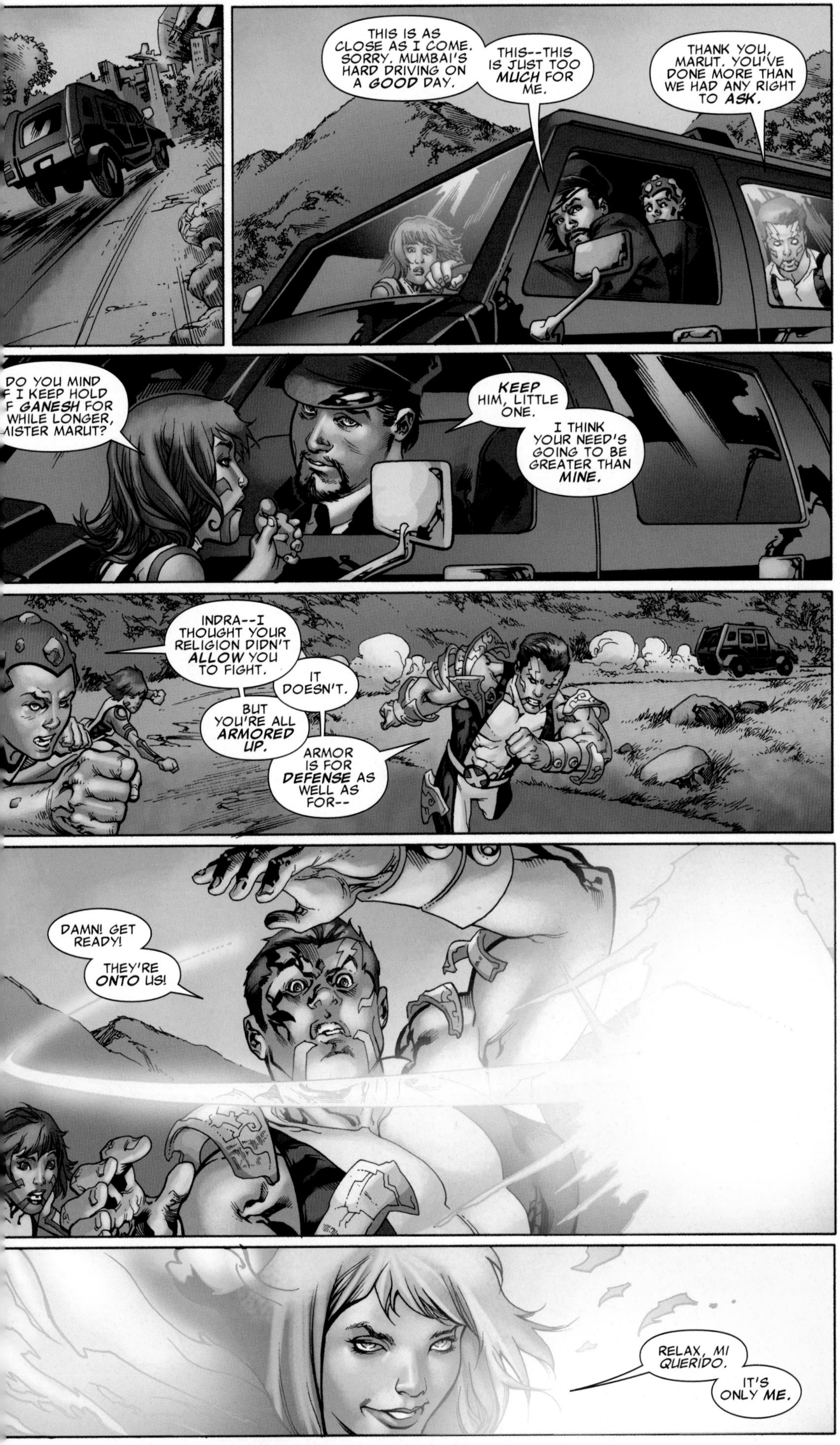

THIS IS AS CLOSE AS I COME. SORRY. MUMBAI'S HARD DRIVING ON A GOOD DAY.
THIS--THIS IS JUST TOO MUCH FOR ME.
THANK YOU, MARUT. YOU'VE DONE MORE THAN WE HAD ANY RIGHT TO ASK.
DO YOU MIND F I KEEP HOLD F GANESH FOR WHILE LONGER, AISTER MARUT?
KEEP HIM, LITTLE ONE.
I THINK YOUR NEED'S GOING TO BE GREATER THAN MINE.
INDRA--I THOUGHT YOUR RELIGION DIDN'T ALLOW YOU TO FIGHT.
IT DOESN'T.
BUT YOU'RE ALL ARMORED UP.
ARMOR IS FOR DEFENSE AS WELL AS FOR--
DAMN! GET READY!
THEY'RE ONTO US!
RELAX, MI QUERIDO.
IT'S ONLY ME.

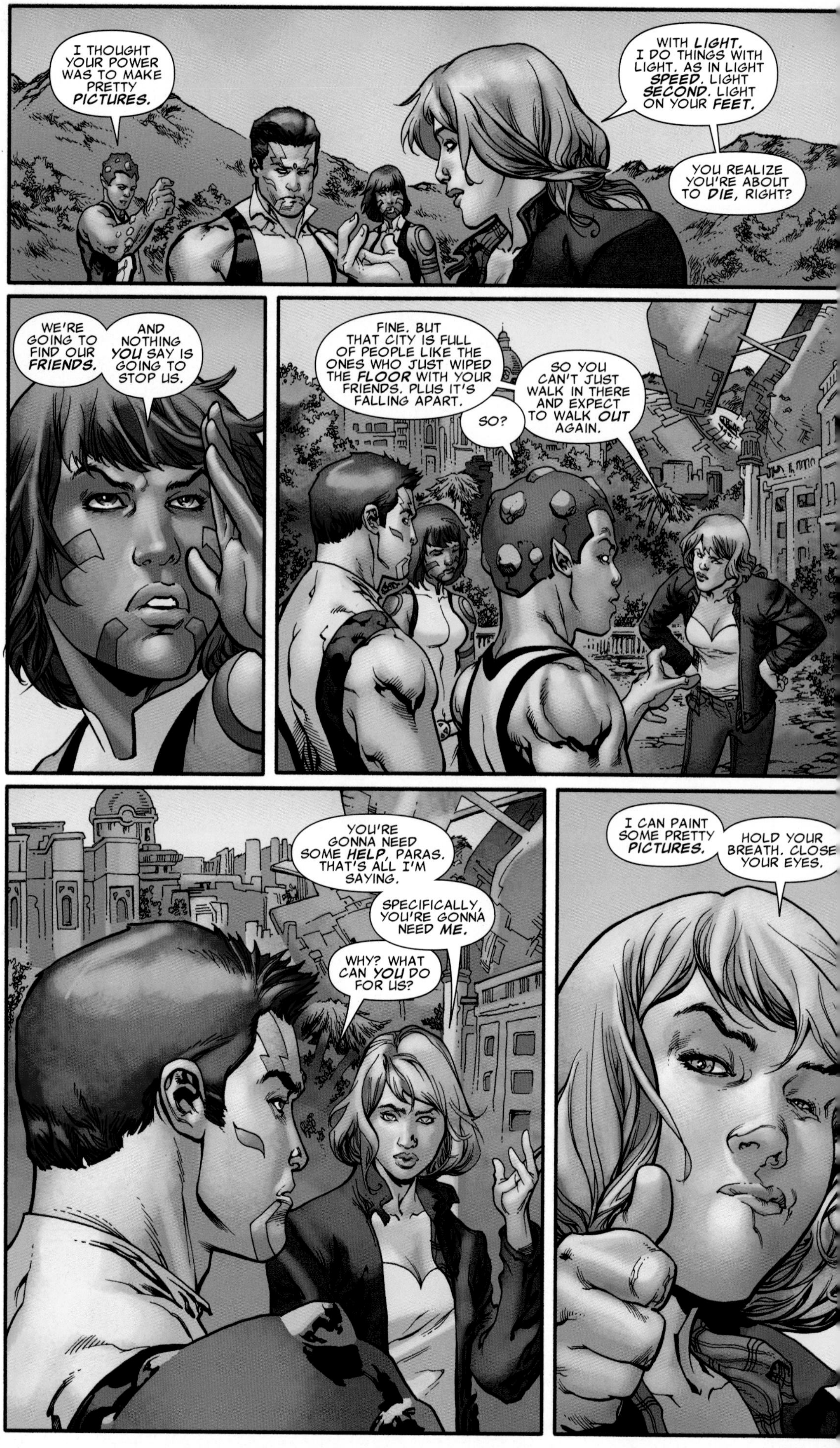
I THOUGHT YOUR POWER WAS TO MAKE PRETTY PICTURES.
WITH LIGHT. I DO THINGS WITH LIGHT. AS IN LIGHT SPEED. LIGHT SECOND. LIGHT ON YOUR FEET.
YOU REALIZE YOU'RE ABOUT TO DIE, RIGHT?
WE'RE GOING TO FIND OUR FRIENDS.
AND NOTHING YOU SAY IS GOING TO STOP US.
FINE. BUT THAT CITY IS FULL OF PEOPLE LIKE THE ONES WHO JUST WIPED THE FLOOR WITH YOUR FRIENDS. PLUS IT'S FALLING APART.
SO?
SO YOU CAN'T JUST WALK IN THERE AND EXPECT TO WALK OUT AGAIN.
YOU'RE GONNA NEED SOME HELP, PARAS. THAT'S ALL I'M SAYING.
SPECIFICALLY, YOU'RE GONNA NEED ME.
WHY? WHAT CAN YOU DO FOR US?
I CAN PAINT SOME PRETTY PICTURES.
HOLD YOUR BREATH. CLOSE YOUR EYES.

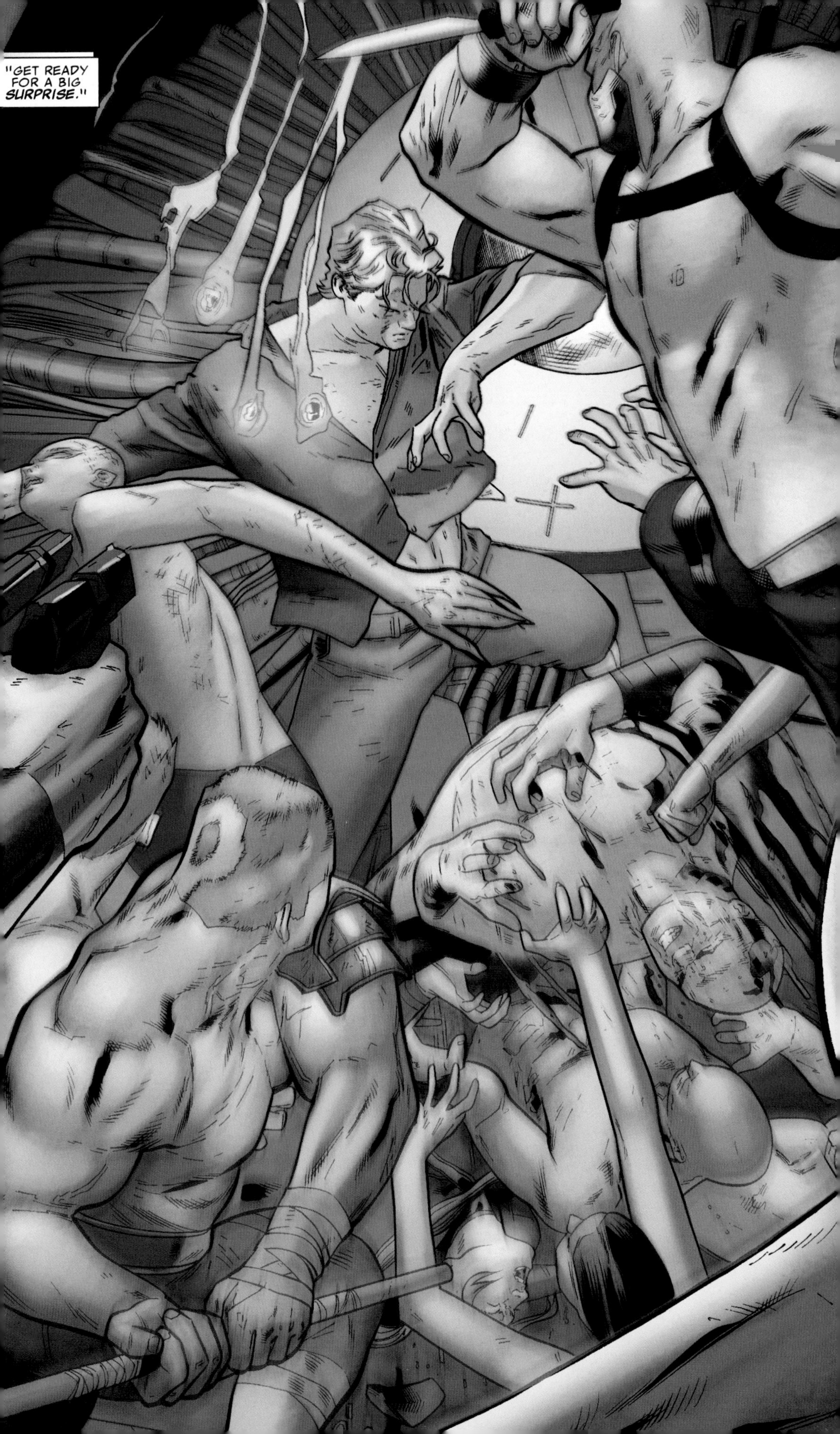
"GET READY FOR A BIG SURPRISE."

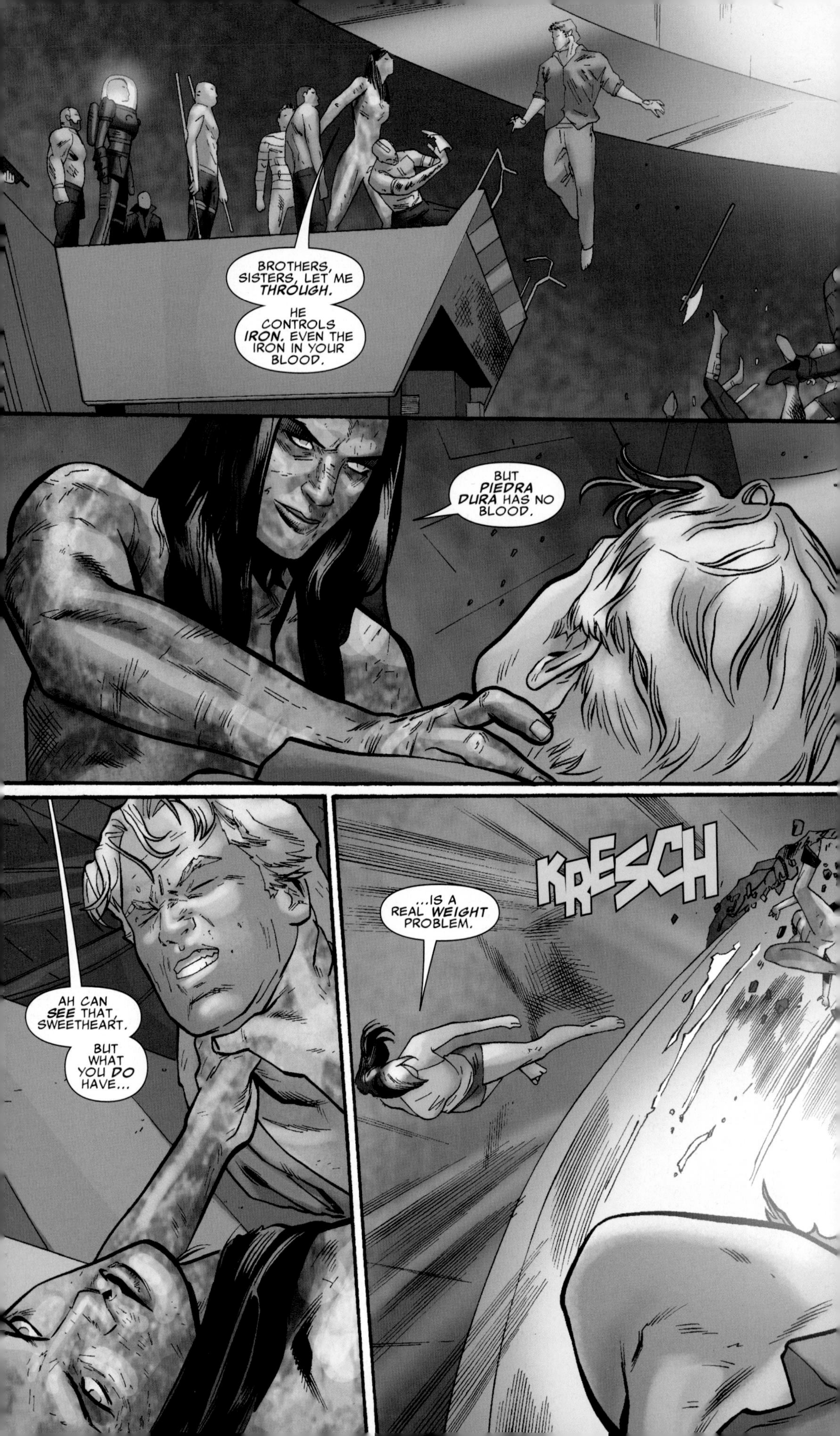
BROTHERS, SISTERS, LET ME THROUGH.
HE CONTROLS IRON. EVEN THE IRON IN YOUR BLOOD.
BUT PIEDRA DURA HAS NO BLOOD.
AH CAN SEE THAT, SWEETHEART.
BUT WHAT YOU DO HAVE...
KRESCH
...IS A REAL WEIGHT PROBLEM.

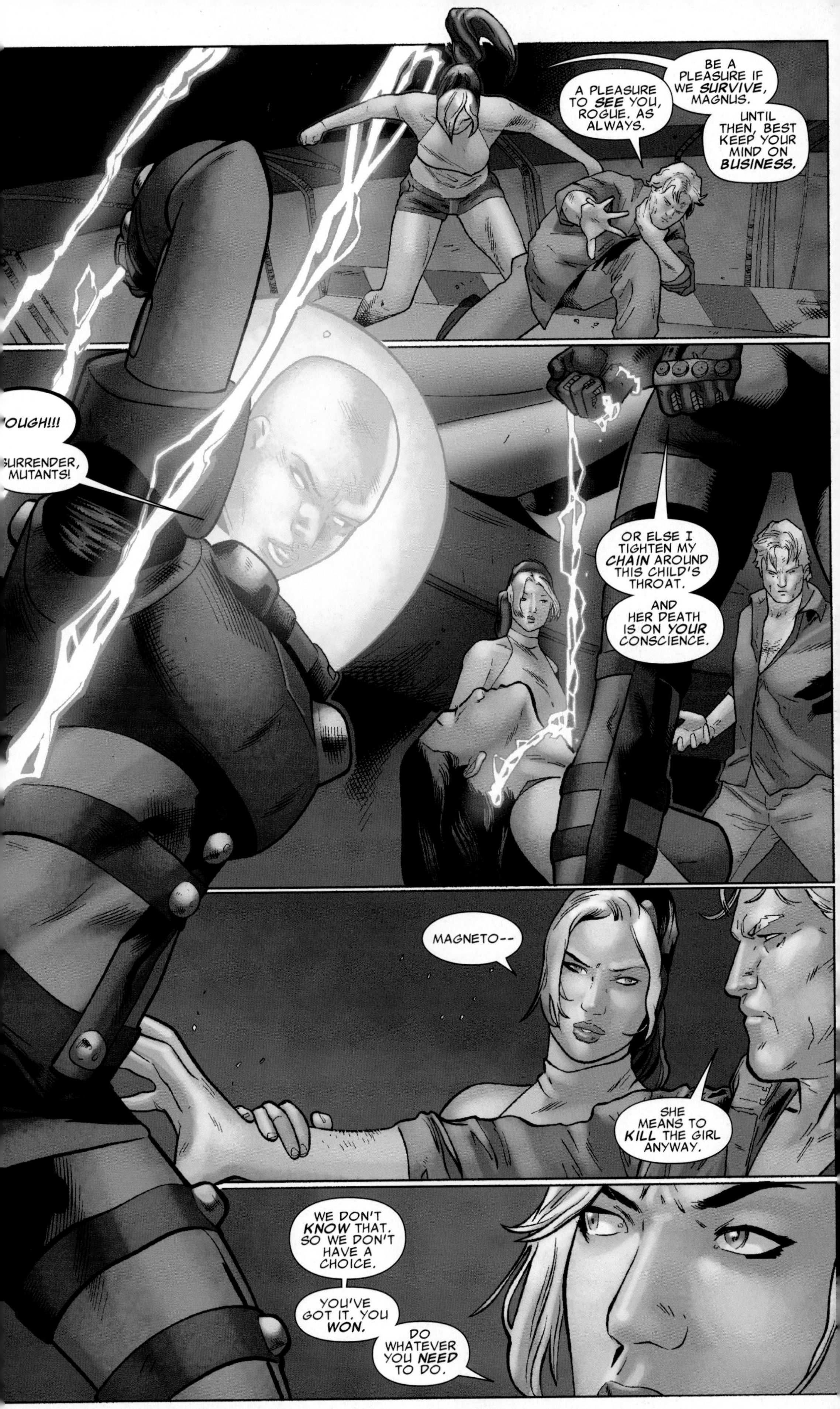
A PLEASURE TO SEE YOU, ROGUE. AS ALWAYS.
BE A PLEASURE IF WE SURVIVE, MAGNUS.
UNTIL THEN, BEST KEEP YOUR MIND ON BUSINESS.
OUGH!!!
SURRENDER, MUTANTS!
OR ELSE I TIGHTEN MY CHAIN AROUND THIS CHILD'S THROAT.
AND HER DEATH IS ON YOUR CONSCIENCE.
MAGNETO--
SHE MEANS TO KILL THE GIRL ANYWAY.
WE DON'T KNOW THAT. SO WE DON'T HAVE A CHOICE.
YOU'VE GOT IT. YOU WON.
DO WHATEVER YOU NEED TO DO.

TAKE THEM. BIND THEM WITH NULL-GAUNTLETS.

YES, CADENA.

THEY'LL D WHEN WE H TIME TO D WITH THE

BUT FIRST, WE MUST RESTORE POWER.

TECHNICIANS, SLAVE THE MAIN ARRAY TO--

CADENA! THEY'RE-- THEY'RE PHASING OUT!

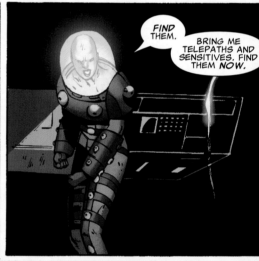

FIND THEM.

BRING ME TELEPATHS AND SENSITIVES. FIND THEM NOW.

YOU'RE NOT WHAT YOU SEEM.

WHO IS, VIEJO? LISTEN, THEY CAN'T SEE US RIGHT NOW.

BUT THEY WON'T TAKE LONG TO FIGURE OUT WE'RE STILL HERE. SO YOU'VE GOT TO MAKE THIS TIME COUNT.

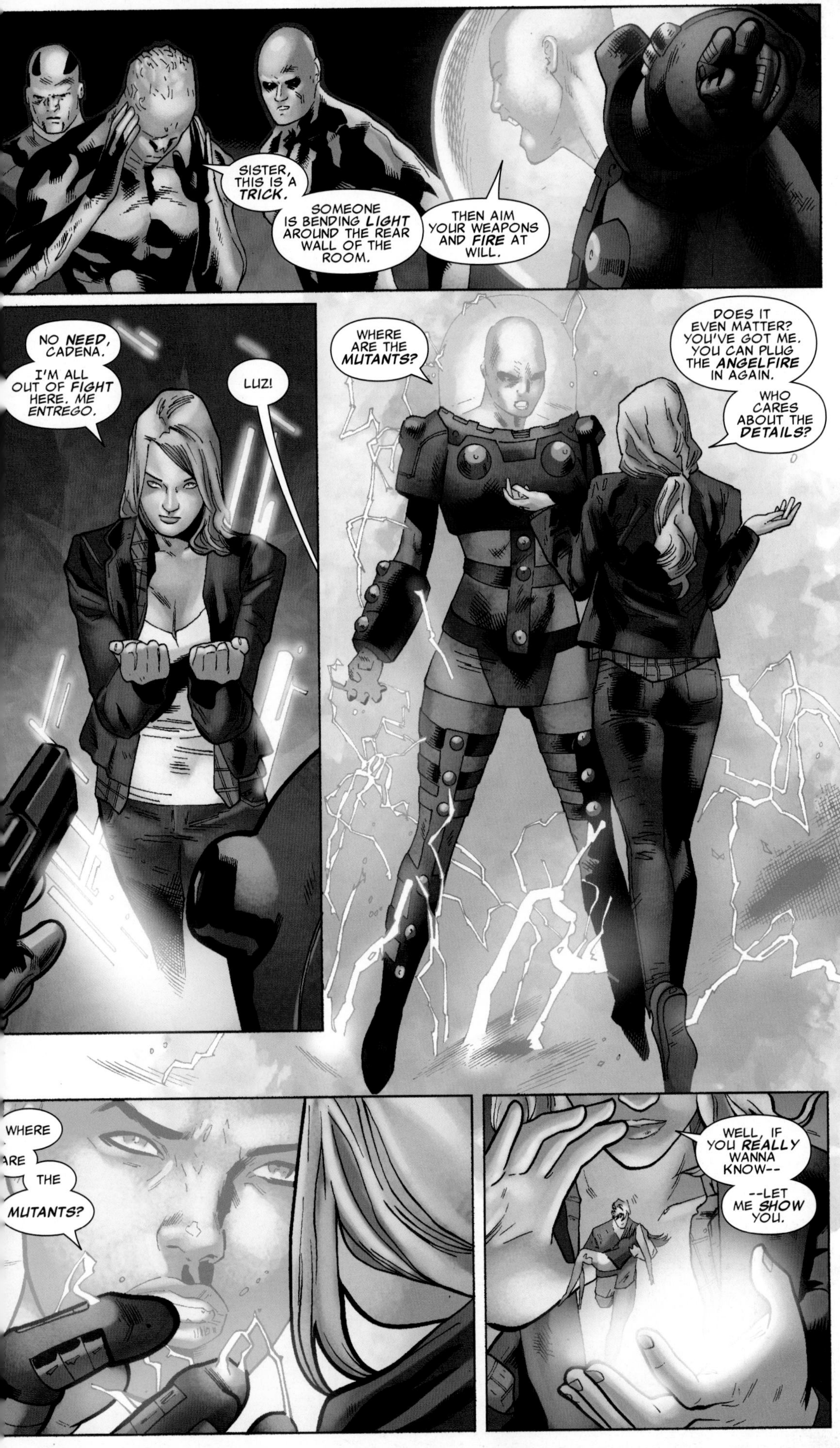
SISTER, THIS IS A TRICK.
SOMEONE IS BENDING LIGHT AROUND THE REAR WALL OF THE ROOM.
THEN AIM YOUR WEAPONS AND FIRE AT WILL.
NO NEED, CADENA.
I'M ALL OUT OF FIGHT HERE. ME ENTREGO.
LUZ!
WHERE ARE THE MUTANTS?
DOES IT EVEN MATTER? YOU'VE GOT ME. YOU CAN PLUG THE ANGELFIRE IN AGAIN.
WHO CARES ABOUT THE DETAILS?
WHERE
ARE
THE
MUTANTS?
WELL, IF YOU REALLY WANNA KNOW--
--LET ME SHOW YOU.

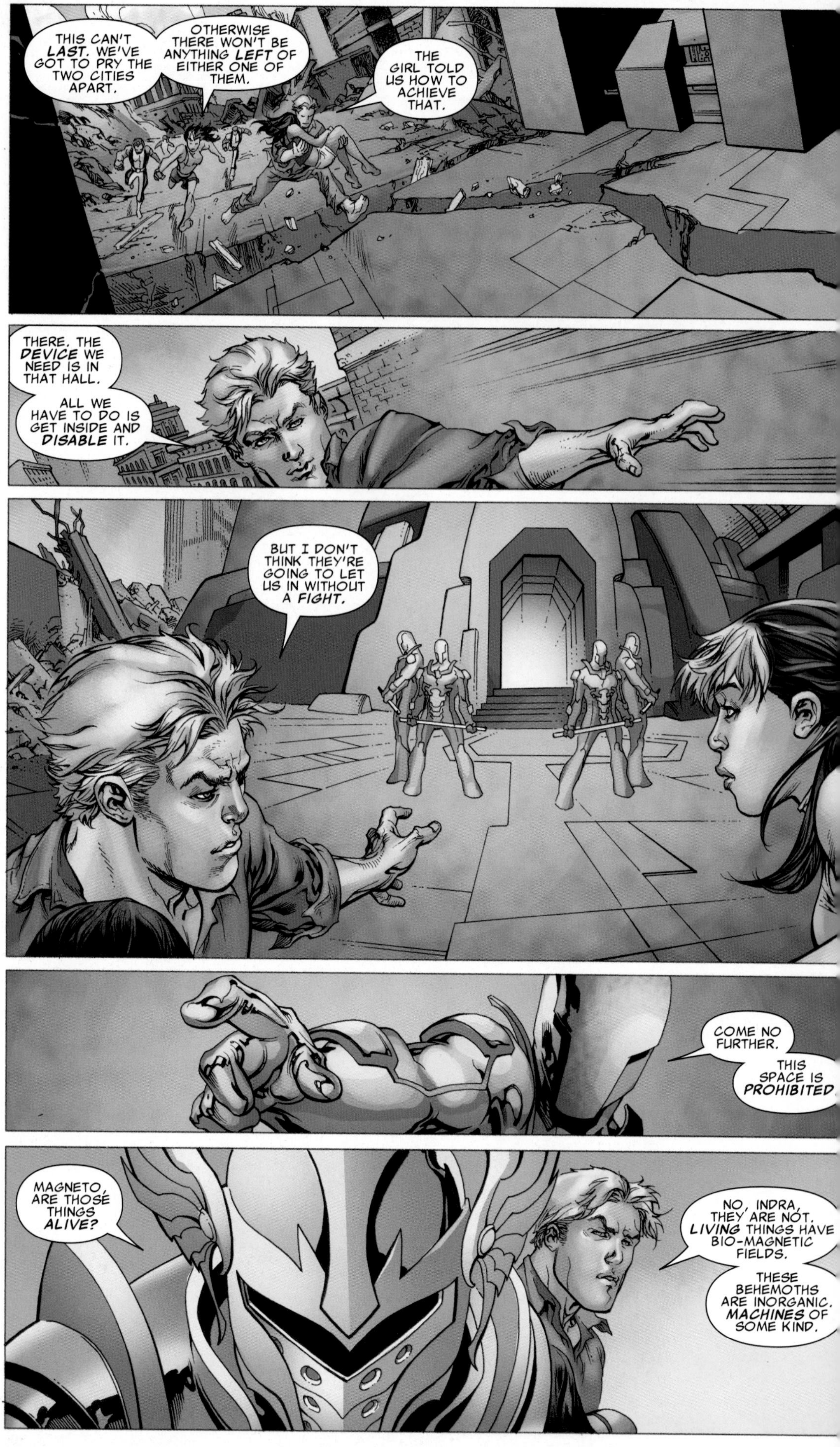

THIS CAN'T LAST. WE'VE GOT TO PRY THE TWO CITIES APART.
OTHERWISE THERE WON'T BE ANYTHING LEFT OF EITHER ONE OF THEM.
THE GIRL TOLD US HOW TO ACHIEVE THAT.
THERE. THE DEVICE WE NEED IS IN THAT HALL.
ALL WE HAVE TO DO IS GET INSIDE AND DISABLE IT.
BUT I DON'T THINK THEY'RE GOING TO LET US IN WITHOUT A FIGHT.
COME NO FURTHER.
THIS SPACE IS PROHIBITED.
MAGNETO, ARE THOSE THINGS ALIVE?
NO, INDRA, THEY ARE NOT. LIVING THINGS HAVE BIO-MAGNETIC FIELDS.
THESE BEHEMOTHS ARE INORGANIC. MACHINES OF SOME KIND.

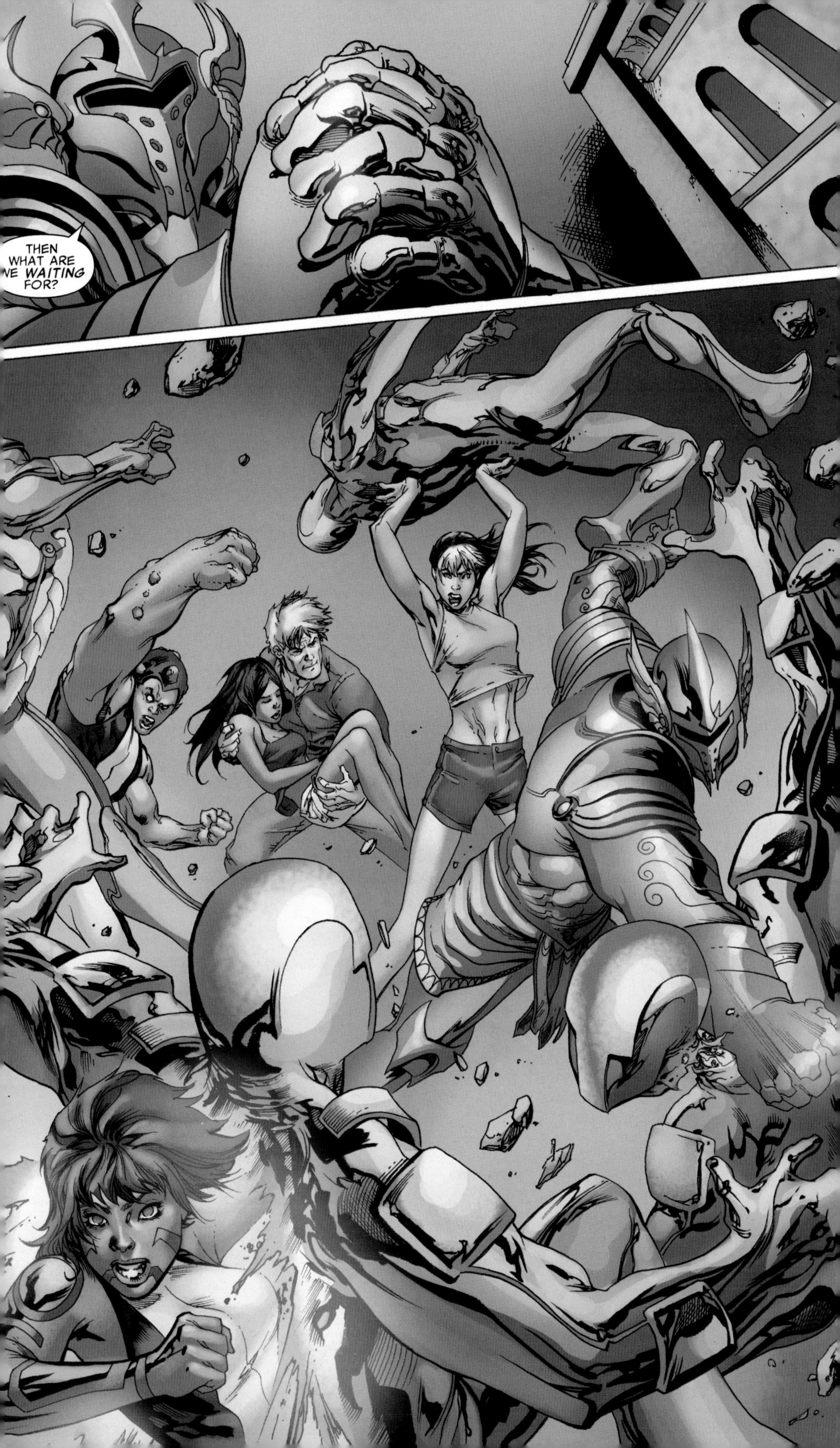
THEN WHAT ARE WE WAITING FOR?

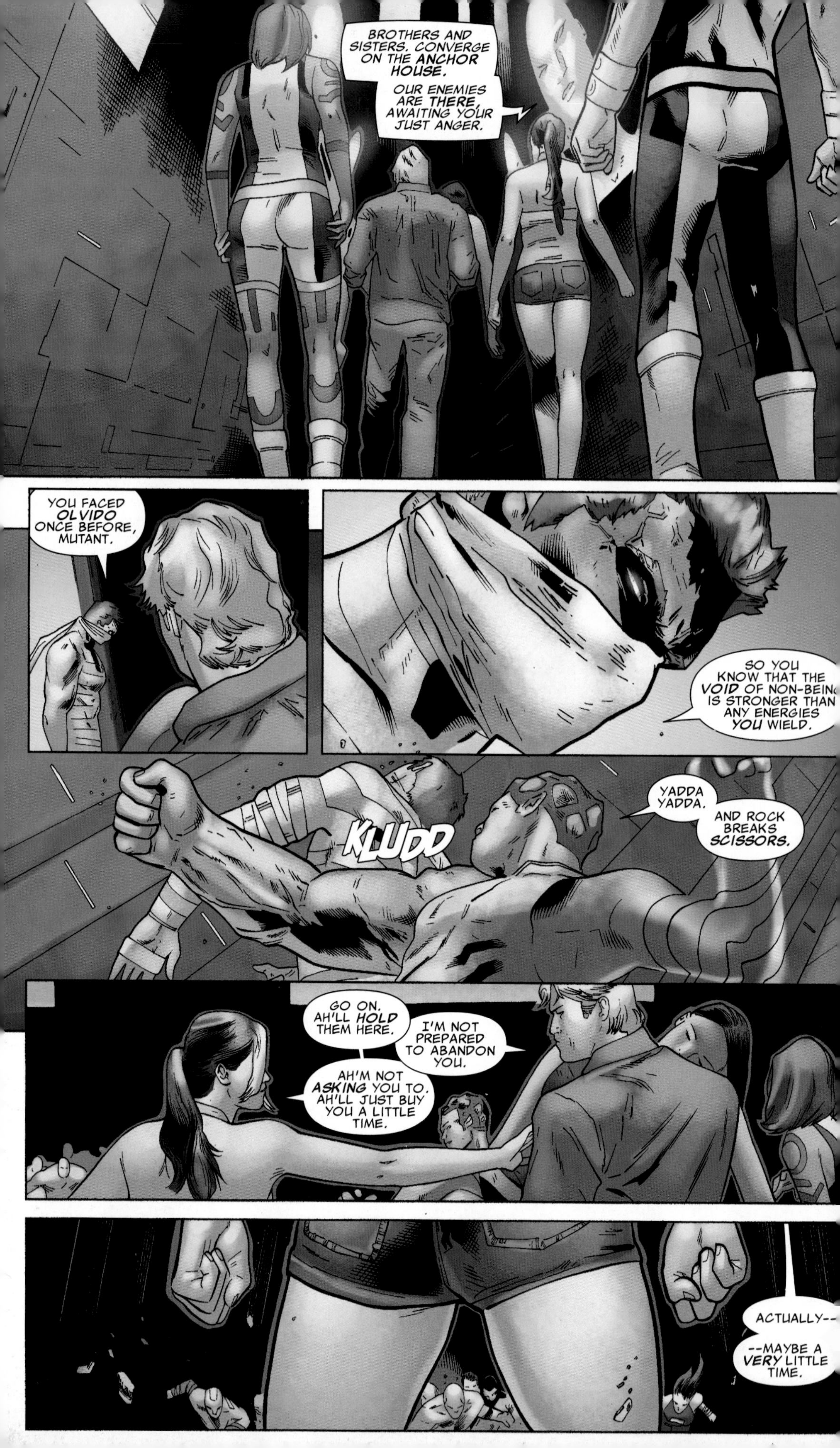
BROTHERS AND SISTERS. CONVERGE ON THE ANCHOR HOUSE.
OUR ENEMIES ARE THERE, AWAITING YOUR JUST ANGER.
YOU FACED OLVIDO ONCE BEFORE, MUTANT.
SO YOU KNOW THAT THE VOID OF NON-BEING IS STRONGER THAN ANY ENERGIES YOU WIELD.
YADDA YADDA.
AND ROCK BREAKS SCISSORS.
KLUDD
GO ON. AH'LL HOLD THEM HERE.
I'M NOT PREPARED TO ABANDON YOU.
AH'M NOT ASKING YOU TO. AH'LL JUST BUY YOU A LITTLE TIME.
ACTUALLY--
--MAYBE A VERY LITTLE TIME.

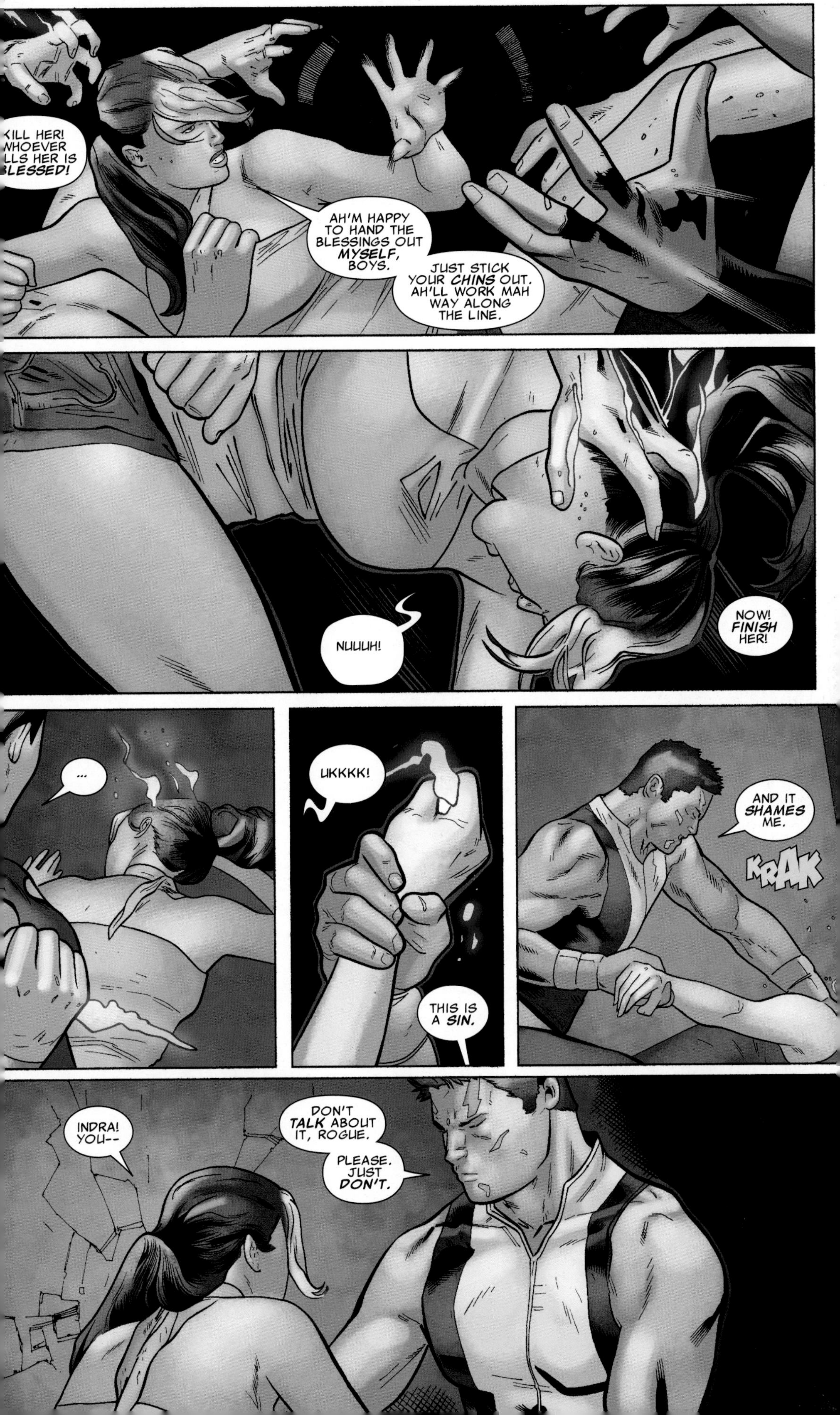
KILL HER! WHOEVER KILLS HER IS BLESSED!
AH'M HAPPY TO HAND THE BLESSINGS OUT MYSELF, BOYS.
JUST STICK YOUR CHINS OUT. AH'LL WORK MAH WAY ALONG THE LINE.
NUUUH!
NOW! FINISH HER!
...
UKKKK!
THIS IS A SIN.
AND IT SHAMES ME.
KRAK
INDRA! YOU--
DON'T TALK ABOUT IT, ROGUE.
PLEASE. JUST DON'T.

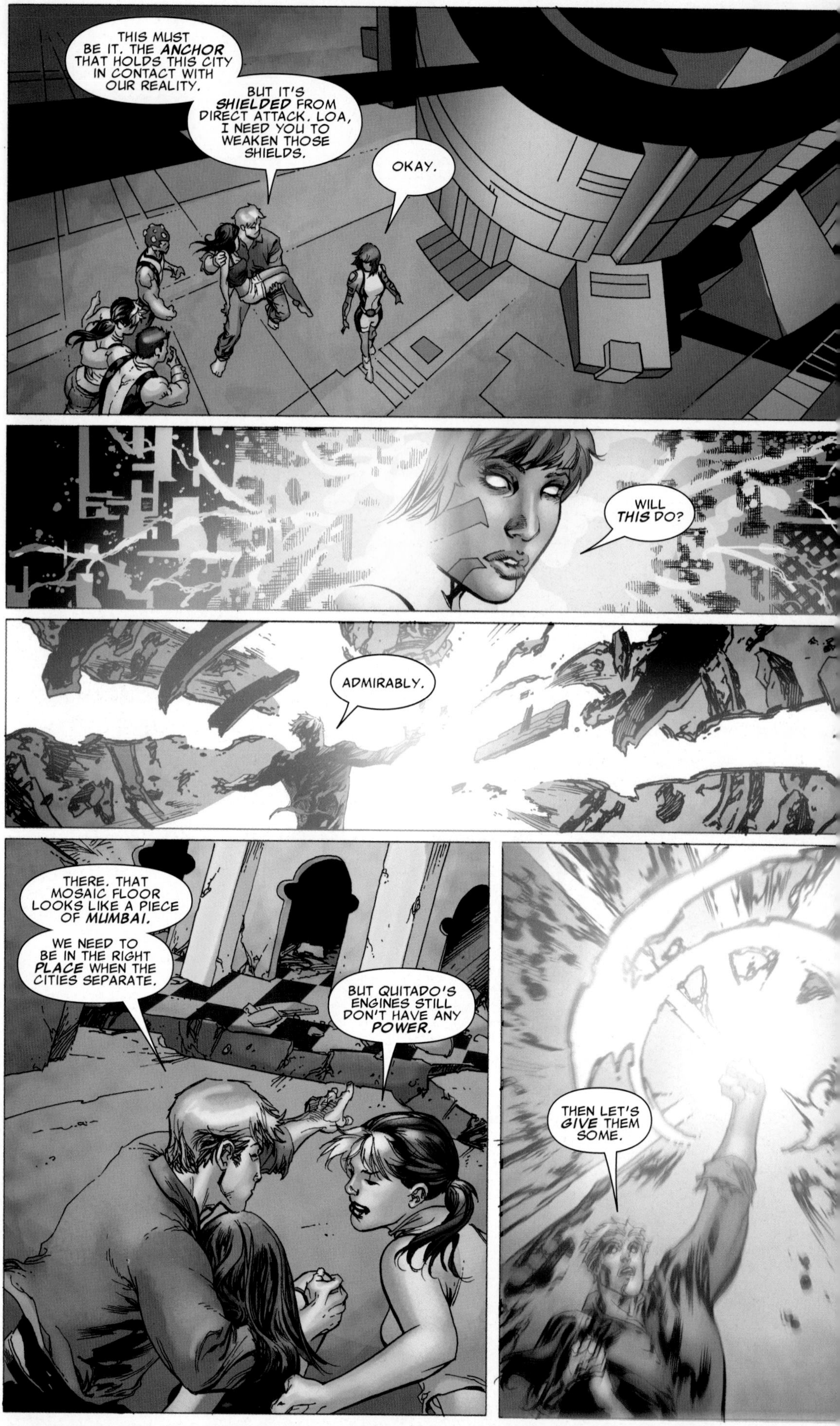

THIS MUST BE IT. THE ANCHOR THAT HOLDS THIS CITY IN CONTACT WITH OUR REALITY.
BUT IT'S SHIELDED FROM DIRECT ATTACK. LOA, I NEED YOU TO WEAKEN THOSE SHIELDS.
OKAY.
WILL THIS DO?
ADMIRABLY.
THERE. THAT MOSAIC FLOOR LOOKS LIKE A PIECE OF MUMBAI.
WE NEED TO BE IN THE RIGHT PLACE WHEN THE CITIES SEPARATE.
BUT QUITADO'S ENGINES STILL DON'T HAVE ANY POWER.
THEN LET'S GIVE THEM SOME.

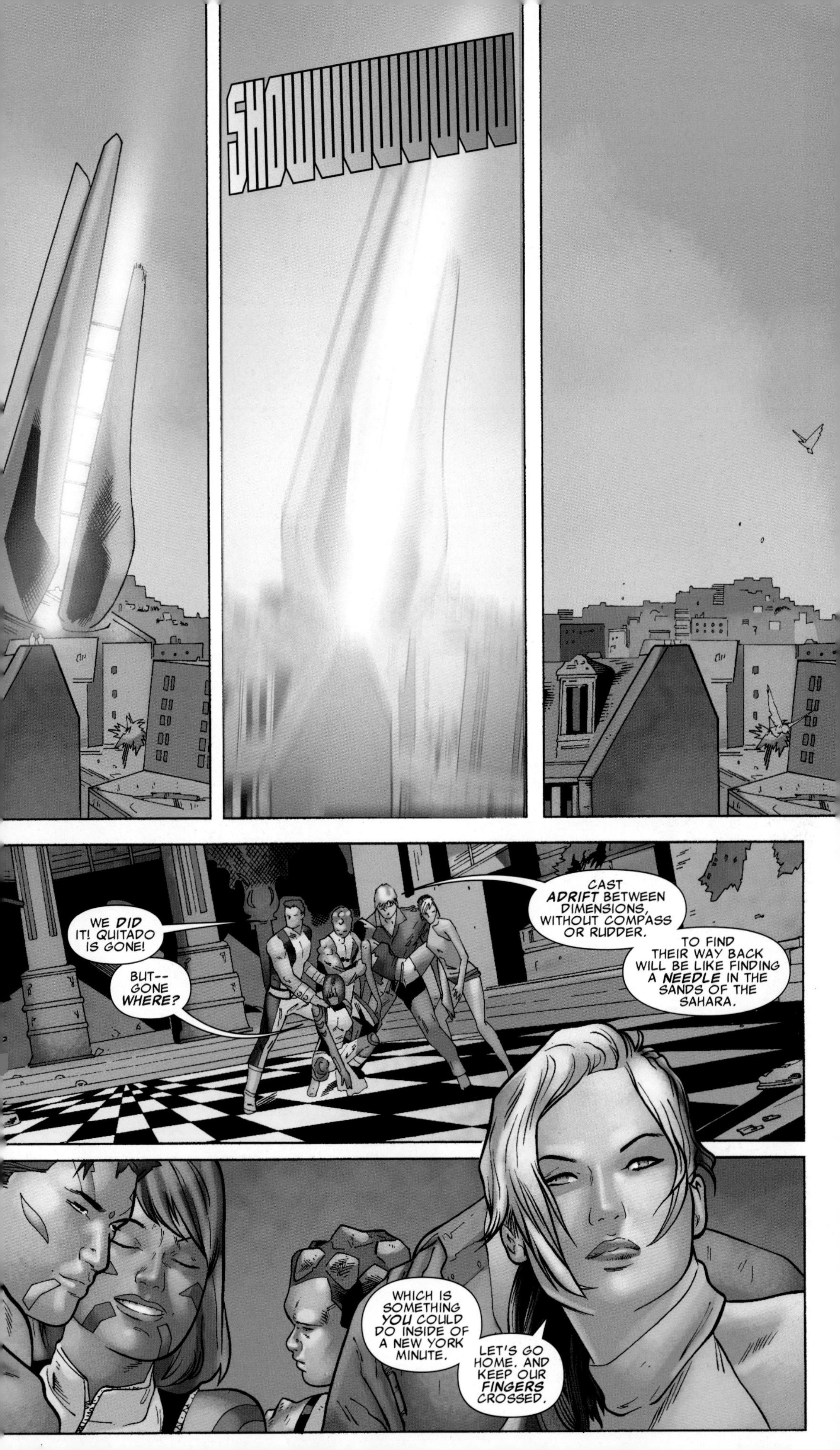
SHOWWWWWWWW
WE DID IT! QUITADO IS GONE!
BUT-- GONE WHERE?
CAST ADRIFT BETWEEN DIMENSIONS, WITHOUT COMPASS OR RUDDER.
TO FIND THEIR WAY BACK WILL BE LIKE FINDING A NEEDLE IN THE SANDS OF THE SAHARA.
WHICH IS SOMETHING YOU COULD DO INSIDE OF A NEW YORK MINUTE.
LET'S GO HOME, AND KEEP OUR FINGERS CROSSED.

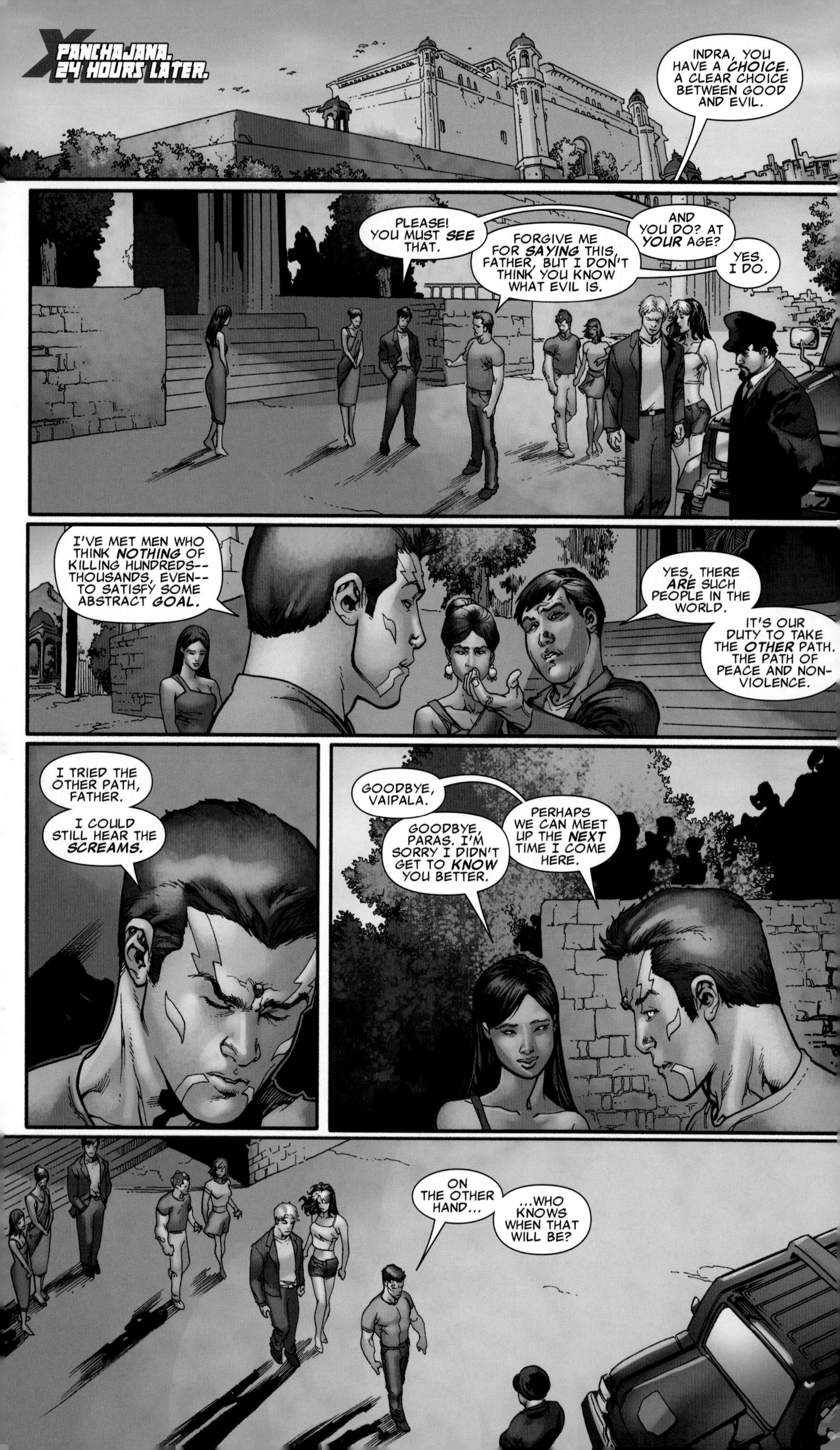
PANCHAJANA. 24 HOURS LATER.
INDRA, YOU HAVE A CHOICE. A CLEAR CHOICE BETWEEN GOOD AND EVIL.
PLEASE! YOU MUST SEE THAT.
FORGIVE ME FOR SAYING THIS, FATHER, BUT I DON'T THINK YOU KNOW WHAT EVIL IS.
AND YOU DO? AT YOUR AGE?
YES. I DO.
I'VE MET MEN WHO THINK NOTHING OF KILLING HUNDREDS-- THOUSANDS, EVEN-- TO SATISFY SOME ABSTRACT GOAL.
YES, THERE ARE SUCH PEOPLE IN THE WORLD.
IT'S OUR DUTY TO TAKE THE OTHER PATH. THE PATH OF PEACE AND NON-VIOLENCE.
I TRIED THE OTHER PATH, FATHER.
I COULD STILL HEAR THE SCREAMS.
GOODBYE, VAIPALA.
GOODBYE, PARAS. I'M SORRY I DIDN'T GET TO KNOW YOU BETTER.
PERHAPS WE CAN MEET UP THE NEXT TIME I COME HERE.
ON THE OTHER HAND...
...WHO KNOWS WHEN THAT WILL BE?

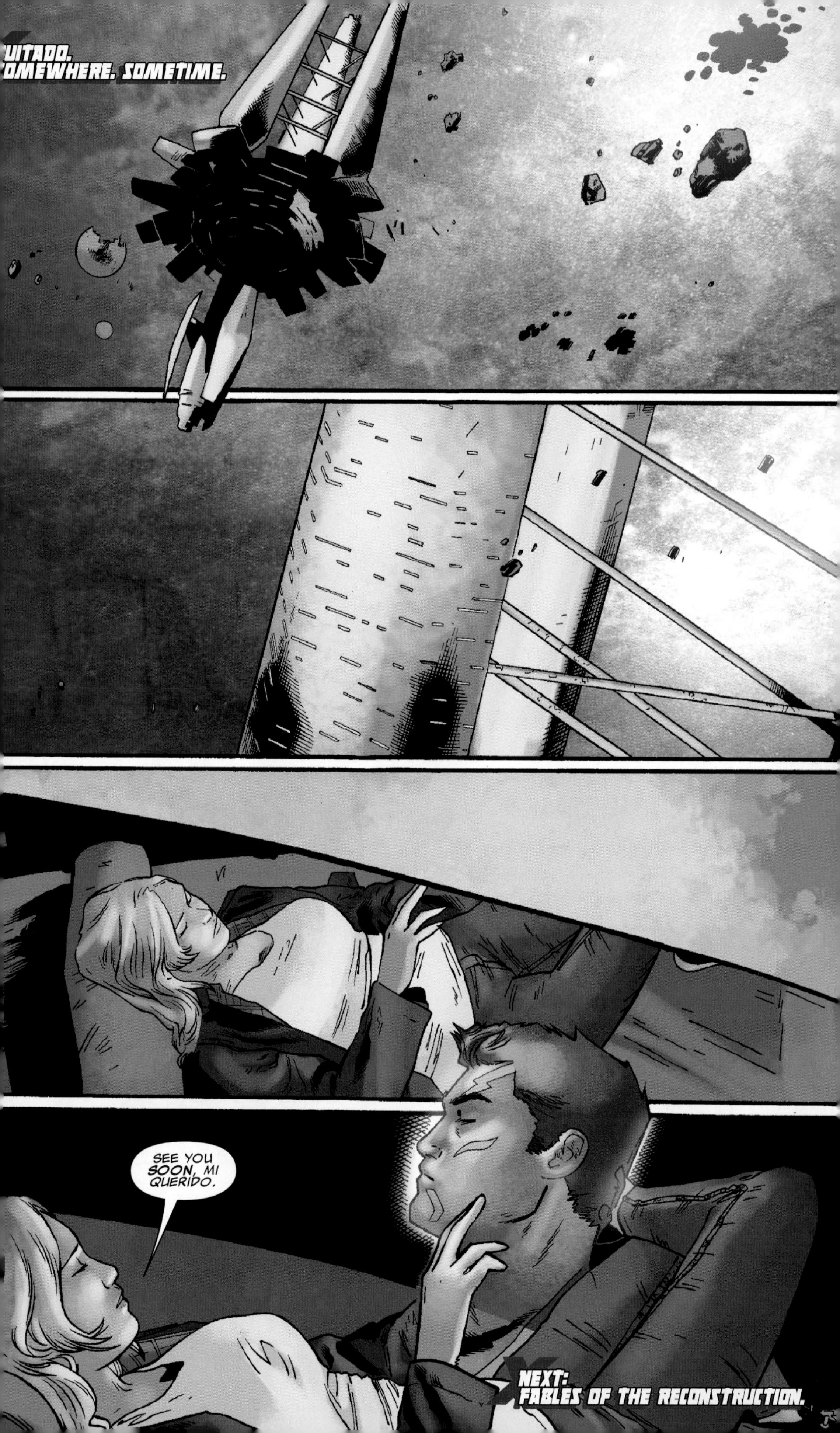

UITADO.
OMEWHERE. SOMETIME.
SEE YOU SOON, MI QUERIDO.
NEXT:
FABLES OF THE RECONSTRUCTION.

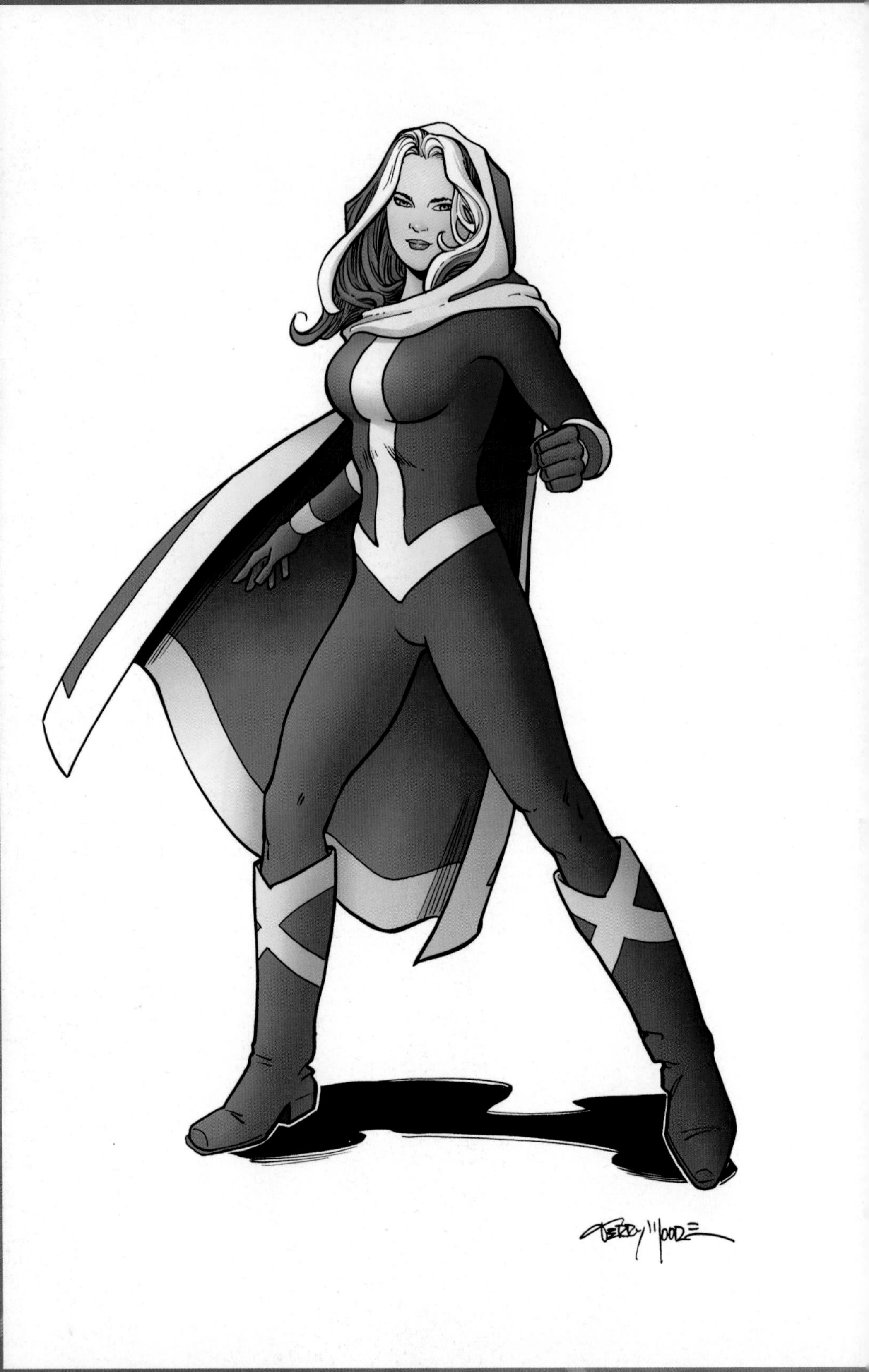
TERRY MOORE

#239 WOMEN OF MARVEL FRAME VARIANT
BY TERRY MOORE & JUNE CHUNG

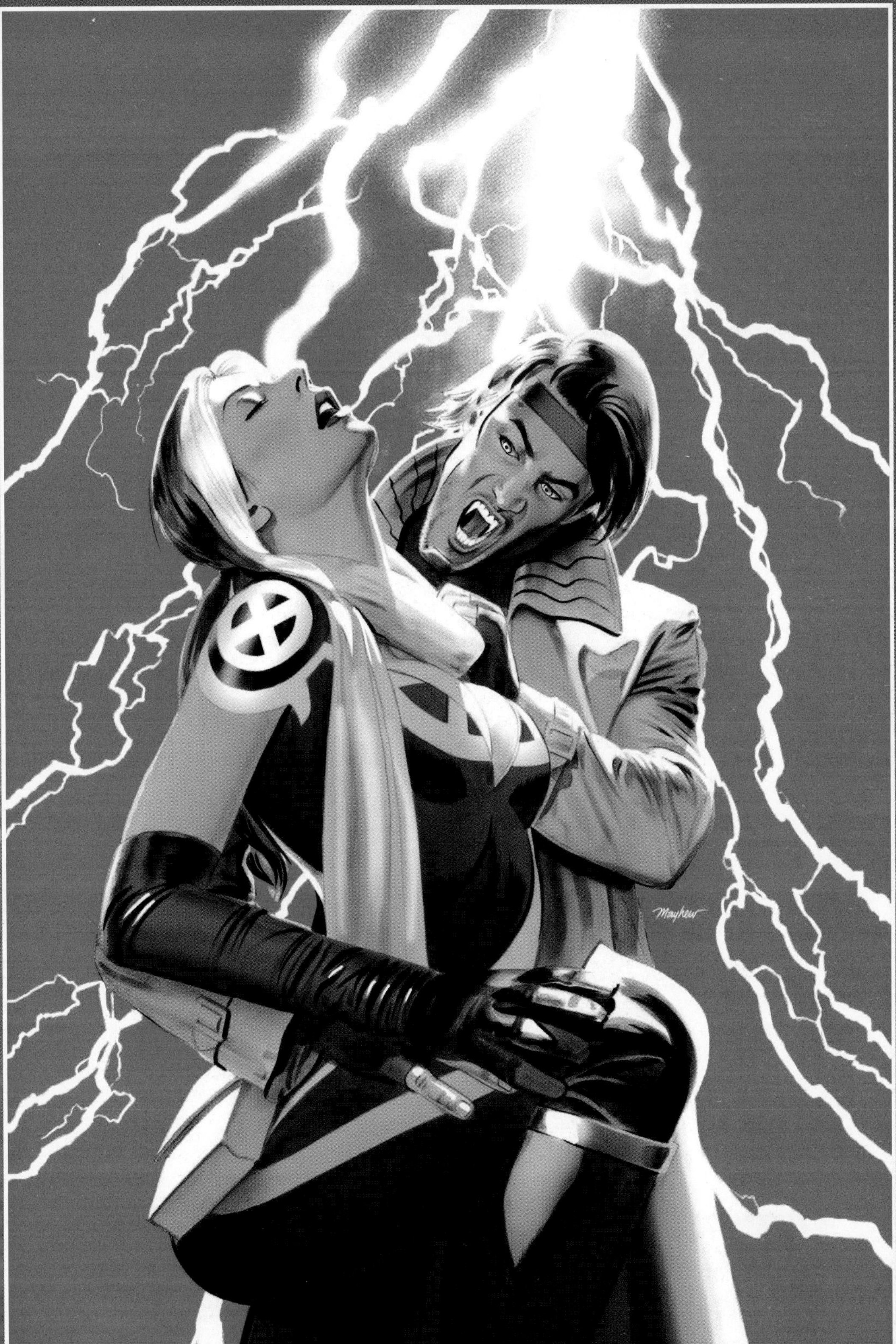
Mayhew

#241 VAMPIRE VARIANT
BY MIKE MAYHEW

REAL NAME: Victor "Vic" Borkowski

ALIASES: None

IDENTITY: Known to authorities

OCCUPATION: Adventurer, student

CITIZENSHIP: USA

PLACE OF BIRTH: Fairbury, Illinois (presumably)

KNOWN RELATIVES: Mr. and Mrs. Borkowski (parents, full names unrevealed)

GROUP AFFILIATION: X-Men-In-Training; formerly Xavier Institute student body/Alpha Squadron

EDUCATION: Various high school level courses at Xavier Institute for Higher Learning

FIRST APPEARANCE: New Mutants #2 (2003); (first name identified) New Mutants #7 (2004); (last name identified) New Mutants #8 (2004); (Anole) New X-Men: Academy X Yearbook Special #1 (2005)

HISTORY: Raised in Fairbury, Illinois, Victor Borkowski lived a happy life, even after his mutant nature manifested, leaving him with a green-skinned, scaly reptilian appearance. Victor often pretended he was one of the heroic X-Men, and his tree house was their mansion headquarters. His parents and close-knit community accepted Victor, but when growing

anti-mutant sentiment reached their town, Victor left for the Xavier Institute for Higher Learning run by mutant telepath Professor X (Charles Xavier) and the X-Men in Westchester, New York, for his safety. Victor continued his education, thoroughly studied the X-Men's history and files, became friends with other mutant youths like Rockslide (Santo Vaccaro), was named best actor by his fellow students, and code-named Anole, after the chameleon species. Initially choosing Wolverine (Logan/James Howlett) as his student advisor, Victor soon realized they were incompatible and asked Karma (Xi'an Coy Manh), whose French class he enjoyed considerably, to be his advisor. Victor's parents continued to be supportive of their son, even attending the school's Parents' Day celebration. Victor was placed on Northstar (Jean-Paul Beaubier)'s Alpha Squadron training group, which included Loa (Alani Ryan) and Indra (Paras Gavaskar), and soon became its student leader. While coming to terms with his sexuality, Victor formed a close bond with the openly gay Northstar. But when a brainwashed Wolverine killed Northstar, Victor was devastated; for a time, he was unaware of Northstar's subsequent resurrection.

After an insane Scarlet Witch (Wanda Maximoff) used her reality-altering powers to strip the majority of mutants of their abilities ("M-Day"), Anole was among the 27 students who retained their mutant genes. After the X-Men's artificial intelligence training room went rogue and threatened the students, co-headmistress Emma Frost disbanded the school's squads, then hosted a battle royale between the students to determine who would join the school's X-Men-In-Training squad, but Anole was not chosen. Later, when the Children of the Vault sent a brainwashed Northstar and his twin sister, Aurora (Jeanne-Marie Beaubier), to attack the Institute, Anole was thrilled to see

ALPHA SQUADRON UNIFORM, PRE-REGENERATED ARM

Northstar alive, though Northstar struck him, an act that deeply upset Anole. Regardless of not being chosen for the training squad, Anole remained at the Institute, where he mourned dozens of depowered students slain by the anti-mutant Rev. William Stryker and his Purifiers, and was present when the X-Men and X-Men-In-Training repelled the Purifiers' subsequent assault on the Institute. Anole was interrogated by Valerie Cooper and the Office of National Emergency (O*N*E), when the X-Men-In-Training left the Institute grounds despite orders not to. Anole refused to offer information on his fellow students, instead coming up with wild, random excuses for their disappearance, which frustrated Cooper, who flagged Anole as a potential problem student. After the drastic student body reduction, Anole and Rockslide developed a close camaraderie filled with teasing each other.

Anole was on Institute grounds during the X-Men's battle with the Hulk (Bruce Banner), who was seeking information from Xavier, shortly before the student body was kidnapped to limbo (Otherplace) by the demonic Belasco, who was seeking his former pupil Magik (Illyana Rasputin). Attacked by demons, Anole's right arm was severed before the students were saved by Magik, in her corrupt Darkchild aspect, who imprisoned the students as she sought student Pixie (Megan Gwynn)'s soul to use against Belasco. During captivity, Anole was surprised his wound was not bleeding and did not hurt, soon regenerating a monstrously proportioned, superhumanly strong arm, which he used to try to save Pixie from the Darkchild, but Pixie's soul was partially taken. The students opposed Belasco's efforts to bring Earth to limbo and witnessed his defeat by the Darkchild before she teleported them back to the Institute. Once on Earth, Rockslide insisted on Anole's admittance to the X-Men-In-Training due to his heroism in limbo. Anole complained of his new arm itching for a time after returning from limbo, and when X-Man Beast (Hank McCoy) suggested all his limbs would regenerate if severed, Rockslide repeatedly tried to convince Anole to cut his other limbs off, so he could grow into 'an awesome dragon guy." While bantering about this, unaware Anole was homosexual, Rockslide called Anole a "sissy," which provoked Anole to beat sensitivity lessons into him. When Rockslide refused to detonate his form for one of Beast's experiments, Anole called him a "sissy" to provoke him; when Beast postulated having someone shatter Rockslide for another experiment, Anole good-naturedly and eagerly volunteered. Following this, seeking to provoke Anole, Rockslide took great joy in announcing Anole's homosexuality to the other students, most of whom already knew.

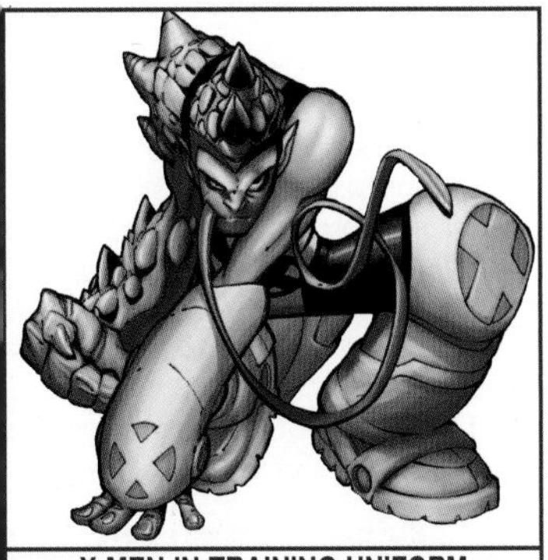
X-MEN-IN-TRAINING UNIFORM

During a massive war over the first post-M-Day mutant birth (Hope Summers), Cyclops (Scott Summers) insisted the X-Men-In-Training not get involved for their own protection. However, the group left to vengefully attack the Purifiers and seek information on the missing baby. They battled with the Purifiers' cyborg Reavers allies and later fought a mutant-devouring Predator X monster that had exhumed deceased students on the Institute grounds for consumption, then began hunting the wounded mutants in the X-Men's infirmary. While fighting the Predator X, Pixie impulsively teleported the students and Predator X to the X-Men for help, arriving during the war's final battle between the X-Men and the mutant-killing Marauders; Anole and the students helped defeat the Marauders and save the baby, who was sent to the future (Reality-80521) with X-Man Cable (Nathan Summers) to grow up under his protection. Following the war, the destroyed Institute was shut down and the students sent home. Despite the warm welcome he received in his hometown, Anole was deeply angered to have been sent home, being let down by his heroes and what he perceived as the theft of his youth by the X-Men. He felt he did not fit in with civilians, suffering a form of Post-Traumatic Stress Disorder. After three months of no communication from Anole, Cyclops sent Northstar to check on him. Seeing Northstar for the first time since he punched Anole while brainwashed, Anole punched Northstar and told him he did not want the X-Men to contact him again; Anole ran away from home, leaving his parents an apology note.

After Cyclops reconvened the X-Men in San Francisco, he recruited former Xavier students Danielle Moonstar and Sunspot (Roberto Da Costa) to gather, teach and train young mutants again; Moonstar located Anole and despite his reservations, she convinced him to rejoin the X-Men-In-Training. Anole was reunited with Rockslide, and with the other trainees, they investigated a group of missing construction workers, ultimately rescuing them from a living island named Krakoa. The trainees then battled the "Y-Men," gang members given superpowers by Leon Nunez, a mutant tattoo artist who could grant powers through his tattoos, and the cyborg Donald Pierce. Anole quickly befriended Jonas Graymalkin, a decades-old mutant who had been released from suspended animation and was struggling to adjust to his new life and his burgeoning homosexuality; Anole helped Graymalkin in both regards. When it appeared his teammate Dust (Sooraya Quadir) was dying, Anole questioned his choice to return, feeling an X-Men-In-Training's role was to serve as cannon fodder for the X-Men, but these feelings seemed to subside when Dust survived. Anole fought against the Neo and the shape-changing alien Skrulls' invasion of San Francisco during their attempted Earth conquest. When Magik returned to Earth, Anole was furious to see her, and when Magik caustically joked about taking part of Pixie's soul, Anole tried to punch her with his enhanced strength arm, but was stopped by Magik's friends Cannonball (Sam Guthrie) and Sunspot.

Anole was later injured stopping riots that followed the proposal of the mutant rights-limiting Proposition X, but recovered enough to stand against corrupt businessman Norman Osborn's forces when they tried to remove the X-Men from Utopia, their newly created floating island sanctuary. While Utopia was being made habitable, Anole repeatedly complained the farming work he was assigned to was not work mutant heroes should be doing. Overhearing this, Magik teleported him to a desert and left him there for five days without food. The experience helped Anole realize even mundane tasks, such as farming, were essential to the island's habitants; upon his return, Anole resumed working without complaint. Later, he was present when the immortal sorceress Selene resurrected an army of mutants in her quest to obtain godhood and sent some of these zombified mutants to attack Utopia.

SUPER-HERO COSTUME
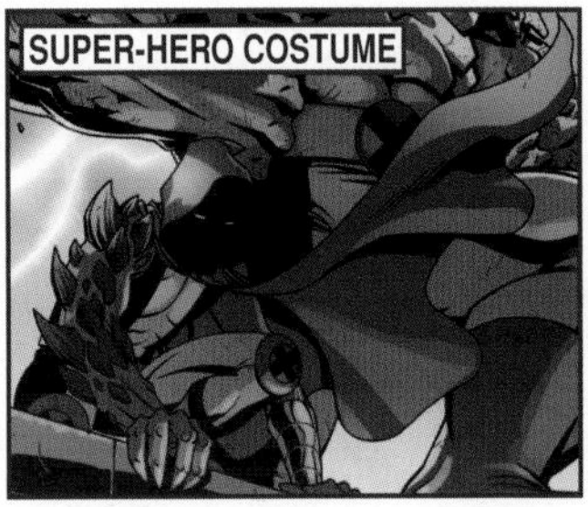

Art by Derec Donovan

Cable and a now-teenage Hope Summers returned from the future, setting off a massive war between the X-Men and the robot-killing Sentinel Bastion's forces. In limiting the X-Men's mobility, Bastion eliminated their teleporters, including banishing Magik to limbo. Despite his initial refusal and self-doubt, Cannonball convinced Anole it was the heroic thing to rescue Magik, no matter his feelings about her. Sometime after Magik's rescue and Bastion's defeat, Anole and Rockslide created super-hero costumes and repeatedly went into San Francisco late at night to fight crime and become heroes, growing a deep appreciation of each other during their outings. However, they soon ran afoul of crimelord Mister Negative when they unwittingly interfered with his criminal operations; Negative subsequently hired the Serpent Society to help him try to kill the boys.

HEIGHT: 5'9" **EYES:** Brown
WEIGHT: 160 lbs. **HAIR:** None; formerly Black

ABILITIES/ACCESSORIES: Anole has multiple reptilian traits, including a spiked carapace on his head; a long, sticky, prehensile forked tongue (extending over five feet) he can control with great accuracy, using it to catch Frisbees and basketballs during sporting events, and restrain the hand of a gun-toting gang member; pads on his hands and feet that allow him to cling to solid surfaces; and apparently retractable sharp fingernails and toenails. He can also change the color of his skin to match the pattern of almost any surface and environment, oftentimes this occurs as an unconscious reflex when he feels threatened. After regenerating his severed right arm, Anole gained enhanced strength, but only in that arm; it has been postulated Anole can regenerate any limb, and they will be similarly superhumanly strong. He is highly athletic and agile, often moving similar to a gymnast in battle, and has some hand-to-hand combat training. Anole sometimes wears a bulletproof Xavier Institute uniform, and a fake mustache with a hooded cloak.

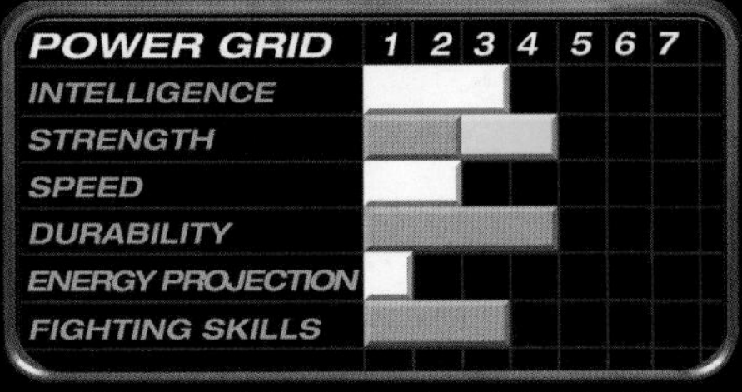
POWER GRID
1 2 3 4 5 6 7
INTELLIGENCE
STRENGTH
SPEED
DURABILITY
ENERGY PROJECTION
FIGHTING SKILLS

YELLOW BAR INDICATES RIGHT ARM RATING

KNOWN MEMBERS: Cadena, Corregidora, Fuego, Luz ("Luisa"), Martillo, Olvido, Perro, Piedra Dura, Rana, Serafina ("Sarah"), approximately 3000 others
FORMER MEMBERS: Aguja, Sangre
BASE OF OPERATIONS: Quitado, Corridor (interdimensional void); formerly Master Mold, Ecuador; Camara Roja Vault ("Red Chamber," aka Conquistador, mobile, originally anchored in international waters between Peru and Chile)
FIRST APPEARANCE: X-Men #188 (2006); (identified) X-Men #190 (2006)

TRAITS: Millennia of genetic drift have transformed the Children of the Vault into a separate human subspecies. The Children's individual post-human abilities are a combination of genetic engineering and tech-based amplification; they are inherent to each member but fueled by power packs worn in their outfits. Although many Children have unique powers and appearances, several "castes" dress identically and serve specific functions, including troops, guards and scientists. The Children reproduce asexually via their advanced technology, which is roughly 6000 years ahead of the modern world and includes teleport devices and esoteric weapons such as black hole-creating "singularity generators" and miniature machines that can alter metal's allotropic nature. When based on Earth, the Children's technology and power packs were fueled by a Suncatcher device, which siphoned solar energy and was powerful enough to briefly dim the sun. All Children can alter their power set to wield the powers of any or all other Children, but in practice this often overloads them; they tend to specialize in one individual power. However, all Children have enhanced strength and can fly and see beyond the visual spectrum. Aguja ("the Needle") generates lines, planes and shapes of non-being that eat through reality, leaving vacuum behind; she wields

**BACK ROW: OLVIDO, RANA & MARTILLO
FRONT ROW: SERAFINA, CADENA & PERRO**

weapons that temporarily neutralize mutants' powers. Cadena ("the Chain"), apparently composed of energy, wears a containment suit and forms energy lariats. Corregidora plants suggestions in people's minds with verbal cantrips; she operates the Children's House of Correction and wields a knife. Fuego ("Fire") shoots flame blasts, senses heat signatures, and absorbs energy around him to fuel his constantly blazing body. Luz ("Light") forms light into coherent and apparently solid images and travels at super-speed. Martillo ("the Hammer") has super-strength and wields an enormous metallic hammer that lets him teleport, analyze his environment and track targets. Olvido ("the Void") is connected to an antimatter universe; he absorbs energy attacks and responds with a negative-energy equivalent. Perro ("the Dog") manipulates gravity in various ways. Piedra Dura ("Hard Stone") is composed of solid rock. Rana ("the Frog") can physically invade opponents' bodies, possessing them or attacking them from within. Sangre ("Blood") transforms his body into liquid and can form bubbles of water around opponents' heads, drowning them. Serafina splices her consciousness into machines via cables that extend from her body. She can hack into computers and human nervous systems with equal ease; she can read, erase or modify computer data, alter people's minds and DNA, and utilize and modify their powers. She can also track residual chemical trails, cloak herself and others, and shield herself and others from the Children's weaponry. The Children are ruled by a Council and speak fluent English and Spanish.

HISTORY: Over 35 years ago, a group of evolutionary biologists teamed with temporal physicist Dr. Bella Pagan to create a new breed of mankind that could repopulate the Earth after a hypothetical extinction-level catastrophe. Deciding to speed up natural evolution, the scientists built a temporal compression unit inside a large Chilean shipping freighter called the Conquistador, populated it with subjects, sealed it and anchored it in international waters. Over the next 30 years,

INORGANIC GUARDS

6000 years passed within the freighter, and a technologically advanced culture evolved, naming themselves the Children of the Vault and genetically engineering a wide range of super-powers. One of the scientists, Dr. Alejandro Casales, eventually felt great remorse about the experiment and hired mutant assassins Sabretooth (Victor Creed) and the force field-generating Pasco to kill all the scientists involved, including himself. After completing the job, Sabretooth and Pasco learned of the Conquistador and investigated, but as they reached the freighter, a global event later known as "M-Day" struck when the insane Scarlet Witch (Wanda Maximoff) used her reality-altering powers to remake the world, ultimately removing the powers of most of Earth's mutants, including Pasco. The energies unleashed by the mass depowering somehow unsealed the Vault, and the Children emerged. Led by Sangre and having monitored the outside world over the years, they planned to wipe out both humans and mutants and claim Earth for themselves. The Children killed the now-defenseless Pasco and badly wounded Sabretooth, who fled. Sabretooth sought shelter with the X-Men, who had offered asylum to all mutants after M-Day, but the Children tracked him as he made his way north. Sangre and Serafina used a singularity generator to vaporize a Mexican bar Sabretooth had visited, leaving false information with a lone survivor to frame the X-Men. Fuego and Aguja attacked Sabretooth, dampening his healing powers, but he escaped again and made it to the Xavier Institute, where the X-Men grudgingly sheltered him.

The Children kidnapped former X-Man Northstar (Jean-Paul Beaubier), who had been brainwashed by the Hand ninja clan, from a SHIELD deprogramming facility, killing all agents and again framing the X-Men. Recruiting Northstar's suicidal twin sister Aurora (Jeanne-Marie Beaubier), Serafina altered the twins' minds and powers and sent them to kill the X-Men. During the battle, Serafina noticed Cannonball (Sam Guthrie) and, curious about sexual reproduction, hacked into the nervous system of the X-Men's comatose patient Lady Mastermind (Regan Wyngarde), using her illusion-casting powers to enthrall Cannonball. Serafina put Cannonball through a time-compressed simulation of romance and married life with her, rewriting the scenario each time Cannonball began to realize its falsehood, but Wolverine (Logan/James Howlett) disrupted the illusion, freeing Cannonball. The X-Men defeated and captured Northstar and Aurora, but Serafina fled, and the Children regrouped.

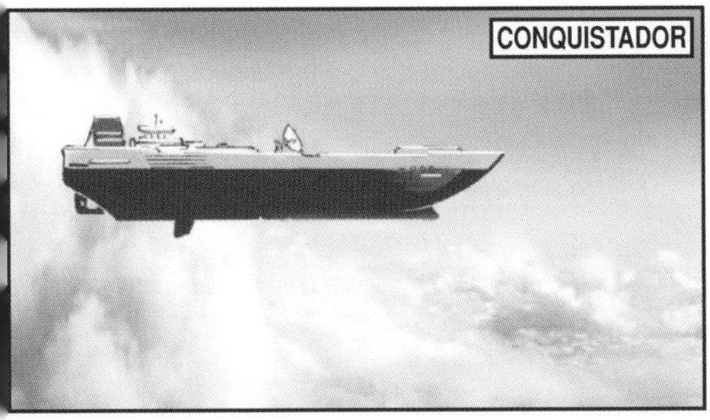
CONQUISTADOR

Equipping the Conquistador with psi-shields, a cloak and flight capabilities, the Children headed for the Institute, but Rogue (Anna Marie) intercepted them with an ad hoc X-Men squad, including Cable (Nathan Summers), Iceman (Bobby Drake), Cannonball and probationary members Mystique (Raven Darkhölme), Sabretooth and the revived Lady Mastermind. However, Fuego vaporized Iceman, and the Children captured most of the other X-Men as the Conquistador arrived over the mansion, easily repulsing the US government-sanctioned Sentinel Squad O*N*E members stationed there after M-Day. As the Conquistador prepared to fire on the mansion, Cable destroyed the Children's Suncatcher, rendering their weapons powerless, and the X-Men broke free and defeated the Children. Lady Mastermind tricked Fuego into fatally blasting Aguja, and Iceman re-formed from moisture in the air, extinguishing Fuego. Sangre tried to crash the Conquistador into the mansion, but Cannonball and the Sentinels caught it. Preparing to fake their deaths and retreat, the Children planted genetically altered animal carcasses in the Conquistador's hold. Mystique shot Sangre with exploding thermite, apparently killing him and starting a fire that gutted the Conquistador, seemingly killing the 3000 Children dwelling inside.

However, the Children had teleported to the Ecuadorian Master Mold Sentinel-building facility, which they took as their new home. Abandoning their goal of eliminating humanity, they built the floating city Quitado in the "Corridor," an interdimensional void, using the Master Mold to create inorganic guards and a labor force of Sentinel robots they named "Servidores." However, the Children soon faced an energy crisis; without a sun to draw fuel from, they powered their generators with the decay of transdimensional particles — but this created radioactive waste, which they vented to Earth near Mumbai, India, causing severe electromagnetic storms. Seeking a better energy source, the Children's scientists invented Angelfire, a device that could be powered indefinitely by the living bodies of 30 of the Children. However, only 29 had useable energy-generating powers — and one of those, Luz, was young and highly rebellious. Seeking adventure, Luz fled to Earth and encountered Rogue and Magneto (Max Eisenhardt), who had brought a group of the X-Men's students to Mumbai to visit the family of fellow student Indra (Paras Gavaskar), whose brother Tejpal was one of many stricken comatose by the Children's radioactive storms. Corregidora sent Servidores after Luz, but when the X-Men defeated the Sentinel robots, Corregidora recognized Rogue as one of their former foes.

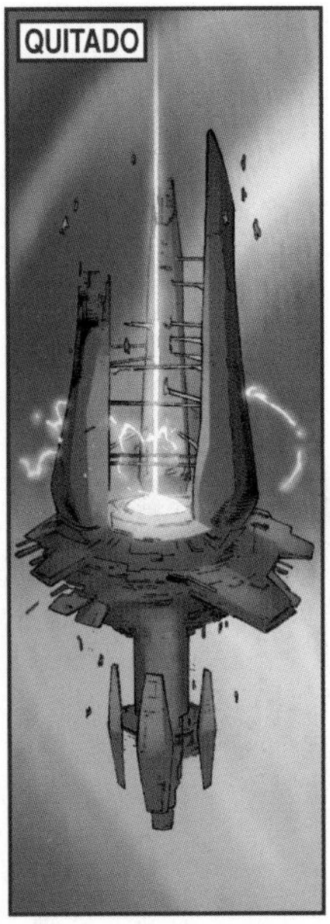
QUITADO

Art by Clay Mann

Luz fell for Indra, but he rejected her, as he was now arranged to be married to Vaipala Rani, his brother's former fiancée. A group of Children teleported to Earth and captured Rogue and Magneto, and Vaipala, who was uncomfortable with the arranged marriage, suggested to Luz the two women switch places. Luz wove light-illusions around both women, and Vaipala, as "Luz," surrendered to save Rogue and Magneto's lives. Returning to Quitado, Corregidora ordered Rogue put to death by Perro in the Sense Forum, a sensory arena the Children could log into and experience remotely, and had Magneto strapped into Angelfire as the 30th energy source alongside "Luz." However, when the scientists activated Angelfire, it malfunctioned and exploded, revealing Vaipala's ruse, and Quitado partially materialized in Mumbai. Luz's feelings for Indra overpowered her urge to escape life with the Children, and she grudgingly agreed to aid the X-Men's students. While Rogue overpowered Perro, Luz and the students infiltrated Quitado and helped Vaipala and their teachers escape the attacking Children. As Luz stayed behind, Magneto destroyed the device anchoring Quitado to Earth, and it faded back into the Corridor — where it now tumbles directionless through the void.

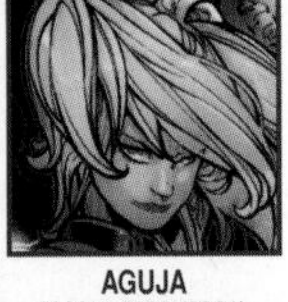
AGUJA
X-Men #188 (2006)

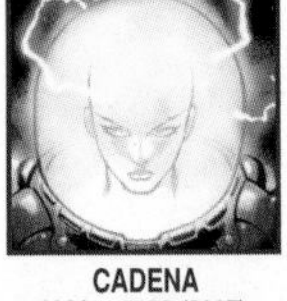
CADENA
X-Men #193 (2007)

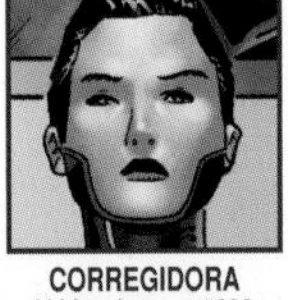
CORREGIDORA
X-Men: Legacy #238 (2010)

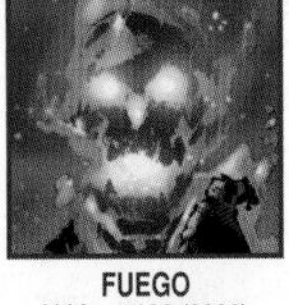
FUEGO
X-Men #188 (2006)

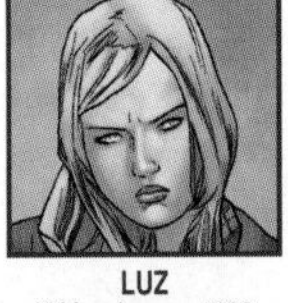
LUZ
X-Men: Legacy #238 (2010)

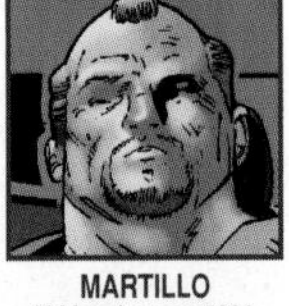
MARTILLO
X-Men: Legacy #238 (2010)

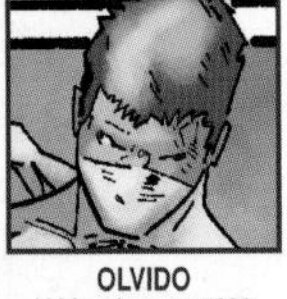
OLVIDO
X-Men: Legacy #239 (2010)

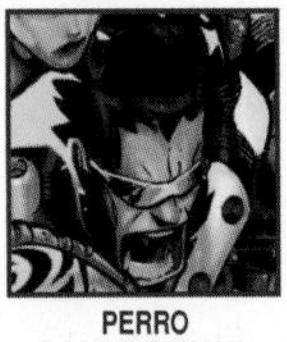
PERRO
X-Men #189 (2006)

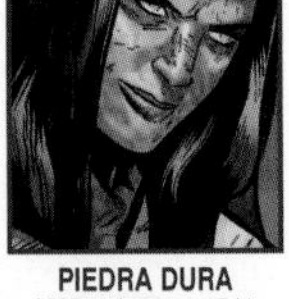
PIEDRA DURA
X-Men: Legacy #241 (2010)

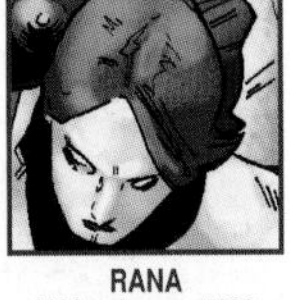
RANA
X-Men: Legacy #239 (2010)

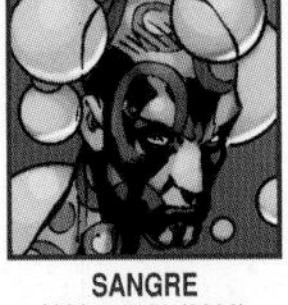
SANGRE
X-Men #188 (2006)

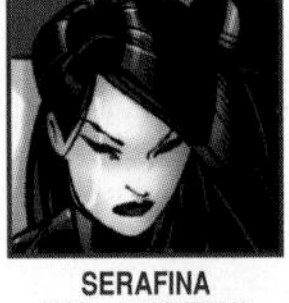
SERAFINA
X-Men #188 (2006)

INDRA

REAL NAME: Paras Gavaskar
ALIASES: None
IDENTITY: Known to authorities
OCCUPATION: Adventurer, student
CITIZENSHIP: India
PLACE OF BIRTH: Mumbai, India (presumably)
KNOWN RELATIVES: Rav (father), Bhakti (mother), Tejpal (brother)
GROUP AFFILIATION: X-Men-In-Training; formerly Xavier Institute student body/Alpha Squadron
EDUCATION: Various high school level courses at Xavier Institute for Higher Learning
FIRST APPEARANCE: New X-Men #7 (2005); (identified) New X-Men: Academy X Yearbook Special #1 (2005)

HISTORY: Paras Gavaskar was born to an Indian family that followed Jainism, a religion that prescribes nonviolence to all living creatures (Ahimsa). Paras grew up a vegetarian on his family's Panchajana Estate outside Mumbai and had an uneasy relationship with his strict father, who Paras felt was compromising Ahimsa by being a lawyer. When his mutant powers manifested, and his purple skin and face markings appeared, Paras attended Charles Xavier's Institute for Higher Learning in Westchester, New York. Paras was placed in Northstar (Jean-Paul Beaubier)'s Alpha Squadron training group, which included Loa (Alani Ryan) and Anole (Victor Borkowski), and at some point took the ironic name Indra (after the Hindu god of war); the group grew close to each other and Northstar. Indra loved science and was named Xavier's most reliable student by the student body. When a brainwashed Wolverine (Logan/James Howlett) killed Northstar, Paras was saddened and remained unaware of Northstar's subsequent resurrection for a time. After an insane Scarlet Witch (Wanda Maximoff) used her reality-altering powers to strip the majority of mutants of their abilities ("M-Day"), Indra was among the 27 students who retained their mutant genes. Co-headmistress Emma Frost disbanded the school's squads, then hosted a battle royale between the students to determine who would join the school's X-Men-In-Training squad, but Indra, who reluctantly participated, failed to be chosen. He was later among students kidnapped to limbo (Otherplace) by the demonic Belasco, but returned to the Institute after Belasco's defeat.

The students realized Indra was potentially Earth's youngest mutant, making him fear he was a target for assassination, and for a time, the students took turns acting as his bodyguard; Beast (Hank McCoy) gave him a bulletproof school uniform, which eased his fears. During a massive war over the first post-M-Day mutant birth (Hope Summers), Indra was saved from a mutant-consuming Predator X monster by Surge (Noriko Ashida). After the war, the Institute was shut down, and the students were sent home. Cyclops (Scott Summers) later regathered the X-Men in San Francisco, and most of Earth's remaining mutants, including Indra, relocated there. When the city erupted in riots over proposed mutant rights-limiting Proposition X, Indra was trying to get home when he was physically assaulted by a HAMMER agent; to protect himself, Indra summoned his armor and struck the agent. Indra was deeply troubled by breaking his nonviolence pact, and when great pain prevented him from summoning his armor, Indra felt the Yakshas (the enlightened ones) had abandoned him for being unworthy. His mentor, Rogue (Anna Marie), felt it was psychological in nature and pushed him to accept the powers he was running away from. Finally doing so, Indra manifested a more threatening version of his armor, as well as numerous bladed weapons for the first time.

When Paras' brother, Tejpal, mysteriously became comatose (due to electromagnetic frequencies caused by the extradimensional Children of the Vault's energy productions), Paras was summoned home and was accompanied by Anole, Loa, and teachers Rogue and Magneto (Max Eisenhardt). Paras' father expressed displeasure at the former terrorist Magneto's presence and told Paras he was to marry Tejpal's fiancée, Vaipala Rani, to fulfill his engagement; out of respect and obedience, Indra reluctantly agreed. Simultaneously, one of the Children, the solid light sculpture-creating Luz, who fled to India to avoid being used as an energy source, encountered the mutants and quickly fell for Indra. A group of Children teleported to Earth and captured Rogue, Magneto, and Vaipala, who was uncomfortable with the arranged marriage and suggested to Luz the two women switch places using Luz's light illusions. To gain his father's permission to rescue his friends, Indra insisted on marrying sooner, but Luz revealed herself before the ceremony was complete, and when Children scientists' machines were destroyed while trying to use energies from "Luz,", Vaipala's ruse was discovered. Indra disobeyed his father and helped rescue his teachers and defeat the Children, using violence on automatons and punching one of the Children to save Rogue. Feeling he could no longer ignore the world's victims of violence, Indra defied his father by returning to San Francisco and the X-Men.

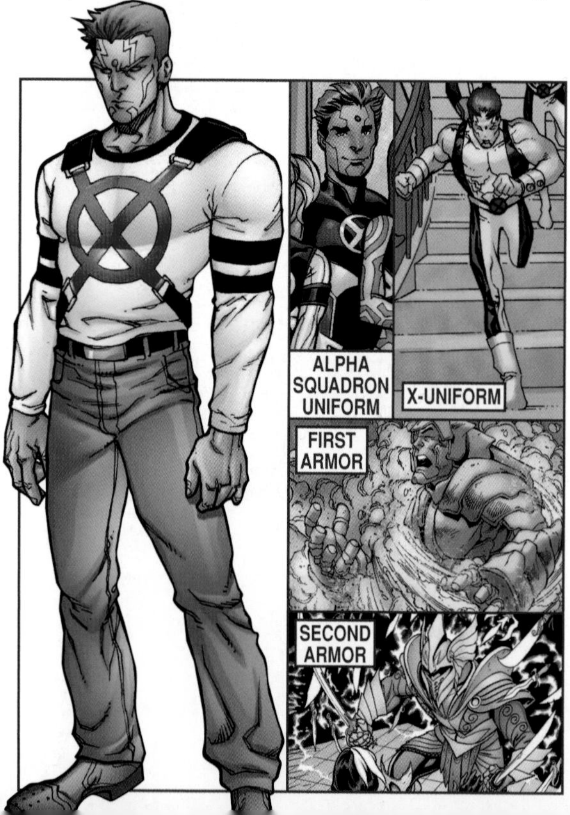

ALPHA SQUADRON UNIFORM
X-UNIFORM
FIRST ARMOR
SECOND ARMOR

HEIGHT: 5'10" (variable when armored) **EYES:** Red
WEIGHT: 185 lbs. (variable when armored) **HAIR:** Red

ABILITIES/ACCESSORIES: Indra can instantly manifest an exoskeleton in the shape of armored plates that can vary in appearance, presumably limited only by Indra's imagination and reluctance to use his powers; the specifications of this armor remain unrevealed, but appear to grant enhanced strength. He can also manifest nearly indestructible bladed weapons that hover about him and can be wielded and thrown like conventional blades; the substance and origin of these blades is unrevealed. Indra wears a bindi on his forehead, and sometimes wears a bulletproof Xavier Institute uniform.

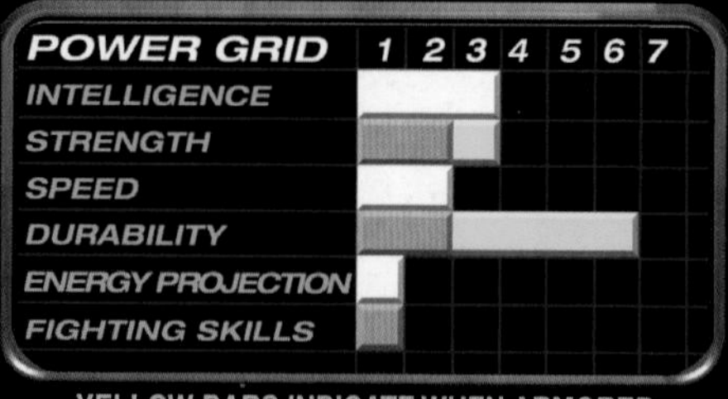

POWER GRID
1 2 3 4 5 6 7
INTELLIGENCE
STRENGTH
SPEED
DURABILITY
ENERGY PROJECTION
FIGHTING SKILLS

YELLOW BARS INDICATE WHEN ARMORED

HISTORY: Alani Ryan's grandmother Alice was the New York City roommate of Betty Dean, the periodic love interest of Atlantean royalty Namor the Sub-Mariner, who gifted Betty with an ancient Atlantean talisman necklace. Before she left for Hawaii with her new husband and son, Alice observed Betty break up with Namor and discard the talisman, which Alice kept. Years later, when Alice's granddaughter Alani, a very laid-back child who loved the ocean, was surfing with her father, they were attacked by albino would-be conqueror Great White and his trained sharks. Saving her father from a shark, Alani jumped through it, her previously dormant mutant power disintegrating the shark and generating tattoo-like markings all over her body; they were subsequently saved by Namor. Afterward, Alani became fascinated by the Atlanteans, studying and reading everything she could find. She enrolled at Charles Xavier's Institute for Higher Learning in Westchester, New York, run by the mutant X-Men, taking the code name Loa (presumably after the Voodoo religion's spirits), and joining Northstar (Jean-Paul Beaubier)'s Alpha Squadron training group alongside Indra (Paras Gavaskar) and Anole (Victor Borkowski); the group grew close to each other and Northstar. When a brainwashed Wolverine (Logan/James Howlett) killed Northstar, Loa was saddened and remained unaware of Northstar's subsequent resurrection for a time.

After an insane Scarlet Witch (Wanda Maximoff) used her reality-altering powers to strip the majority of mutants of their abilities ("M-Day"), Loa was among the 27 students who remained mutants. Co-headmistress Emma Frost disbanded the school's squads, then hosted a battle royale between the students to determine who would join the school's X-Men-In-Training squad; Loa failed to be chosen. She was later present when the anti-mutant Reverend William Stryker and his Purifiers killed dozens of depowered students and invaded the Institute, and when the Hulk (Bruce Banner) attacked while seeking information from Xavier. She was among students kidnapped to limbo (Otherplace) by the demonic Belasco, who sought former Xavier student Magik (Illyana Rasputin). While there, Loa tried to save Pixie (Megan Gwynn) when Magik tried to steal her soul as a weapon, but Magik defeated her; the students returned to the Institute after Belasco's defeat. Feeling anxiety about the experience and the dark times mutants were going through, Loa sought out Elixir (Josh Foley) to make out; the two subsequently began dating.

Following a massive war over the birth of Hope Summers, the first post-M-Day mutant birth, the Institute was shut down and the students sent home. Cyclops (Scott Summers) later reassembled the X-Men in San Francisco, and most of Earth's remaining mutants, including Loa, relocated there. When the city erupted into riots following the proposal of anti-mutant Proposition X, Loa helped stop rioters on Telegraph Hill, then assisted repelling corrupt businessman Norman Osborn's forces when they tried

REAL NAME: Alani Ryan
ALIASES: None
IDENTITY: Known to authorities
OCCUPATION: Adventurer, student
CITIZENSHIP: USA
PLACE OF BIRTH: New York City, New York
KNOWN RELATIVES: Alaka'i Ryan ("Ben," father), unidentified mother, Ben Ryan (grandfather, presumably deceased), Alice Terrel Ryan (grandmother, deceased), Alaka'i Terrel (great-grandfather, presumably deceased)
GROUP AFFILIATION: X-Men-In-Training; formerly Xavier Institute student body/Alpha Squadron
EDUCATION: Various high school level courses at Xavier Institute for Higher Learning
FIRST APPEARANCE: New X-Men #5 (2004); (identified) New X-Men: Academy X Yearbook Special #1 (2005)

to force the X-Men off Utopia, an artificial island sanctuary off the coast of California. One of Utopia's earliest citizens, Loa was injured by reanimated members of Magneto (Max Eisenhardt)'s Acolytes sent by the immortal sorceress Selene in her quest to obtain godhood. Rescued by the visiting Deadpool ("Wade Wilson"), Loa was disturbed to learn Deadpool had read her diary and was traumatized when he used her as a weapon to destroy the attacking zombies. Three weeks after her grandmother died and gifted Alani the talisman, the Aqueos, a sub-aquatic vampiric race, was unintentionally awakened by now-X-Man Namor, who asked Loa to research Atlantean tomes for Aqueos information. While underwater to deliver the key information that led to the vampires' defeat, Loa began drowning when her diving helmet was destroyed by a vampire, but her talisman began glowing and mystically allowed her to breathe underwater. Later, seeking answers about the amulet, Alani swam to New Atlantis, where she was welcomed by Namor, and told the talisman had somehow interacted with her X-gene, apparently turning her into a full-time water breather, much to Loa's dismay.

ALPHA SQUADRON UNIFORM

AMPHIBIOUS, WITH AMULET

X-UNIFORM

HEIGHT: 5'3"   **EYES:** Blue-green
WEIGHT: 125 lbs.   **HAIR:** Auburn

ABILITIES/ACCESSORIES: Loa can become intangible, able to pass through solid objects, but doing so causes whatever she traverses to crumble. Loa can breathe underwater; originally she needed to wear her talisman to do so, but her bronchi have adapted to process water, making her fully aquatic; any other sub-aquatic attributes Loa has gained are unrevealed. Loa sometimes wears a bulletproof Xavier Institute uniform. Loa is an experienced surfer.

POWER GRID	1	2	3	4	5	6	7
INTELLIGENCE							
STRENGTH							
SPEED							
DURABILITY							
ENERGY PROJECTION							
FIGHTING SKILLS							

REAL NAME: Max Eisenhardt
ALIASES: Magnus, Erik Lehnsherr, "Master of Magnetism," "Lord of the Electromagnetic Fire," Erik the Red, Grey King, White King, Michael Xavier, Creator, White Pilgrim, Prisoner #214782, others
IDENTITY: Secret
OCCUPATION: Would-be conqueror, mutants right activist; former recluse, ruler, teacher, adventurer, headmaster, terrorist, Nazi hunter, orderly, carpenter, prisoner of war
CITIZENSHIP: Germany
PLACE OF BIRTH: Unrevealed location in Germany
KNOWN RELATIVES: Magda Eisenhardt (wife, presumed deceased), Anya Eisenhardt (daughter, deceased), Wanda Maximoff (Scarlet Witch, daughter), Pietro Maximoff (Quicksilver, son), Lorna Dane (Polaris, daughter), Zala Dane (apparent daughter), Jakob Eisenhardt (father, deceased), unidentified mother (deceased), Ruthie Eisenhardt (sister, deceased), Erich Eisenhardt (uncle, deceased), Vision (son-in-law, deceased), Crystalia Maximoff (Crystal, ex-daughter-in-law), Luna Maximoff (granddaughter), William "Billy" Kaplan (Wiccan, alleged grandson), Thomas "Tommy" Shepherd (Speed, alleged grandson), Joseph (clone, deceased)
GROUP AFFILIATION: X-Men; formerly the Genoshan "Excalibur," Acolytes (leader), the Twelve, Hellfire Club (New York Inner Circle), New Mutants (headmaster), Savage Land Mutates (creator), Brotherhood of Evil Mutants (founder), Sonderkommando
EDUCATION: Some public schooling, unspecified advanced training in genetic engineering and robotics
FIRST APPEARANCE: X-Men #1 (1963)

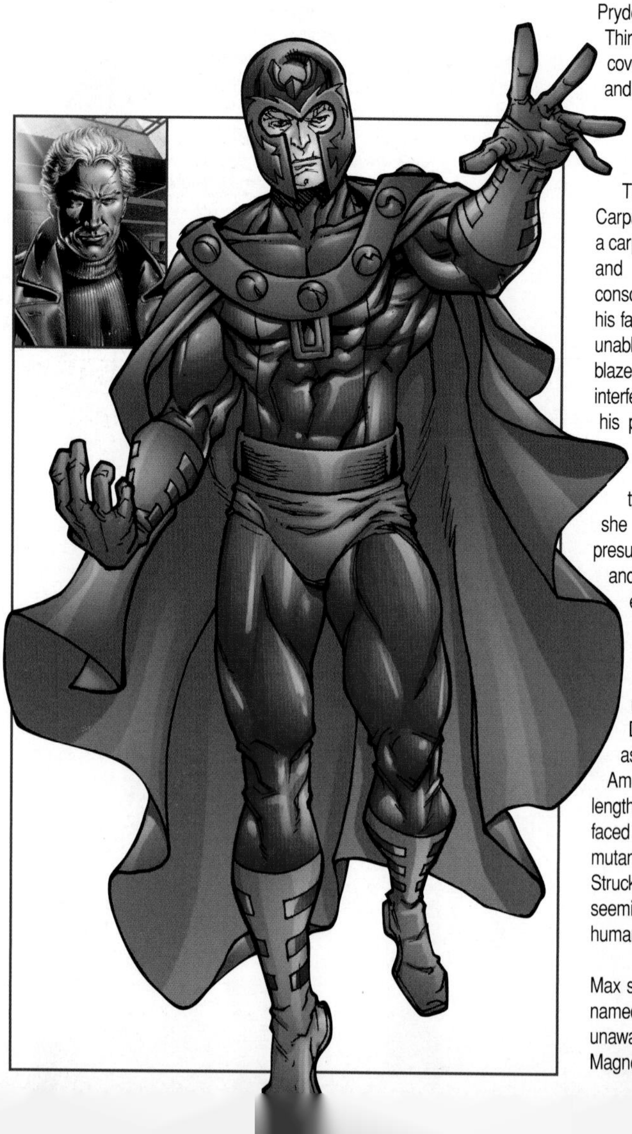

HISTORY: Max Eisenhardt grew up in Germany during the Third Reich's consolidation of power in Europe. Bullied at school, his only friend was a young girl named Magda. Despite his weaker stature, Max excelled at javelin throwing, unaware this was thanks to his latent mutant magnetic powers. Accused of cheating and expelled from school, Max and his family fled to Poland to escape Nazi oppression. After the Nazis invaded Poland and began rounding up Jews for mass extermination, Max's family tried to escape but were captured by Nazis, lined up and shot. Only Max survived by subconsciously using his powers to alter the bullets' trajectories to miss him. The strain rendered him unconscious, and he was left in a mass grave. Upon waking, Max returned to Warsaw but was soon captured and sent to Auschwitz concentration camp. One of the first prisoners there, Max sought to avoid the medical examinations conducted by a mysterious albino geneticist (the future Mr. Sinister) and so joined the Sonderkommando, tasked with cleaning out the crematorium's furnaces. There he discovered the twisted bodies of those who had endured the albino's "medical exams," which sought to catalyze the mutator gene. Growing to manhood within the camp, Max used his Sonderkommando status to help and inspire others to continue their fight for survival, including the Shulmans, Chava Rosanoff (nee Prydeman, relative of future X-Man Kitty Pryde), and Magda. As the Third Reich faced defeat in the war, they sought to kill all prisoners to cover their atrocities. When a guard threatened Magda, Max killed him and fled Auschwitz with her days before the Soviets liberated the camp. At some point, Max began suffering repeated headaches as his powers developed.

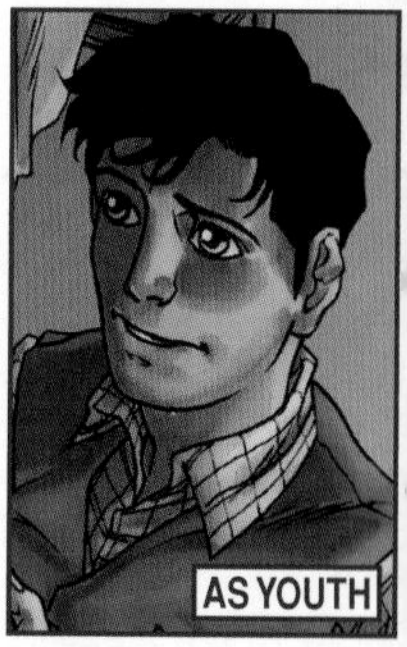
AS YOUTH

They settled in a small village in the Carpathian mountains where Max became a carpenter. Falling in love, the pair married and had a daughter, Anya. Max first consciously used his mutant powers when his family was trapped in a burning house; unable to rescue his daughter from the blaze due to his inexperience and the interference of authorities, he unleashed his powers to slaughter the humans. A terrified Magda fled; finding herself pregnant, she gave birth to mutant twins at Wundagore Mountain, who she left in the care of her midwife, the cow-woman Bova; Magda presumably died in unrevealed circumstances after leaving Wundagore, and it would be many years before Max learned of his children's existence. Meanwhile, to shake off his pursuers, Max had master forger George Odekirk create the false identity of Sinte Gypsy "Erik Magnus Lehnsherr" for him. Max was unaware at some point he sired another daughter that would eventually become the magnetic-wielding X-Man Polaris, and allegedly a fourth child, Zala Dane. Max eventually made his way to Israel where he worked as an orderly in a psychiatric hospital near Haifa. He befriended American mutant telepath Charles Xavier, with whom he shared lengthy debates, hypothesizing what would happen if humanity were faced with a race of super-beings. The pair ultimately revealed their true mutant natures to each other when they prevented Baron (Wolfgang von) Strucker from obtaining a large cache of Nazi gold. Causing a cave-in that seemingly killed Strucker, Max realized his and Xavier's views on mutant/human relations were incompatible and he left with the gold.

Max subsequently worked for a covert agency as a Nazi hunter, code-named "Magneto." When he captured former Nazi Hans Richter, he was unaware Richter was working with the same agency. For this failure, Magneto's handler sought to kill him but failed. Enraged, Magneto took an aggressive stance against humanity, wanting to lead mutants into becoming Earth's dominant life form. He began amassing resources to further his cause, notably an orbital base dubbed "Asteroid M." He formed the terrorist Brotherhood of Evil Mutants (the "Evil" part having been added to their name by the media), recruiting the teleporter Astra, the agile Toad (Mortimer Toynbee), the illusionist Mastermind (Jason Wyngarde), and mutant twins Scarlet Witch and Quicksilver (actually Magneto's long-lost children, though none of them knew it). Magneto ruled the Brotherhood through fear and intimidation, and his constant abuse twisted Toad into a sycophant who blindly worshipped him. Magneto met with Xavier and his then-lover Amelia Voght at the former Auschwitz camp, where Xavier failed to talk him out of his planned war on humanity. Magneto subsequently sought an alliance with German mutant telepath Whisper (Karl Reifschneider), whom Magneto believed to be a fellow Auschwitz survivor; however, upon learning Whisper had actually been a guard at Auschwitz, Magneto ignored Whisper's claims of reformation and slew him.

CREATOR

After a falling-out with Astra led to her quitting the Brotherhood, Magneto attacked the Cape Citadel military base and was opposed by Xavier's own mutant group, the X-Men. Magneto then conquered the South American nation of Santo Marco and prepared for the X-Men's inevitable arrival by setting a nuclear device that would destroy the country. Defeated by the X-Men, Magneto and the Brotherhood fled, but not before Quicksilver helped the X-Men save countless innocents by defusing the bomb. When the enigmatic alien Stranger arrived in New York, both Magneto and Xavier sought to recruit him to their respective causes, leading to another clash between their teams.

The Stranger ultimately departed, capturing Magneto and the Toad as specimens for study on his laboratory planet. Escaping back to Earth, Magneto sought to create an army of mutants but was again opposed by the X-Men, who summoned the Stranger back to Earth to reclaim his prize specimen; Magneto soon escaped back to Earth again. Discovering Quicksilver and the Scarlet Witch had reformed and joined the Avengers during his absence, Magneto tried to manipulate them into rejoining his cause. After learning of Xavier's apparent death, Magneto was regretful he was not the one to have killed him.

Later attacked by the X-Men, Magneto soundly defeated them and controlled their minds, inciting them to battle the Avengers. When they broke free of his control, Magneto sought to flee — but his escape was sabotaged by the Toad, who had endured enough of Magneto's abuse. Magneto seemingly died in an explosion, but survived by burrowing through the ocean floor into a series of caverns that led him to the secluded Antarctic prehistoric jungle the Savage Land. He used his genetic engineering knowledge to mutate several natives into super-powered beings he dubbed the Savage Land Mutates. Soon after, Magneto again battled the X-Men, his mutate-creating device was destroyed, and he was lost in another explosion. Surviving yet again, he fell into an underground river that carried him to the ancient Savage Land civilization known as the "Land of the Dead," where he discovered a mind-numbing gas he intended to use against humanity. He projected his astral self to the native Nhu'gari people, manipulating them into building an airship filled with the gas. The X-Men foiled his plans again, and he jumped from the airship into the ocean.

Rescued by the Mutate Amphibius, Magneto was taken to an island where energy vampire Sauron was developing a machine to tap the region's geothermal energies. Realizing this device could restore his then-ailing powers, Magneto sought to ally with Sauron, who rejected him and left him to die inside a volcano. Fighting his way back to the surface, Magneto was rescued by Namor the Sub-Mariner, who took him to sub-aquatic Atlantis. Magneto goaded Namor into declaring war on the surface world and, while Namor clashed with the Fantastic

Art by John Byrne

Four, subjugated the Atlantean army and took control of New York City; however, the Fantastic Four's Reed Richards created a feedback machine to trap Magneto in a cone of his own power and then turned him over to the US military. Escaping his human captors, Magneto attacked the Royal Family of the Inhumans before again clashing with the X-Men and the Avengers. Defeated, Magneto was placed in an energy bubble at the Earth's core where the planet's magnetic lines of force negated his powers; however, a slight fluctuation in the Earth's magnetic field allowed him to escape.

Discovering the remains of an ancient advanced civilization, Magneto used technology abandoned by Inhumans Phaeder and Maelstrom to create Alpha, the "Ultimate Mutant." Alpha eventually turned on his creator, reducing Magneto and the Brotherhood to infancy. Xavier took the infant Magneto to Muir Island where geneticist Moira MacTaggert manipulated his DNA to correct a genetic defect she believed

X-MEN TRAINING UNIFORM

Art by Mary Wilshire

responsible for his maniacal cruelty. Magneto was later restored to adulthood by the Shi'ar Eric the Red (Davan Shakari), with whom he forged a failed alliance to destroy the X-Men. Magneto then formed a new Brotherhood consisting of Burner, Lifter, Peeper, Shocker (Randall Darby) and Slither; however, when they failed to recruit the symbiotic mutant Mr. One and Mr. Two due to Captain America (Steve Rogers)'s intervention, Magneto abandoned them. Magneto then captured a new incarnation of the X-Men and imprisoned them deep within an Antarctic volcano. After the X-Men escaped and defeated him, Magneto retreated to Asteroid M where his mind began to heal, and MacTaggert's genetic manipulation began to restore his sanity; he soon sought to force the world's governments to disarm their nuclear stockpiles, destroying a Russian city (after warning the population to evacuate) and sinking the Russian submarine Leningrad with all hands onboard in self defense.

Clashing with the X-Men once more, Magneto almost killed the young mutant Kitty Pryde, an act that shocked him into reevaluating his life. Shortly thereafter, he learned Quicksilver and the Scarlet Witch were his lost twin children Wanda and Pietro, but the twins remained wary of their long-lost father despite his claims of reformation. After the Technarch Warlock's inadvertent destruction of Asteroid M, Magneto was rescued from the ocean by fishing boat captain Aletys "Lee" Forrester, who took Magneto to his island base within the Bermuda Triangle to recuperate. She experienced Magneto's "human" side, and the pair had a brief romance. After aiding Earth's heroes against the threat of the Beyonder, a remorseful Magneto turned himself over to the World Court to be tried for his crimes; he would have been found guilty if not for an attack by Baron Strucker's vengeance seeking children Fenris. During the battle, Xavier's extraterrestrial lover Lilandra Neramani arrived to take Xavier, whose body was dying due to multiple recent injuries, to be healed by advanced Shi'ar technology; Xavier made Magneto promise to take over as headmaster of his school. Magneto reluctantly agreed, supervising the fledgling New Mutants and joining the X-Men on missions.

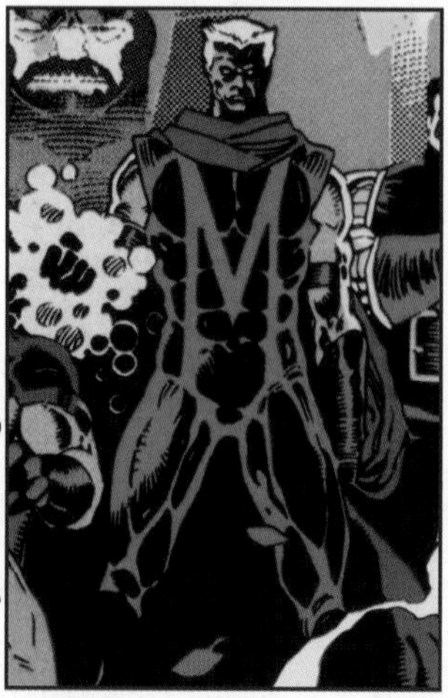

Art by Mike Mignola

Later seeking an alliance with the Hellfire Club against ever-increasing threats to mutants, Magneto and the X-Men's leader Storm (Ororo Munroe) briefly shared the position of White King within the Club's Inner Circle, before philosophical differences between Magneto and the Club's Black King Sebastian Shaw resulted in Shaw being deposed as leader and Magneto assuming the position of "Grey King," which alienated him from the New Mutants. Magneto subsequently sought to reassert his influence over the Scarlet Witch after she collapsed into a near-catatonic state following the dismantling of her android husband the Vision and the loss of her twin children. Wanda recovered in Magneto's care, though her attitude grew more malicious and bloodthirsty. Magneto welcomed Quicksilver back to their alliance as well, but Pietro helped the Avengers seize the Scarlet Witch and defeat Magneto, who again seemingly died in an explosion.

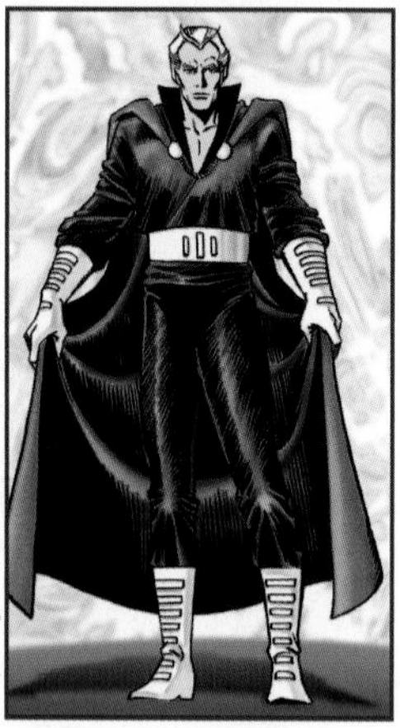

Art by John Romita Jr.

Magneto returned to the Savage Land, where he encountered the former X-Man Rogue (Anna Marie). An attraction quickly grew between the two, interrupted when they teamed up with the Savage Land's protector Ka-Zar (Kevin Plunder) and a United Nations task force led by Nick Fury to oppose the threat of Zaladane (Magneto's alleged daughter Zala Dane). Among the UN task force was Colonel Yuri Semyanov, whose son had died aboard the Leningrad and who had secretly conspired with Zaladane to eliminate Magneto; Semyanov shot Magneto, allowing him to be captured by Zaladane's forces. Zaladane tried to absorb Magneto's energies, but was interrupted by Magneto's allies. Magneto slew Semyanov in self-defense and, despite Rogue's protests, apparently slew Zaladane as well.

Magneto retired to a rebuilt Asteroid M, where his solitude was interrupted by the arrival of the mutant Acolytes, who begged him to assist in the civil war between mutants and humans on the island nation of Genosha. Magneto agreed, and when the X-Men intervened, the Acolytes captured them and Moira MacTaggert; learning Moira had genetically manipulated him during his second infancy, an outraged Magneto had Moira use the same procedure to "reprogram" the X-Men. The process failed, however, and Magneto was severely injured during the ensuing battle. The Acolyte Fabian Cortez, who claimed to be healing Magneto, was actually using his power-amplification ability to mask Magneto's pain, weakening him in the process. Cortez further betrayed Magneto when he triggered the nuclear missiles Magneto had set up around the asteroid. Magneto's power kept the base safe, but the damage was too severe. While the X-Men escaped, the asteroid crashed to Earth. After recovering, Magneto returned with a more fanatical following of Acolytes and co-opted

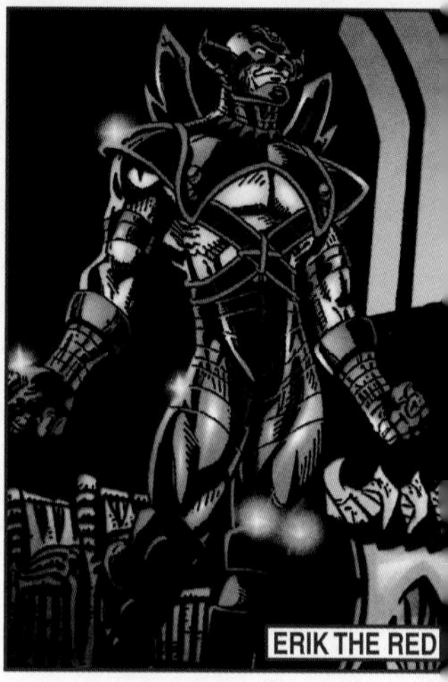

ERIK THE RED

the remains of the space station Graymalkin into a new orbital base h named Avalon, intended to be a safe haven for mutants. Magneto ser his Acolyte Exodus to Earth to recruit mutants to his cause before invitin Xavier and the X-Men to join. To Xavier's dismay, one of his X-Men – Colossus (Piotr Rasputin) — accepted Magneto's invitation. Opposin Magneto's recruiting drive, the world's governments activated th Magneto Protocols, a satellite network that created an electromagnet web around the globe beneath which Magneto would be powerles In retaliation, Magneto unleashed a global electromagnetic pulse th caused hundreds of deaths. Xavier, the X-Men and Quicksilver invade Avalon to confront Magneto. In the ensuing clash, Magneto serious injured Wolverine (Logan/James Howlett) by magnetically removing th Adamantium from his skeleton. In response, Xavier wiped Magneto' mind and left him comatose. When a battle between Holocaust of Earth 295 (the "Age of Apocalypse") and the Acolytes' new leader Exodu destroyed Avalon, Colossus placed Magneto in an escape pod, whic crashed to Earth.

Astra discovered the pod and sought revenge on Magneto by using alie technology to clone him, then pitted the clone against Magneto. Realizin the clone was more powerful, Magneto knocked him unconsciou and fled. For a time, the clone (dubbed Joseph) was believed to be rejuvenated Magneto and joined the X-Men. When the X-Men returne to Earth from an intergalactic mission, Magneto forced their spaceship t crash in Antarctica near his old base. Posing as Erik the Red, he staged mock trial of Gambit for his role in the infamous mutant Morlock massacre causing dissent in the X-Men's ranks. When the Israeli Mossad late jeopardized his forged Lehnsherr identity, Magneto slew Odekirk befor they could question him. He then built a new cybernetic assistant name Ferris who oversaw construction of a new magnetic North Pole base t house an amplification conduit that would give Magneto control over th Earth's bioelectric magnetosphere. Magneto then sent Ferris to the UN t issue an ultimatum to the world — cede him authority to create a have for mutants on Earth, or suffer a crippling global electromagnetic puls In response, the UN launched a tactical nuclear strike against Magnet Astra attacked Magneto, destroying his machines, forcing him to absor more electromagnetic energy than he could wield safely, energy th would permanently damage Earth's atmosphere if left uncontrolle Astra had Joseph attack Magneto; however, the X-Men's arrival disrupte Astra's influence over Joseph, who sacrificed his life to repair Earth's magnetosphere. The UN subsequently granted Magneto sovereignty over Genosha in the hope the country's turmoil would distract him fro his world conquest ambitions.

Magneto began consolidating his political power on Genosha, despit his now-severely weakened powers. He recruited his former Acolyt Fabian Cortez to provide him with power boosts in exchange for a sea in his newly formed cabinet. Magneto soon faced opposition from the renegade Mutate Zealot as well as Quicksilver and Rogue, and after he defeated the Zealot, Magneto had Voght, now an Acolyte, manipulate Quicksilver into joining his cabinet. Soon after, Magneto was revealed to be one of the Twelve, a group of mutants supposedly destined to usher in a prophesized golden age for mutantkind. Eternal mutant Apocalypse (En Sabah Nur) captured Magneto and the rest of the Twelve, seeking to usurp their power for himself; however, Magneto's weakened powers short-circuited Apocalypse's machine. In the ensuing clash, Magneto discovered he could use the magnetic powers of former X-Man Polaris to tap into the Earth's magnetic field and thus mask his weakened state. After Apocalypse was defeated, Magneto returned to Genosha with Polaris and began teaching her to expand her control, while using her as a front for his own failing power. Genosha soon began to flourish under Magneto's rule, but a rebellion in Carrion Cove plagued him. The rebels had discovered genetic manipulation technology in the city that they felt could not be allowed to fall into Magneto's hands, which would enable him to restore himself to full power. Though the UN, rogue Acolytes, Cortez, the Avengers, Quicksilver and Polaris all opposed him, Magneto destroyed the city as a distraction to allow him to access the chamber and restore his power. He then slew Cortez for his treachery and exiled both Quicksilver and Polaris, though they later slipped back into the country to join the rebellion against Magneto.

With an army of mutants at his disposal following the curing of the Legacy virus, Magneto declared war on mankind. The X-Men opposed him yet again, and Wolverine severely injured Magneto in the ensuing clash. Recuperating, Magneto was powerless to prevent Sentinels controlled by Xavier's genetic twin Cassandra Nova from decimating Genosha and executing 16 million mutants. Magneto was again believed dead; after a recording purported to contain his last words was found, mutant supremacist ideals became widespread in the mutant community with some adoring him as a martyr to the mutant cause. Later, Kuan-Yin Xorn was transformed (apparently by the increasingly delusional Scarlet Witch) into a duplicate of Magneto. Believing he was the real Magneto, Xorn co-opted the Xavier Institute's Special Class and secretly turned them into his new Brotherhood and attacked Manhattan. The X-Men mounted a resistance, and during a confrontation with "Magneto," Xorn killed Jean Grey with a massive electromagnetic attack before being killed in turn by Wolverine. The true Magneto was secretly still in Genosha, where he joined Xavier in rebuilding the shattered nation; while together, the two discussed the frequent headaches Magneto suffered since his powers developed. Together, they faced threats including Unus' band of survivors, Magistrates, the Dark Beast's scavengers, and Earth-295's Sugar-Man. Magneto and Xavier also restored the humanity of cybernetic Omega Sentinel Karima Shapandar and organized a mutant alliance known informally as "Excalibur." When the Scarlet Witch went insane and attacked her Avengers teammates, apparently killing some, her mind was apparently shut down by Dr. Stephen Strange's magic; when Magneto learned of this, he was granted custody of the Witch by the demoralized Avengers; the Avengers subsequently disbanded. When the X-Men and a new Avengers team later met to decide the Witch's fate, Quicksilver pressured her into altering reality into a world where mutants were the dominant species and lived openly without fear, with Magneto as Earth's ruler (Reality-58163/ "House of M"), with most living unaware of their previous reality.

When Magneto regained his memories, he was furious with Quicksilver for what he did in Magneto's name, and slew him. The Witch attacked Magneto and resurrected Quicksilver. In her delusion and frustration over her father repeatedly choosing the mutant-human struggle over his children, the Witch lashed out at Magneto by speaking the words "no more mutants" as she restored Reality-616, but with the majority of mutants stripped of their mutant gene, including Magneto, Quicksilver and Polaris; a global phenomenon dubbed "M-Day." Magneto became a recluse on Genosha until the arrival of the Collective, a coalescence of mutant energies displaced by M-Day led by Xorn's essence. This energy subsequently possessed American mutant Michael Pointer as its human host and repowered Magneto. While Magneto resisted the Collective, he was rendered comatose by a tremor within his brain caused by super-powered SHIELD agent Daisy Johnson. As SHIELD transferred Magneto into their custody, he seemingly died in a helicopter explosion.

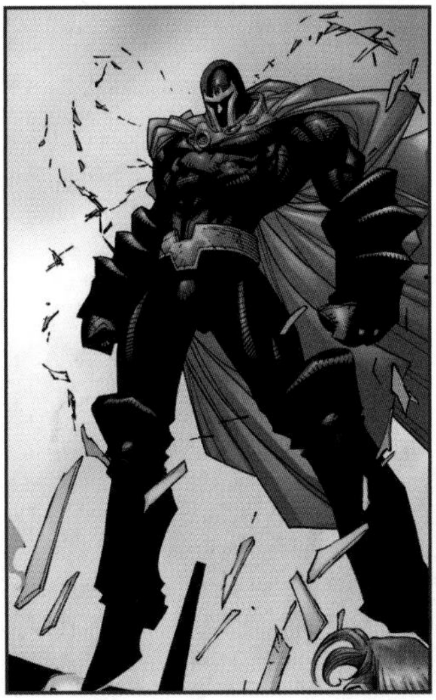
Art by Leinil Yu

Former Acolyte Exodus sought Magneto's aid restoring Xavier's mind after renegade X-Man Lucas Bishop unintentionally shot him in the head. Magneto succeeded with Omega Sentinel's assistance. For this act, Exodus sentenced Magneto to death and would have killed him if not for Xavier defeating Exodus. Magneto later rejected former Xavier student Hellion (Julian Keller)'s request to become his disciple because of Hellion's arrogance. At some point, Magneto became aware of the only mutant birth since M-Day, and that the baby was sent to the future for safekeeping, to be raised by X-Man Cable (Nathan Summers).

Searching for a way to restore the mutant gene, Magneto allied himself with the master geneticist High Evolutionary (Herbert Wyndham). Wearing a suit designed by the Evolutionary that replicated his lost powers, Magneto assaulted the X-Men in their new San Francisco home to distract them while the Evolutionary extracted a portion of the nearby Dreaming Celestial's brain, an enigmatic, near-omnipotent extraterrestrial Celestial, from it creating a device to restore mutant powers. After returning to the Evolutionary's ship, the Evolutionary restored Magneto, but the machine was destroyed and nearly killed Magneto. During his time in the Evolutionary's space station, Magneto became aware of a 10-mile long projectile that had been launched by Earth's enemies, but was prevented from destroying Earth by Kitty Pryde's phasing powers, who became trapped in it; Earth's prominent minds and scientists were unable to stop the projectile and rescue Pryde. Focused on restoring mutantkind, Magneto memorized the projectile's unique metal for a later time.

During this time, X-Men leader Cyclops (Scott Summers) led the X-Men to gather Earth's remaining mutants and created a floating island nation named Utopia, fashioned from the remnants of Magneto's former satellite base. Impressed that Cyclops had united and led the mutant race, a goal Magneto had long sought, Magneto laid his helmet at Cyclops' feet, a symbolic gesture of submission. Despite not trusting him, Cyclops allowed Magneto to remain upon Utopia. During an attack upon Utopia by mutant-consuming Predator X creatures, Magneto helped the X-Men defeat them, but learned extended use of his powers would rapidly overexert him.

When Utopia began sinking, the X-Club, the X-Men's science team, approached Magneto, hoping to use him as an electromagnetic power source to keep the island afloat; Magneto agreed to work with the Club. However, they soon realized Magneto would have to operate at peak capacity for 19 hours a day to maintain the island, an impossible feat, so Magneto secretly worked with Namor, now an X-Man, to build a pillar

HOUSE
OF M

Art by Aaron Lopresti

that would support the island, as well as give Namor's scattered sub-aquatic Atlantean people a location to rebuild a home. However, when Magneto revealed the pillar's completion, Cyclops was frustrated at Magneto's failure to follow the chain of command. Explaining he wanted to be of help and gain Cyclops' trust, Cyclops refused to give it. Realizing he needed to offer an article of faith to the X-Men, Magneto focused on the projectile's metals imprisoning Kitty Pryde and magnetically recalled it to Earth, an act that left Magneto greatly strained.

Around the same time, Magneto's former Hellfire Club ally, the immortal sorceress Selene, resurrected millions of deceased mutants in her quest to obtain godhood. Magneto accompanied a group of X-Men to Muir Island, his powers proving instrumental in defeating the reconstituted energy being Proteus (Kevin MacTaggert) but at a continued cost to his health. During this mission, Magneto expressed interest in Rogue once more, who rejected his affection, recalling his previous murders. Rogue was now point person for all the young mutants on Utopia, so Magneto took interest in helping Rogue with this task, but she still refused to trust him.

When the first post-M-Day baby (now a teenager named Hope Summers) returned to the present, a massive war erupted between the X-Men and mutant-hunting Sentinel Bastion's forces. During the war, dozens of Nimrod Sentinels were sent to destroy Utopia and slay all mutants. Despite being hospitalized for his repeated power expenditures, Magneto destroyed a number of Nimrods, protecting other hospitalized mutants and Utopia's population. After the war, Magneto helped Rogue and a number of her wards battle the extradimensional Children of the Vault in India and learned two members of the Young Avengers, Wiccan (William Kaplan) and Speed (Thomas Shepherd), may somehow be the Scarlet Witch's lost children, therefore his grandchildren. Despite being warned to stay away from the boys by now-Avenger Wolverine, Magneto sought them out and with the Young Avengers embarked on a quest to locate the missing Witch, battling the Avengers and Quicksilver along the way and leading them to would-be world conqueror Victor von Doom's Latveria.

NOTE: *Magneto once told Geist his wife had died in the Nazi concentration camp Geist had visited. Magneto's wife, Magda, survived well beyond World War II. It is unclear whether Magneto was attempting to deceive Geist, or whether he was referring to Magda's spirit dying, or if the account was simply in error.*

HEIGHT: 6'2"   **EYES:** Bluish-gray
WEIGHT: 190 lbs.   **HAIR:** Silver (formerly black)

ABILITIES/ACCESSORIES: Magneto can control all forms of magnetism, shaping and manipulating magnetic fields, whether natural or artificial. Magneto's power is practically limitless. He can completely assemble complicated machines within seconds, erect highly impenetrable magnetic force fields around himself, manipulate the iron content of blood so as to control others' actions, achieve flight by gliding along natural magnetic lines of force, alter his perceptions to see the world as electromagnetic energy, or even usurp control of an entire planet's electromagnetic field. Further, he can use his powers in more than one way simultaneously. It is unclear whether Magneto draws magnetic force from external sources (if so, then he could do so over vast distances) or whether he can generate magnetic force from within himself. Nor is it clear whether Magneto's power is psionic or purely physiological in nature. Magneto's ability to wield his superhuman powers depends largely on his physical condition. When severely injured, his body cannot withstand the strain of manipulating major magnetic forces.

Although Magneto's primary power is control over magnetism, he can also project or manipulate any form of energy within the electromagnetic spectrum, including visible light, radio waves, ultraviolet light, gamma rays and X-rays. He can manipulate gravitons to create an anti-gravity field, and do so whenever he levitated a nonmagnetic object. Hence, Magneto may be living proof of the long-sought Unified Field Theory that all forms of energy are related; however, Magneto almost always uses only magnetism, since it was more difficult for him to manipulate other forms of energy. He has also exhibited powers of astral projection and telepathy and has claimed he can control the minds of others, though his abilities along these lines appear to be minimal. Since his repowering, it is unclear to what extent these non-magnetic abilities still exist.

An excellent strategist and tactician as well as a skilled leader, Magneto is trained in hand-to-hand combat. He has mastered many technologies and is an expert on genetic manipulation and engineering, with knowledge far beyond that of contemporary science. He is regarded as a genius in these fields. He can mutate humans in order to give them superhuman powers, or create adult clones of human beings and then manipulate these clones' genetic structures during their development. He has also learned how to create artificial living beings. Magneto's inventions include complex robots (such as the caretaker Nanny and his assistant Ferris), computers, magnetically powered generators and vehicles, even entire space stations. His helmet is specially designed to prevent telepathic intrusion and repel psionic attacks. He has also used special uniforms to mimic his mutant powers when his own powers were lacking.

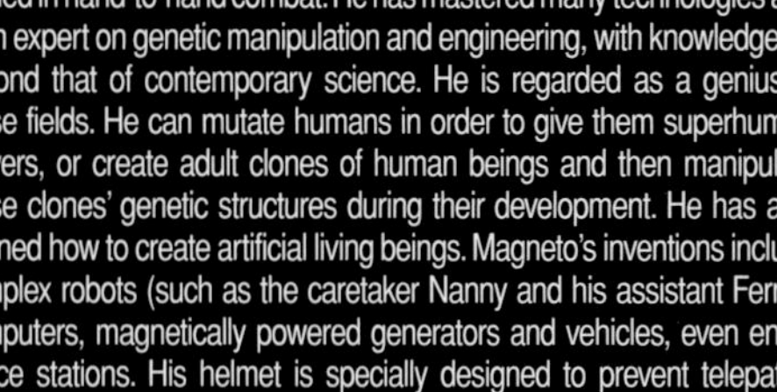

POWER GRID	1	2	3	4	5	6	7
INTELLIGENCE							
STRENGTH							
SPEED							
DURABILITY							
ENERGY PROJECTION							
FIGHTING SKILLS							

ROGUE

HISTORY: Born in a commune near the Mississippi River, Anna Marie led a happy life until her parents became involved in a plan to find the mythical "Far Banks." During a mystic ceremony, Anna's mother crossed over, leaving her and her father alone. He asked his sister-in-law Carrie to help raise Anna; however, Carrie's strict nature led Anna to rebel, earning her the nickname "Rogue," and she eventually ran away from home. In the nearby swamps, the shape-shifting mutant Mystique (Raven Darkhölme) found Rogue and offered to take her in. Accepting, Rogue went to live with Mystique and her lover, the blind mutant seer Destiny (Irene Adler). Rogue soon came to regard Mystique as a surrogate mother.

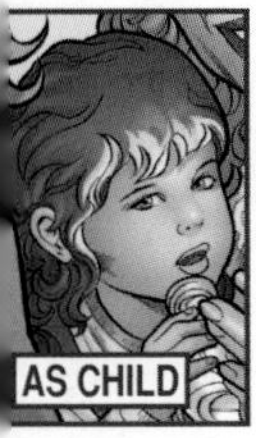
AS CHILD

Rogue's mutant power to imprint abilities and memories via touch manifested when she kissed fellow teenager Cody Robbins. Her mind was filled with his memories as Cody fell into a coma, and the terrified Rogue fled. Chased by an angry mob, she escaped a lynching through a chance encounter with the mutant cyborg Cable (Nathan Summers). Mystique and Destiny taught Rogue how to use her powers, but couldn't teach her how to control them. Realizing she could never live a normal life, Rogue began participating in Mystique's criminal endeavors. She befriended mutant memory manipulator Blindspot, whose similar powers negated Rogue's, allowing them to touch. After a mission together in Japan alongside local mutant Sunfire (Shiro Yoshida), Mystique's mistrust for Blindspot caused her to end their association. Blindspot erased all memory of herself from those involved for her own protection. Eventually, Rogue joined Mystique's Brotherhood of Evil Mutants. When Destiny foresaw the hero Ms. Marvel (Carol Danvers) was somehow tied to a tragedy which might one day cost Rogue her soul, Mystique tried to destroy Danvers, hoping to spare her foster daughter; however, hoping to please Mystique and not wanting her foster mother to fight her battles for her, Rogue attacked Ms. Marvel in San Francisco; during this fight, the inexperienced Rogue permanently absorbed Danvers' powers and memories, including the emotional ties associated with them; though not immediately obvious, trying to live with these stolen memories was the tragedy Destiny had foreseen. The transfer also altered Rogue's physiology to become an amalgam of her own mutant human make-up and Danvers' human/Kree hybrid form, giving Rogue lasting superhuman physical powers such as flight and strength.

Mystique then sent Rogue against the Avengers as a diversion while she freed the other Brotherhood members from prison; however, the Avengers recaptured the prisoners while Mystique and Rogue fled. Soon after, while visiting Mystique's civilian persona in the Pentagon, Rogue encountered Danvers, who was helping the X-Men on a mission. After a brief clash, Rogue escaped. She and Mystique then again tried freeing their teammates as they were transferred to Windhurst Prison, Virginia, but were partially foiled by the Spaceknight Rom, freeing only Destiny. The three women briefly allied with the alien Dire Wraith-human Hybrid (Jimmy Marks) against Rom, but after learning of Hybrid's plan to enslave the Earth, Rogue and her teammates opposed him; Rogue showed unprecedented heroism during the battle, using her powers to weaken Hybrid enough for Rom to seemingly destroy him.

Mystique set Rogue against Angel (Warren Worthington), hoping she could find the X-Men through him; though Rogue refused to absorb Warren's memories, not wanting to risk developing a physical mutation like Angel's wings, her attack led to a series of battles with Angel's then-love interest Dazzler (Alison Blaire) until Dazzler finally achieved a decisive victory, causing Rogue to develop a grudge against her. Increasingly upset over her inability to control her powers, fearing she was going insane due to her inability to rid her mind of Danvers' psyche, and frustrated with Mystique and Destiny's inability to help her, Rogue desperately sought aid from their enemies, Professor Charles Xavier and his X-Men. Convinced of her sincerity, Xavier accepted her onto the team despite the X-Men's objections; however, the team's friend Carol

REAL NAME: Anna Marie (surname unrevealed)
ALIASES: Anna Raven, Dr. Kellogg, Carol Danvers, "Ace," Mutate #9602, Irene Adler, Miss Smith
IDENTITY: Secret
OCCUPATION: Adventurer; former mechanic, waitress, terrorist
CITIZENSHIP: USA
PLACE OF BIRTH: Caldecott County, Mississippi
KNOWN RELATIVES: Owen (father), Priscilla (mother, deceased), Carrie (aunt), Raven Darkhölme (Mystique, unofficial foster mother), Kurt Wagner (Nightcrawler, unofficial foster brother), Graydon Creed (unofficial foster brother, deceased)
GROUP AFFILIATION: Formerly X-Men, X-Treme Sanctions Executive, X-Treme X-Men, Brotherhood of Evil Mutants
EDUCATION: College-level courses at Xavier's School, partial law degree
FIRST APPEARANCE: Avengers Annual #10 (1981)

Danvers, who had then recently become the cosmic-powered Binary, assaulted Rogue and angrily cut her ties with the X-Men upon learning of Xavier's decision. It wasn't until Rogue risked her life to save her teammate Wolverine's fiancée Mariko Yashida that she began to gain the X-Men's trust.

After Xavier consulted geneticist Dr. Richard Palance about Rogue's condition, Palance became obsessed with her absorption power. He secretly sampled her DNA, then spliced it with a viral agent and infected himself, granting him a power similar to Rogue's. After Mystique tried to bring Rogue home, Rogue asked Mystique to respect her decision and let her stay; Rogue then won further acceptance from her new teammates by risking her life to save Colossus (Piotr Rasputin), severely injured battling the Brotherhood. Later, Rogue aided Colonel Mike Rossi, Danvers' former lover, who was surprised to find Rogue acting and even

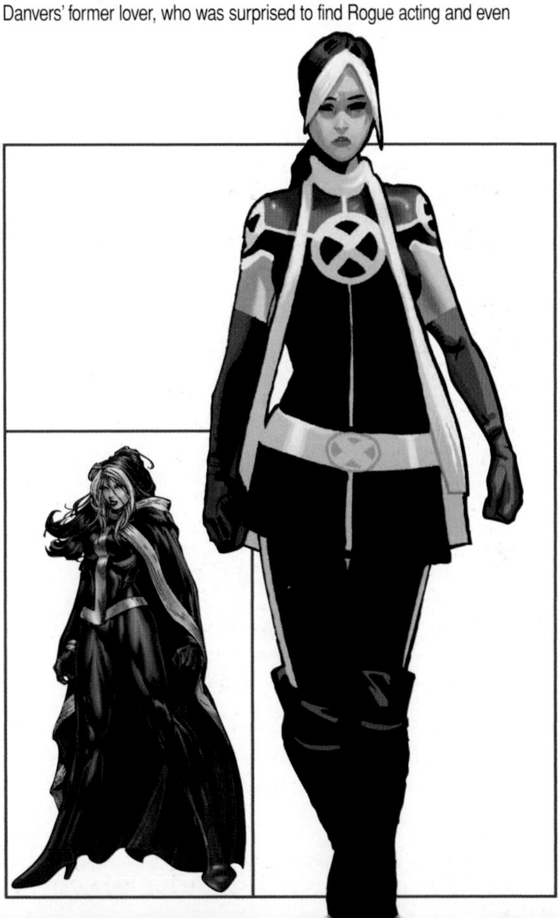

Art by Karl Moline, Igor Kordey, John Romita Jr. & Cynthia Martin

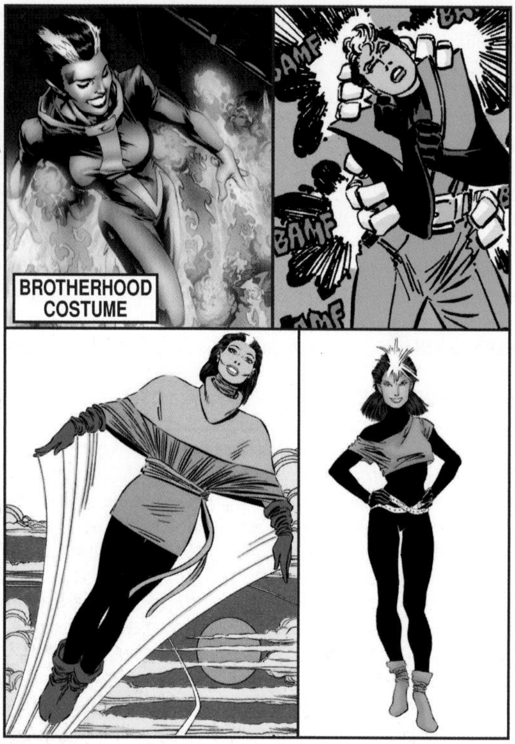

BAMF
BROTHERHOOD COSTUME

speaking like Danvers. Rogue had unwittingly allowed Danvers' psyche to take control and, upon reasserting her own psyche, she came to realize the full extent of what she had done to Danvers and fled home to the Mississippi. Wrongly accused of murder, Rogue was targeted by federal agent Henry Gyrich, armed with a prototype weapon meant to neutralize Rogue's powers. Rogue's teammate Storm (Ororo Munroe) came to her aid and inadvertently took the shot meant for Rogue, losing her powers. The X-Men were then attacked by the Earth-811 ("Days of Future Past") future's advanced Sentinel Nimrod. To defeat it, Rogue risked disfigurement by imprinting several teammates' powers simultaneously. To her relief, the attributes faded soon after. When Dazzler joined the X-Men, she and Rogue resolved their differences after they saved each other's lives during a battle with the Marauders.

When the world believed them dead following a battle with the Native American Adversary, the X-Men settled in an abandoned Australian outback town. When the X-Men opposed agents of the mutant-enslaving island nation Genosha, Rogue and Wolverine were captured and their powers temporarily nullified, allowing Genoshan soldiers to torture Rogue. Withdrawing into her mind, Rogue learned that left over psychic energy from past imprints remained there. She encountered Danvers' psyche and made a pact with it to temporarily share her body, gaining Danvers' skills as a covert agent to escape. Danvers' psyche exhibited the ability to control Rogue's power, suggesting that Rogue's lack of control was psychological in nature. At times, Rogue resisted the Danvers psyche, prompting it to forcibly take control. Rogue ultimately made peace with it, and after a battle against an amalgamation of Nimrod and the Steven Lang-programmed Master Mold, Rogue entered the Siege Perilous, a mystical gateway that granted those who pass through it a second chance at life. The gateway's magic separated Rogue and the Danvers persona, giving each a body to inhabit but with only enough life force to sustain one. The Danvers construct attacked Rogue, who fled to the Savage Land. Not wanting to repeat her past mistake, Rogue surrendered to Danvers, but they were both rendered unconscious by Magneto (Max Eisenhardt), who used a device to transfer Danvers' powers back to Rogue, essentially killing the Danvers construct. Rogue remained with Magneto for a time and began falling in love with him until she witnessed his brutal murder of Savage Land priestess Zaladane. Rogue then briefly fell under the sway of the Shadow King until his defeat by the X-Men and X-Factor.

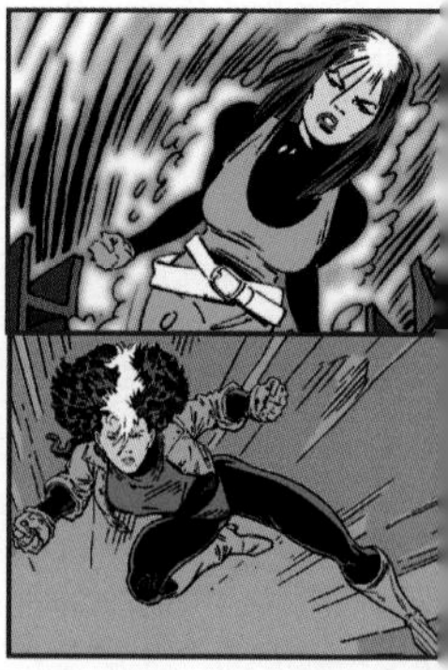

Rejoining the X-Men, Rogue became attracted to a new recruit, the mutant thief Gambit. The pair quickly fell in love, and Rogue's feelings for Gambit grew even after learning of his estranged wife, Bella Donna Boudreaux. Rogue later unwittingly imprinted Bella Donna's memories of her relationship with Gambit. As a result, during one of Rogue's annual visits to the comatose Cody Robbins' hospital bedside, Bella Donna orchestrated Cody's kidnapping. During the ensuing conflict, Cody died, so the Thieves' Guild mystic Tante Mattie allowed Rogue to meet with Cody on the astral plane where she learned he held no grudge against her. Rogue and Gambit eventually shared a kiss, whereupon she imprinted his memories, learning of his past involvement with evil geneticist Mr. Sinister. Subconsciously running from the truth, Rogue moved to South Carolina and worked as a waitress until she was attacked by the anti-mutant Operation: Zero Tolerance's forces. Saved by the young Magneto clone Joseph, she joined him in helping the X-Men battle the psionic creature Onslaught and then remained with the team. Rogue's attraction to both Joseph and Gambit caused friction between them. Joseph discovered a way to modify Xavier's Z'nox Chamber, originally used to shield minds from detection, to shield himself from Rogue's power, allowing him to give her a friendly kiss. Later, Magneto captured Rogue and Gambit intending to put Gambit on trial for his past. With their powers nullified by an inhibitor field, the pair spent their first intimate night together. At the trial, the X-Men learned of Gambit's past, leading to Rogue rejecting Gambit and abandoning him in Antarctica, partly due to Gambit's own residual personality in her mind seeking atonement for his sins. Afterwards, Rogue learned of the Agee Institute, an organization that could permanently remove mutant powers. Seeing a chance for a normal life, Rogue sought to undergo the procedure; however, fearing the unscrupulous use of the device to depower others against their will she destroyed the machine. Initially unable to locate Gambit, she was tenuously reunited with him upon his return to the X-Men, and Joseph's subsequent death ended the tension between them.

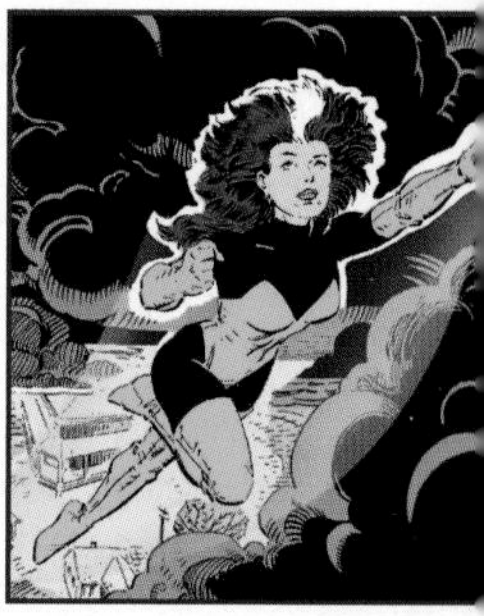

After Earth was deemed an intergalactic prison, Rogue imprinted the shape-shifting alien Skrull Zcann. The resultant mixing of her already amalgamated physiology with that of Zcann's caused her to spontaneously manifest past imprinted powers, which she eventually controlled via meditation. When a seemingly crazed Mystique threatened humanity with a modified version of the mutant-killing Legacy virus, Rogue confronted her but was wounded. Soon after, Rogue and others formed a splinter X-Men group to search for the now-deceased Destiny's diaries, which predicted mutantkind's future. During their quest, the team opposed an attempted invasion of Earth by the interdimensional warlord Khan. To help repel the invaders, Rogue had her teammate Sage "jumpstart" her powers to allow her to consciously activate any past imprinted powers, but exposure to an interdimensional energy and being stabbed by the villain Vargas left her temporarily powerless. Gambit had also been left powerless, so the pair seized the opportunity to try and

MUIR ISLAND COSTUME

SPLINTER GROUP UNIFORM   **ANNA RAVEN**

complete absorption of another instantaneous, but fatal. After Pandemic's defeat, Rogue's immune system collapsed and she fell into a coma. She was hospitalized on her teammate Cable's island Providence shortly before it was attacked by the sentient Shi'ar weapon the Hecatomb. Cable realized Rogue was the key to its defeat and forced her awake, whereupon she absorbed the Hecatomb's 8 billion stored memories, an act that threatened to overwhelm her mind. Mystique then betrayed the X-Men to the Marauders, shooting and kidnapping Rogue as part of the plan to save her. After the birth of the first mutant baby since "M-Day," the X-Men, the Marauders and the anti-mutant Purifiers all sought its whereabouts. Ultimately, the Marauders abducted the infant and took it to Sinister, whom Mystique betrayed so she could use the infant's power to heal Rogue, remove the death touch and purge all residual psychic energy. Before learning this, Rogue angrily tried to execute Mystique with her death touch, which left Mystique the only other imprint in Rogue's mind for a time. Needing time alone, Rogue returned to the Australian outback where she was approached by the artificial intelligence Danger, who sought to use Rogue as the conduit for its revenge against Xavier. Rescued by Xavier and Gambit, Rogue's fractured mind was repaired by Xavier which allowed her absorptive power to redevelop again at a more natural pace, granting her control. After this, Rogue and Gambit rejoined the X-Men in their San Francisco location, where Rogue accepted an offer to be a mentor to young mutant students in the X-Men's care, then becoming a guardian of sorts to the mutant baby (now a time-traveling teenager named Hope), to help protect her from anti-mutant forces.

live a normal life together in mutant-friendly Valle Soleada. After aiding the X-Men against mutant predator Elias Bogan, they rejoined the team.

After fully recovering and her powers returning, Rogue was placed on active duty and assigned a squad of students to teach. She later sought out the Far Banks to be reunited with her mother's spirit, and regained the memories of her youth. In an effort to attain some stability in their relationship, Rogue and Gambit undertook professional therapy conducted by their teammate Emma Frost; however, they found that they couldn't even touch on the astral plane without Gambit's astral form being drained. After Rogue's past mission with Mystique, Sunfire and Blindspot became public knowledge, she investigated, leading to Sunfire being crippled and her being captured by Lady Deathstrike. Rogue was then reunited with Blindspot who restored Rogue's memory of her and forced contact between Rogue and Sunfire, making Rogue absorb Sunfire's powers long-term. Blindspot then removed a portion of Rogue's memory, making her believe she was still in the Brotherhood. As a result, Rogue attacked the X-Men; however, she soon realized something was amiss and forced Blindspot to restore her memories.

Mystique sought to separate Rogue and Gambit by seducing Gambit in the form of an attractive young mutant student named Foxx, but Gambit resisted, and after her Foxx cover was exposed Mystique petitioned for membership in the X-Men. To Rogue's chagrin, she was voted in, and after most of the world's mutants were depowered on "M-Day," Mystique took up her membership, bringing with her mutant thief Pulse (Augustus Madison), whose disruption power negated Rogue's. Mystique considered Pulse Rogue's perfect match, much to Gambit's dismay; however, Rogue ultimately rejected Pulse's advances. When mutant conqueror Apocalypse (En Sabah Nur) attacked the X-Men, he revealed Gambit had been transformed into his Horseman Death. Initially failing to sway him, Rogue was forced to battle him until the love he felt for her began breaking through. Gambit subsequently left to clear himself of the brainwashing's effects.

Knowing from Destiny's diaries that Rogue faced great peril in her future, Mystique set in motion a plan to save her, and she secretly joined the Marauders. After Rogue became an X-Men field leader, she chose Mystique as a member of her roster. Rogue was soon captured by Dr. Palance, now Pandemic, who believed Rogue's ability was a way to attain immortality. He used her as a test for the Strain 88 virus, which made

HEIGHT: 5'8"   **EYES:** Green
WEIGHT: 120 lbs.   **HAIR:** Brown with white streak

ABILITIES/ACCESSORIES: Rogue can imprint the memories, abilities, personalities, mannerisms, outward physical characteristics and superhuman abilities of others through skin-to-skin contact, which often causes the other being to be rendered unconscious. She can absorb multiple beings simultaneously. Upon imprinting another's memories, Rogue also gains any associated emotional ties, which she can typically control, however, absorbing psyches more powerful than her own has resulted in her psyche being supplanted for the duration. Prior to gaining control of her power, extended contact typically resulted in permanent absorption, and fragments of the any psyche she temporarily imprinted remained in her subconscious; the current extent of these aspects is unrevealed.

Previously, Rogue imprinted and retained the powers of Ms. Marvel (Carol Danvers), giving her super-strength (Class 50), near-invulnerability, flight, and an amalgamated mutant human/alien Kree physiology that had some immunity to poisons, above normal reflexes and psychic "seventh sense" that enabled her to subconsciously anticipate an opponent's moves, though only while under great stress. While Rogue possessed Danvers' psyche, her "double" consciousness made her resistant to telepathic probes, allowed access to Danvers' extensive military training, and at times, Danvers' psyche could control Rogue's body. Following brief power amplifications, Rogue could reactivate past imprinted abilities and could also tap into the psyches of past imprints to determine their current status and relive past events from their perspective. For a time, Rogue retained Sunfire's ability to absorb solar radiation and convert it into plasma, surround herself with an aura of heat intense enough to melt steel, see in the infrared spectrum, and fly by creating thermal updrafts. Rogue can speak fluent French.

POWER GRID	1	2	3	4	5	6	7
INTELLIGENCE							
STRENGTH							
SPEED							
DURABILITY							
ENERGY PROJECTION							
FIGHTING SKILLS							

YELLOW BARS INDICATE POTENTIAL POWER RATINGS

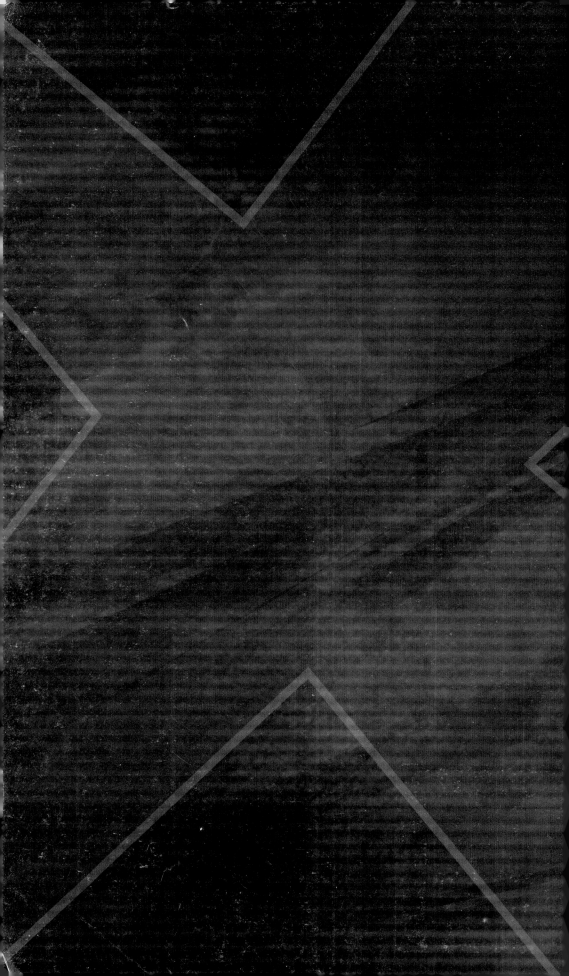